DIGITAL IMAGES FOR THE INFORMATION PROFESSIONAL

For Os, Anthony and the Mishkin

Digital Images for the Information Professional

MELISSA M. TERRAS
University College London, UK

ASHGATE

Published by

Ashgate Publishing Limited
Gower House
Croft Road
Aldershot
Hampshire GU11 3HR
England

Ashgate Publishing Company
Suite 420
101 Cherry Street
Burlington, VT 05401-4405
USA

www.ashgate.com

British Library Cataloguing in Publication Data

Terras, Melissa M.
Digital images for the information professional
1. Digital images 2. Electronic information resources
3. Digital libraries - Management 4. Digital libraries -
Collection development
I. Title
025.1'77

Library of Congress Cataloging-in-Publication Data

Terras, Melissa M.
Digital images for the information professional / by Melissa M. Terras.
p. cm.
Includes bibliographical references and index.
ISBN 978-0-7546-4860-4
1. Digital images. 2. Digital preservation. 3. Photography--Digital techniques. 4. Electronic information resources. I. Title.

TA1637.T45 2008
025.3'44--dc22

2008019105

ISBN 978-0-7546-4860-4

Printed and bound in Great Britain by
MPG Books Ltd, Bodmin, Cornwall.

Contents

Preface

> Photography is certainly not what it was! Indeed, along with the new industrial revolution of which much is heard today, a new photographic revolution is in progress. We have gone far since the days when a handful of pioneers made tentative experiments with messy chemicals, manipulated cumbersome wet plates and subjected their sitters to exposures lasting as long as ten minutes. Pictures that until a few years ago were an impossible challenge to the camera are now at the beginner's fingertips! (Kodak Limited 1961, 6, *How to Make Good Pictures*)

Images are an integral part of human history, culture and society. From daubing on rocks, to chiselling out woodcuts, to inventing printing and photographic techniques, to digitizing print material, humans have continually improved the technology available to enable them to create, share and disseminate visual information. Since its birth, 150 years ago, photography has been used by artists for expression, by journalists to record events, by scientists to record data and by everyday people to faithfully record the world, their life, their travels and their family. Photography, and the creation and dissemination of images, is an established part of culture, heritage, the media, and both work and home life, but the technology which provides the means to produce, manipulate and share such images has changed rapidly over the past decadc.

Today, with the ever decreasing cost of digital capture equipment and storage facilities, and increasing speeds of accessing the Internet, creating, sharing and storing digital information is easy and becoming ever more common. The means by which we create and share image information is rapidly changing, as digital photography stands poised to replace its film-based predecessor.

> Humans have a voracious appetite for information in visual form, and the digital image has such overwhelming technical and economic advantages as a way of meeting this demand, that it seems certain to succeed the photograph as our primary medium of visual record – much as the photograph itself succeeded the hand-drawn and painted image. Unlike silver-based photographic film, the digital image does not consume scarce, non-renewable resources. It does not require a time-consuming and expensive chemical development process. It can be stored compactly, accessed by computer, manipulated freely, and transmitted to remote locations within seconds of creation (Mitchell 1992, 19).

This raises issues for the information professional – defined here as an individual working in a library, archive, museum, cultural heritage or information environment whose aim is to maintain, and often improve, access to the ever growing amount of information generated from within the culture and heritage industry, the media, and, increasingly, by the general public. In order to best preserve and safeguard the escalating amount of digital image information currently in general circulation, or in private or public archives, it is necessary to understand the artefact that we are dealing with: the digital image itself.

The aim of this book is to provide an overview of the changing information environment and maturing technologies, which underpin digital images. By placing them in their historical, technical and cultural framework, exploring computational processes, and giving overviews of how and why they are created, developed, used, searched, found, manipulated and appropriated in both 'memory institutions' and in personal collections. This book aims to provide an information professional with the tools needed to understand many prime issues surrounding digital images.

This is not a book about how to manage and carry out a digitization programme. There are many publications which exist detailing the planning, funding, instigation and management of digitization initiatives, the majority of which deal with the production of two-dimensional digital images. (Although it is becoming increasingly achievable to digitize archives of moving images and sound, the majority of primary historical sources fit comfortably on a scanner bed or before the lens of a camera.) This book is not an attempt to reproduce the guidelines and textbooks already written on setting up and carrying out digitization projects: seminal texts are recommended at the end of each chapter. However, many of the books regarding digitization initiatives in a library, archive, culture and heritage sectors, focus on management issues: including budgeting, collections management, selection of objects to be digitized and digital preservation. Most have a slim chapter on the digital object they are creating: the digital image. The aim of this book is to flesh out the details and answer the questions that a curious, information professional may be asking themselves about how digital images function, how they are appropriated in a library, archive and 'memory institution' sector, and the wider cultural and historical background and impact of digital imaging technologies.

Publishing constraints mean that this is a book about digital images without any images. Where it is useful or necessary, pointers to individual images, diagrams or essential literature are given within the text.

A subject such as this is in danger of becoming rapidly technically obsolete. To avoid this, this book concentrates on the principles and historical framework of the technology and discipline, rather than up to date product implementations. This is not a book about cameras, scanners or other peripheral devices, as the technology changes rapidly (and there would be too much to say on the subject, that is another book in itself). Instead, plenty of helpful pointers are given to sources which are updated regularly about current recommendations regarding the available technology. Usually online, these sources, such as the Technical Advisory Service for Images (www.tasi.ac.uk), often feature purchasing recommendations for those about to embark on digitization and imaging projects.

This book aims to be a reference and guide for those who use or create digital images for various applications in the library, archive, museum, culture and heritage sectors, or for those who wish to understand more about the digitization environment and issues regarding the format and longevity of both institutional and personal digital image data.

In 1998, when I began my doctorate in the Robot Vision Lab in Oxford University's Engineering Department, I was plunged into a world of zeroes and ones. I could find very little that explained to me – the humanities graduate – the background, workings and underpinnings of digital images. Since then, due to cheaper technologies and faster networking capacity, digital image production has grown exponentially. Nearly 10 years later, researching and teaching in a library department, I still see the need for an accessible book that would explain in non-technical language the fundamentals of digital imaging, the background to imaging technologies and the main issues regarding access to and preservation of digital image data. This is the book I wished someone else had written for me. I have written it for Os, the Mishkin and the Bump (who turned out to be Anthony).

Dr Melissa Terras,
Senior Lecturer in Electronic Communication,
School of Library, Archive and Information Studies,
University College London.

Acknowledgements

I am indebted to Andrew Ostler, who gave each chapter a thorough proofreading and challenged and informed my understanding of the topic while making sure I was looked after: thank you, Husband. Edward Vanhoutte (Centre for Scholarly Editing and Document Studies, Royal Academy of Dutch Language and Literature, Ghent) was extremely helpful as a careful proofreader and the source of much encouragement: *dank u wel.*

Chapter 1
Introduction

> … the soul never thinks without an image (Aristotle, *De Anima* Book III, Part 7).

> The illiterates of the future will be the people who know nothing of photography rather than those who are ignorant of the art of writing (László Moholy-Nagy 1932, quoted in Jeffrey 2006, 111).

Images have been part of human society, psychology and imagination since the earliest times, before the dawn of written language. In the closing stages of the twentieth century, digital images emerged as the dominant medium to capture, create, store, share and disseminate visual information. For those working in the information profession, such as librarians, archivists, curators, knowledge managers and information specialists, understanding our changing information environment and changing approach to image-based material can facilitate the creation of, access to, and long-term sustainability of digital image material.

This chapter explores some basic underpinnings which inform the rest of the book: What do we mean by 'image', and why are they so important to humans? What are digital images, how are they created, and for that matter, what is meant by the term 'digital'? This text focuses on issues surrounding bitmaps, rather than vector graphics, and the reasons for this approach are explained, as is why such a text (with a focus on issues pertinent to information professionals) is necessary. Finally, an overview of the remaining content of the book is presented, detailing its scope and aims.

Images

The creation of images has been a human activity since the beginning of human society: our early ancestors painted or carved rocks with depictions of their lifestyles and beliefs. Rocks are not very portable, however, and humans like to share their images, and the knowledge contained within them. Much investment in technology has focused on the ability to create, replicate and disseminate visual information, from early print materials, to later attempts at photography and the ability to capture 'an artificial imitation or representation of the external form of any object' (OED 1989a) via means of recording patterns of light. Indeed, the OED definition of 'image' includes light as a particular source of images: an image can be:

> An optical appearance or counterpart of an object, such as is produced by rays of light either reflected as from a mirror, refracted as through a lens, or falling on a surface after passing through a small aperture (ibid.).

The complete definition of an 'image' is wide, however, and there is no room in this book to address the complex philosophical, historical and linguistic debate regarding what images actually are: as well as the physical manifestation of light falling on photosensitive paper or light-sensitive arrays:

> We speak of pictures, statues, optical illusions, maps, diagrams, dreams, hallucinations, spectacles, projections, poems, patterns, memories, and even ideas as images, and the sheer diversity of this list would seem to make any systematic unified understanding impossible (Mitchell 1984, 504).

The focus of this book is the image at its most literal: 'a graphic, pictorial representation: a concrete material object' (ibid. 521), a 'non-moving representation of visual information' (Anderson et al. 2006, 7) which has a physical manifestation, even if it is just a file which resides on a computer's hard drive or on a web server.

Two-dimensional images are an important means of communication, source of information, and focus of both social interaction and scholarly activity in modern society. Images play an important role in cultural and social history, can contain valuable historical information, and are used more and more in academic research, which aims to study culture in its widest sense: focusing on artefacts and cultural produce. It is becoming popular for interpretations of visual material to be incorporated into academic reasoning: this is partly to do with the more exotic or interdisciplinary themes emerging in modern research 'like the history of smells, or witchcraft. Studying themes like this, all sorts of sources, previously not often used by historians – images, literature, plays – are consulted' (van den Berg 1992, 8).

Digital images are now the media of choice for creating, sharing, accessing and manipulating image material. Digitization projects in libraries, archives, museums and other 'memory institutions' are merrily creating image representations of their holdings for display, sharing and distribution via the Internet. Individuals are creating, manipulating, utilizing and sharing vast collections of digital images in ways which would not have been possible with traditional photographic media. The increasing prevalence and pervasive nature of digital imaging technologies requires engagement and understanding by those working within the information sector.

Images and Humans

The word 'image' stems from the Latin *imaginem* or the later French *imagene*, expressing ideas of imitation, copy and likeness, but also of thought, conception and imagination. This reflects the fact that the human perception and understanding of images is both a physiological and conceptual process. It is not entirely understood how the human eye-brain system functions.

Physically, the vertebrate eye is complex. Light passes through the opening in the front of the eye, the pupil, and the lens focuses the image on the retina, a sheet of layers of neural tissues that line the back of the eyeball. Photoreceptors generate a neural signal when they detect light, and this signal is sent via the optic nerve to the brain (Gregory 1998; Livingstone 2002). What happens next is not clear:

> The eye is a simple optical instrument. With internal images projected from objects in the outside world, it is Plato's cave with a lens. The brain is the engine of understanding. There is nothing closer to our intimate experiences, yet the brain is less understood and more mysterious than a distant star (Gregory 1998, 1).

Human perceptual and cognitive systems have limited capacities for processing information, but much of it is devoted to dealing with visual input. Being biological systems, and not identical, the cortex area devoted to processing images varies greatly from human to human (Andrews et al. 1997), but a relatively large proportion of brain activity, estimated at above 50 per cent, is devoted to vision. Research into how we see, perceive and interpret the world around us, and our reaction to images, is wide, varied and spans an interdisciplinary reach encompassing psychology, biology, physiology, chemistry, physics, philosophy and beyond (Bruce et al., 1996, introduce many of the theories and debates postulated so far). What is certainly true is that the human brain can process complex visual information quickly, it does so by various mechanisms which are not fully understood, and that humans can be stimulated in various emotional, intellectual, physical and behavioural ways by imagery and image content (Lang et al. 1993, 1998). Our enjoyment of visual art is an extension of this complex physical and perceptual activity (Molnar 1997; Livingstone 2002). 'We humans like images: our brains are specially adapted to interpret them' (Trefethen and Embree 2005, 8): it is little wonder, then, that the ease of producing, manipulating and disseminating them afforded by digital media and networks has resulted in an exponential increase in image material for personal and cultural consumption.

It is important to note that the human visual system suffers from many limitations. It can detect light and interpret the consequences of light stimulus – within a specific range of wavelengths – but has limited ability to perceive certain colours, being more sensitive to green and yellow, then red, rather than blue. Small variations in colour are virtually impossible for the human eye to detect: our visual system merges small details into a unified whole, being set up to view the global information of a scene or a smooth, continuous tone image, rather than individual constituent properties. The human visual system is much more sensitive to changes in luminance (light) values than changes in colour. Additionally, individuals perceive colour differently. Colour blindness affects 8 per cent of men and less than 1 per cent of women (Birch 2001, 33), where some individuals see certain pairs of colours as being identical, those with normal vision would see them as different, but aside from this, the perception of colour is subjective:

> the similarities and differences between your experience of red and mine lie somewhere between the classes of cells activated in our retinas, thalamuses, and visual cortices, and the similarities between the memories activated in our frontal lobes (Livingstone 2002, 33).

Computer digital imaging and multimedia technologies often exploit these limitations in the human visual system, or try and recreate human perceptual processes, in order to present material to us effectively. For example, computer monitors generate colours by mixing three additive primaries of red, green and blue light onto small, individual points on the screen. The refresh rate with which the screen is repainted varies from 1/25th to 1/80th of a second, depending on the device, which is enough to fool an eye into seeing a still image, or continuous motion if the image is changing frame by frame. The size of the individual points is set to be below our perception threshold, so we see a continuous tone image. Our visual systems blend the image chromatically, spatially and temporally:

> Chromatically in that we do not see only various shades of red, blue, and green, but all the colours in between. Our visual systems blend colours … Spatially, because the individual pixels are too small to be resolved by the photoreceptor spacing in our retinas, unless we are looking very closely at a very large monitor … [and] Temporally in that we see neither the scan pattern nor the fact that the image is presented at a rate of thirty frames per second … a rate our visual systems are unable to resolve (Livingstone 2002, 192).

In addition to this, certain approaches to compressing images, which make file sizes smaller (see pp. 50–58) exploit the way the human eye system deals with variation in colour and replicates this mathematically. JPEG compression, in particular, was designed to discard colour information that the human eye just does not readily perceive (see pp. 76–79), efficiently creating a smaller file which looks much like the original. The way that digital imaging technologies work is closely related to our own physiology and physical limitations.

Defining 'Digital'

The ordinary, or 'real' world of our senses, exists in a continuous flowing stream of signals across time and often space. A sound, a movement, a photographic print or a line drawn from a pencil all exist in analogue, where a varying signal represents a continuous range of values. In order to record, copy, transmit or analyse such a complex signal using computational power, it is necessary to translate this into a form which is more simple, predictable and processable. All telecommunication systems have one thing in common: the information to be sent is converted into signals, which can be transmitted and reassembled on reception, to be converted into something we can perceive as a fair copy of the original.

Digital systems are those which rely on a sequence of discreet numeric values, rather than the unconstrained and continually varying qualities of analogue signals. Numeric values are used in digital systems for processing, display, transmission and input: often sampling values from analogue sources. The term 'digital' comes from the Latin for finger *digitus*, as these systems use counting and discreet, or separate and distinct, numeric values for calculating, reflecting the way we often use our own fingers for counting or, as was common in the past, as a unit of measurement.

The most common digital systems are those used in computing and electronics which rely on the binary numeric system. This is a system which represents all numbers using only two symbols, typically 0 and 1. This is represented in a fairly straightforward manner in electrical or optical systems: typically 1 is denoted by an electronic pulse present, 0 by its absence. A string of zeroes and ones can represent numbers (1 is 'one'; 10 represents 'two'; 11 represents 'three'; 100 represents 'four'; etc.). These zeroes and ones are known as binary digits, or more commonly as the shortened derivation: 'bits'. Any number of bits can be combined to represent a set of values. A set of 8 bits is called a 'byte' (a unit settled on in the 1960s due to the popularity of 8-bit microprocessors). A long string of bytes, such as an entire file, is often referred to as a 'data stream'.

Strings of bits can represent text: text encoding formats assign a set of binary numbers to represent letters of a language alphabet. The ASCII (American Standard Code for Information Interchange) is a standardized 7-bit character code for the transmission of data, which describes the codes of the 128 different characters which can be described in 7 bits: from 0000000 to 1111111. The character D, for example, is number 68 in the specification, so is represented in the binary string 01000100. As long as the computer can recognize this binary string as ASCII it can process and display large strings of bits as 'plain text' (the operating system will usually examine the file and determine what format it is and how it should be displayed).

Strings of bits can also represent images. The overall purpose of this book is to describe in detail how this functions; but for the moment, imagine a black and white chessboard. If we take white to be 1 and black to be 0, the chessboard could be represented by a string of bits, from the top left white square: 1010101001010101 … etc. This creates a 'bitmap': the bits of the data stream are mapped, one by one, to colours in the image. As long as the computer had some way of knowing that 8 bits represented one line (the 'scan line' length, which is the type of information provided within a file header in an image format, see p. 65), then a representation of the chessboard could be stored in bits and easily copied and transmitted to other computers and painted onto computer screens. An alternative way to store graphical data would be to use ASCII text to create a list of instructions to a computer 'One white square. Then one black square. Repeated four times. Next row. One black square …' etc. A program could read this set of instructions and paint the resulting image onto the screen in a series of shapes called vectors (see pp. 7–8). However, describing photographic content in this manner is complex, and the sampling method of describing an image as solidly toned squares is most useful for complex image data.

Strings of bits can also represent sound and moving images: as the information to be represented grows more complex, more bits are required to represent it, and more complex mechanisms are used to store, display and process the information contained within the data stream.

Providing numeric, textual, image, sound and video-based data in digital format, whether they have been translated from an analogue signal into bits or 'born digital' by being created with computational technologies in the first place, has various advantages. These strings of bits can be easily replicated, transmitted, accessed and processed. Saving the data in a structured, predetermined format means it may be device independent and can be transferred from system to system with minimal problems. Data can be manipulated by dedicated computer programs, allowing new versions of the information to be generated. Data can also be processed: mathematically sorted through to show hidden relationships, new arrangements, different views and expanded, contracted or concatenated knowledge.

It should be noted that digital is not always best, and that there is still a place for analogue technologies in this world. Analogue devices pre-date digital and are still effective in representing information: wristwatches, gas meters, odometers in cars, etc. Human eyes and ears can sometimes distinguish between continuous analogue signals and bit by bit digital approximations. Digital media are at their most effective when their constituent parts – samples – are not detectable by human senses.

The Digital Image

A digital image is a representation of an image stored in numerical form, for potential display, manipulation or dissemination via computer technologies. Digital images store graphical information in small, discontinuous, non-homogenous, numerical elements.

On one level, a digital image is like any other computer data file: just a long code of ones and zeroes, using information as its raw material. Digital images are captured through a process of creating, storing and manipulating numbers in a computer. Once created, this sequence of numbers becomes infinitely malleable, but is usually rendered into visual form which the human eye can see. Output devices generate a representation of the image data from the mathematical detail contained within a file – although the majority of output devices (screens, prints) are actually analogue.

There are more complex three-dimensional imaging technologies – but we shall concentrate on two-dimensional images. In particular, this text concentrates on bitmap, or raster, images: those which consist of discreet numerical units called 'pixels' (see pp. 35–37) which combine to make a continuous tone image, rather than vector graphics which consist of a set of instructions to the computer regarding spatial primitives (squares, circles, etc.) and how these relate to one another. Bitmap graphics are by far the most popular type of image used to create representations of objects for use in memory institutions, they are the type of image output by digital cameras, and are the most popular types of image on the Internet.

Types of Digital Images: Vector and Bitmapped Graphics

There are two distinct classes of digital images: vector graphics and bitmap images. Although digitization projects and cultural and heritage institutions will be most likely to produce and deal with bitmap images (and the focus of this book is on their growing prevalence and use) it is useful to contrast and understand the different function of the two types of images and to see why bitmaps are the preferred format for storing photographic and detailed pictorial information.

Vector graphics were the first type of computer graphic to be implemented in the 1950s. They use a series of geometric drawing commands, such as lines, curves or shapes and solid or graduated colour, to represent an image (for example, draw a green triangle inside a blue rectangle and fill the triangle body in green), giving precise mathematical descriptions of the position, size and relationship of the different components. Computer monitors and laser printers can display vector graphics by redrawing this mathematical representation (all early computer displays drew images onto Cathode Ray Tube monitors following these type of instructions, using a 'random scan display') but the format has two main drawbacks. Images of paintings and photographs would require tens of thousands of drawing commands to represent them in vector format – can you imagine trying to describe a Jackson Pollok painting or an ancient document, in terms of lines and shapes? Determining which commands to use to represent the painting or document would be a monumental task. Second, complex vector images take a long time to display and have very large file sizes. They also function best on vectored output display devices, such as plotters and random-scan displays: if displayed on raster devices (the majority of today's display technologies, which paint the picture onto the screen scan line by scan line and pixel by pixel), they need high resolution displays to display them as effectively and the processing power to 'render' the image onto the raster display: where a two-dimensional bitmap image is computed, pixel by pixel, from a chosen viewpoint of the vector image.

There are benefits to vector formats, and they are the approach of choice for creating representations of objects and space in fields such as product design, architecture, engineering, construction, geography and archaeology. They are the basis of Geographical Information Systems and certain Virtual Reality systems. Because each line or shape is defined and drawn individually from others, it is easy for drawing programs to add, delete and modify individual elements without disrupting other elements of the image. Because the image is composed of defined objects, vector graphics can be scaled up or down with no effect on the image's quality: they are scale independent. It is also simple to perform transformations, where the position or direction of the viewpoint is changed, creating new views of the scene, changing such features as perspective and scale, and enlarging or shrinking the image seamlessly. Vector graphics are good for images requiring spot colour, when a uniform colour is used in a defined region, such as in images of logos or diagrams, where one colour floods an entire area. Images created in vector format can be rendered to create a bitmap image at the desired scale and size (it is almost impossible to create a vector description of a bitmap image, however, as it is difficult to define instructions to reconstruct an image from its bitmap representation). Vector graphics are entirely suited to images which consist of simple shapes, such as charts, graphs, logos and diagrams, and are useful for architectural, engineering and archaeological plans which map spatial data.

The alternative approach to image representation is to use a bitmap, also referred to as raster representation. The image is broken into a grid by the capture device, with the light value (lightness, darkness or colour) of each piece of the grid – a pixel – recorded individually.[1] The resulting two-dimensional array of numerical values, where each array element represents a colour to be displayed at a specific location, could easily be displayed, copied and transmitted. Bitmap representation is by far the most commonly used digital imaging method nowadays: it is interesting to note that the increased emphasis on bitmap graphics technology, from the 1980s onwards, corresponds to the massive upwards shift in the output of digital image information. Bitmaps are relatively easy to implement and, within limits, work for any image: they can record just about any conceivable image or view of a scene since any image can be broken up into a grid (and as far as the human eye is concerned, if that grid is small enough we see it as a continuous tone image).

There are various advantages to using bitmapped images. First: image quality. Bitmap representation works well for images with complex variations in colours, shades or shapes, such as photographs, paintings or screenshots (modern computer

1 In older usage, the terms pixelmap, graymap and pixmap were also used to describe images which had many bits of colour data assigned to each individual pixel, with the term bitmap referring to an array or 'map' of single bits, each bit corresponding to a pixel. Nowadays, the term 'bitmap' refers to an array of pixels, whatever the type, and the bit depth (see pp. 44–49) specifies the size of memory devoted to colour information of the pixel.

screen displays originate in bitmap format and are therefore most easily recorded in the same way). Additionally, the representation translates well to output devices, such as screens, projectors and printers. High resolution images – when the grid is made suitably small, containing thousands, or even millions, of individual colour samples – are capable of capturing minute, complex or pictorial detail. Bitmap image data is easily captured, shared and disseminated.

One drawback of bitmap representation is the size of files produced: colour and high resolution image files can require many megabytes of memory to process and display (see pp. 49–50), and manipulating such large volumes of data can also place heavy demands on the processing power of the device handling the image. For that reason, the issue of how to make the file sizes smaller through compression techniques (see pp. 50–58) is a very significant issue when dealing with bitmap formats. A further drawback is their lack of flexibility: bitmap data must be manipulated at an individual colour sample level. It is not possible to decide to 'change the colour of that dog to black': each individual pixel has to be selected manually. Individual pixels have no intrinsic connection to each other, and the computer retains no contextual information regarding shape. A final problem is found when resizing bitmap images: changing the image size can change the image in an unacceptable manner. For example, if an image is enlarged the individual pixels can become large enough to reveal themselves, producing blocky representation (called pixelation, aliasing or stair-casing). This can be avoided by inserting or deleting pixel information through a mathematical operation called interpolation (see pp. 38–40).

Neither bitmap nor vector graphics methods are better than the other: they simply have different functions and uses. Vector representation has many more limitations, but is more efficient and flexible for many applications. Desktop application programs (such as word-processing software) are increasingly able to deal with both vector and bitmap images, and some metafile formats (such as PDF, see pp. 95–96) can deal with both types of data in the same file. However, the majority of digital images created by the home or professional user are bitmaps. Memory institutions creating digital image representations of documents and artefacts will be doing so using bitmap formats. The majority of images appearing online are bitmaps. Bitmap formats are the representation of choice for complex, pictorial, detailed and image information. As a result, this text focuses on bitmap images.

The Creation of Digital Images

Due to changes in the information environment, including the lowering costs of computing and digital imaging technologies, and the increase in available network speeds (see Chapter 2), digital images have become the most popular way to share and disseminate both personal and institutional image information. Bitmap images can be created in two fundamental ways. They can be 'born digital': existing only in digital format after being captured on digital imaging equipment, such as cameras, mobile phones and webcams, or created using a digital imaging software package. Alternatively, they can be the result of 'digitization', where a representation of an analogue object is captured (via camera or scanner) to provide a surrogate, digital image of the picture, document or artefact in question:

> digitisation is the method of creating a digital image from an original book or manuscript utilising an electronic capture process. A digital camera (one equipped with an electronic light-sensitive device in place of the photographic film) captures the optical characteristics of an original. It records the data, not on chemical-based photo-sensitive film but in an electronic file format. The resulting data file can be enhanced for various desired visual effects, is easily stored in databases, can be reproduced multiple times without generational degradation of quality, and can easily and quickly be transmitted across the Internet to anywhere in the world (Grycz 2006, 33).

Digitization, then, involves the creation of a binary representation of an object which already exists, rather than the creation of new and novel pictorial information:

> Digitization is a process which is cannibalising and regurgitating photographic (and other) imagery, allowing the production of simulations of simulations (Willis 1990, 199).

Most personal digital image collections (see Chapter 6) are born digitally: produced by increasingly affordable and pervasive digital camera technologies. Digitization of cultural and heritage image-based material is predominantly an institutional effort (see Chapter 5), although there are plenty of individuals scanning-in old photo albums, or creating digital image representations of their personal collections (see Chapter 6). Digitization of archival, manuscript, photographic and pictorial information is commonly undertaken by memory institutions to facilitate access to their collections (see Chapter 5) and although other media, such as sound and moving images, can be digitized, the most common output of digitization programs is digital images and their corresponding documentation (see Chapter 7). As a result, those working in the information industry, undertaking digitization initiatives and dealing with digital images, should be aware of the many issues surrounding the creation, appropriation, use and usefulness of digital images themselves.

Why 'Digital Images for the Information Professional'?

The creation, storage and transmission of digital image data is a focus of much effort in cultural institutions, and changes in technology and the information environment are having a profound impact in many areas. Cultural heritage is becoming readily available to a wider audience, holding potential for both teaching and research. Additionally, imaging technologies are becoming increasingly popular in general society, and there is a need to understand how people are using the technology outside institutional boundaries, so that we can communicate using the same technology within our institutions. Those working within the information community also have a role to play in educating the general public about the sustainability and fragility of their digital image collections (see Chapter 6). The 'information professional': an individual managing, developing and deploying information services within an organization or community, is now faced with rapid developments in technology and corresponding changes in society, which have to be understood, accommodated and often facilitated:

> Technology today does not evolve in a clear linear pattern. It shifts and mutates in great leaps and bounds, and often in unexpected directions. Because of this, the future holds more questions than answers … How will these advances change our notion of what photography can or should be? What will happen as modeling software becomes increasingly capable of generating photo-realistic imagery that cannot be distinguished in any way from real life? The only things we can be sure of is that the human desire to understand the world through representation will propel the process of making images through greater and greater changes in the years to come (Lipkin 2005, 10).

There is a clear need for the information professional to be aware of these technological developments, and the flow of digital image information that accompanies it. Understanding digital imaging technologies is the first step to being able to create, use, store and provide access to digital images with confidence in our changing information landscape.

In many ways, this book was born out of frustration: for those working with digital images in the library, archive, museum and information sector there are various texts detailing the management and managerial aspects of digital imaging projects (see pp. 137–139 for further reading) but often these texts place little focus on the actual medium commonly used to present and provide image data which emanates from a digitization initiative. This book aims to provide an overview of different, pertinent aspects of digital images which will be of relevance to those working with digital media environments, providing a common understanding of the principles and issues that pertain to the creation and distribution of both individual digital images and digital image archives as a whole.

This book aims to provide a basic, thorough, outline of digital image technologies and related issues, placing the processes in their historical and contextual framework, explaining common methods and standards, using a vocabulary and approach that librarians, archivists and other information professionals will understand.

Chapter Overview

This chapter has introduced definitions of imaging, digital technologies and introduced the focus of the text: digital, bitmapped images, which are a subject of interest for those in the information profession due to the growth in use of digital imaging technologies in today's society.

Chapter 2 provides an overview of the history of digital imaging technology. Although digital images have seemed to become popular relatively recently, the technology has been in development for a surprisingly long time, and this chapter demonstrates how the culmination of years of research into imaging, home computing and networking technologies has led, in recent years, to an exponential increase in digital image content being made available, by both institutions and the general public.

Chapter 3 looks at the digital image in detail, examining important features of bitmapped graphics, such as pixels, resolution, interpolation, bit depth, compression and image manipulation. An understanding of these basic technological underpinnings is necessary to frame the topics presented in the remainder of the book, and this chapter aims to approach these topics in such a way as to explain them thoroughly, without recourse to obfuscating technological or mathematical jargon.

Chapter 4 explores digital image file formats and how digital image information is created, stored and rendered by computing systems. The chapter discusses why file formats are necessary, why so many image file formats came to be in existence, and the difference between proprietary and non-proprietary formats. The most popular bitmap image formats used within memory institutions (GIF, PNG, JPEG and TIFF) are discussed in detail, to give an understanding of how and why these became the formats of choice. Additional information is presented about less commonly used formats which may also be of interest to projects dealing with legacy data or dealing with newer, digital camera-based formats.

Chapter 5 provides an overview of how digital images have been used within the library, archive and cultural and heritage sector. In particular, the developing and changing role of digitization within memory institutions is explored, with an emphasis on the creation of digital image surrogates. Current issues regarding the use and usefulness of digital images are explored, as is the approach of institutions to new and developing imaging and Internet technologies.

Chapter 6 discusses the growth in use of digital imaging technologies by the general public, exploring the changing information environment and the transforming role of photography in modern society. In particular, the nature and role of personal collections of digital images is explored. However, the long-term viability of many of these collections is questionable, and this chapter also seeks to explore the role that information professionals may have in educating and informing the general public about the long-term sustainability of their digital image collections.

Chapter 7 examines the type of information which should be stored alongside digital imaging files to aid in their management, long-term sustainability and retrieval: image metadata. Particular emphasis is given to available metadata schemas which are used to describe digital images, and the structured vocabularies and terminologies which can be used to describe the content of images to facilitate use of digital collections. These are juxtaposed with alternative means of searching and retrieving images: folksonomies (tags) and Content Based Image Retrieval techniques.

The final section of the book, Chapter 8, scopes current issues in digital imaging which are pertinent to those working within the information profession. The essential, yet complex issue of colour reproduction and accuracy is addressed, giving pointers to best practice in creating image surrogates which faithfully represent original documents or artefacts. This leads on to issues of quality, and the ways in which institutions may control, or benchmark, digital image fidelity and accuracy. Wider issues regarding digital image manipulation and the changing information environment are presented. Legal issues, such as copyright and rights management are explored. Finally, questions of sustainability and the longevity of digital image collections are noted.

This text is geared towards the type of questions an information professional may ask about the technologies detailed, and framed in such a way as to be of use in library, archive, cultural and heritage information environments. Technologies in common use are given preference over those at the 'leading edge'. Pointers to reference material, appropriate guidelines, standards and applications in the relevant information sectors are given throughout the text where necessary. In addition, each chapter provides further reading and references, for those who wish to learn more about specific topics.

Chapter 2
The History of Digital Images

> Professor Bell is convinced that in the near future it will be possible to see by telegraph, so that a couple conversing by telephone can at the same time see each other's faces. Extending the idea, photographs may yet be transmitted by electricity, and if photographs, why not landscape views? Then the stay-at-home can have the whole world brought before his eyes in a panorama without moving from his chair (All the Year Round 1894, 330, quoted in Marvin 1988, 260 n. 22).

We have seen that the primary aim for converting an image into a numeric or digital format is to facilitate copying, transmission and processing of that pictorial information. Delivering an image in an encoded format is easier than trying to transmit the continuous, analogue representation of a photograph, drawing or document. Encoding images in this way, and for this purpose, has been done for a surprisingly long time, and an understanding of the development and history of digital images can aid in understanding their fundamental characteristics.

Visual imagery is a powerful communicator and the development of digital imaging technologies is tied to the development of communications technology, itself dependent on complex relationships between various scientific discoveries and the culture which encouraged them. Digital photography did not just materialize in the late twentieth century: scientists and technologists had been working for over a hundred years to understand how to use the power of electricity to communicate across long distances and how to use automated computational power to carry out mathematical analysis, eventually finding ways of capturing, distributing, then storing and processing digital information, including images. In turn, the growth in information communications technologies (ICT) has led to the increased production and use of digital images in all areas of life and culture in the developed world.

The aim of this chapter is to explain the genesis and development of digital imaging technologies, in order to impart an understanding of the converging technologies and changing modern environment which have allowed and encouraged increased access to and production of digital information in general, and digital images in particular.

The Age of the Telegraph

Electronic communication between two distant places was possible from the end of the eighteenth century. The social and political upheaval of France's Great

Revolution resulted in a strong need for the French Government to keep in touch with provincial centres: Napoleon realized that rapid communications would give him advantages in turbulent times. A young mechanic from Normandy named Claude Chappe, after experimenting with electricity and a clockwork-like device, developed a system of 'optical telegraphy' which communicated messages via automated semaphore signalling, demonstrating it to the National Convention in 1792. The first line between Paris and Lille was opened in 1794, and eventually reached as far as Rotterdam and Venice. However, operational problems, such as losing the static charge because of high humidity, meant that the performance could be rather erratic.

It was not until the invention of the electrochemical cell battery (by Alessandro Volta in 1800) and further understanding of the relationship between electricity and magnetism, allowing a low electronic current to transmit signals (by Hans Christian Oersted and André Marie Ampère in 1819) that communicating electronic signals over distances would become feasible. Experiments were carried out by many scientists working independently across Europe to construct systems which would allow this to happen, some allowing transmissions of up to a mile before the signal would fade (see Larson 1977; and McConnell et al. 1999, for an overview).

In the early 1830s, the young, but noted, sculptor and portrait painter Samuel Morse, knowing nothing of previous scientific investigation into constructing a long distance system for electric communication, began experimenting with electrical transmission to increase the speed in which messages could be sent and received. His interest came from personal tragedy: while travelling overseas, a letter telling him of his wife's illness did not reach him before her untimely death. Yet Morse had problems in transmitting electrical signals over long enough distances to make his system useful. In 1835, Joseph Henry (a Professor of Mathematics and Natural Philosophy) invented the electromagnetic relay device, a form of electrical amplifier which gave the means of transmitting electrical impulses over short distances, and passing the weak current at the end of the range onto another length of cable which could, in turn, pass the signal on, again and again, avoiding the problem of trying to transmit a signal long distances. Morse eventually asked Joseph Henry for advice, and relays were incorporated into their telegraph (from the Greek 'communicating over distance') system. The first telegraph message was sent in 1837, electrically spelt out in code used by the United States Navy, after which Morse composed his long and short dashed-based code to allow faster transmission of information. By 1844 a telegraph line between Washington and Baltimore had been completed, by 1851 another was laid across the Channel, linking Great Britain to the Continent, by 1854 London and Paris were connected, 1861 saw a line stretch from New York to San Francisco and, in 1866, at the second attempt, a line was successfully laid 2,600 miles across the Atlantic, stretching from Valentia in Ireland to Heart's Content in Newfoundland. The Victorian world had its own network, capable of communicating information through dots and dashes, and increasing the rapidity of information exchange and dissemination (although this did not eliminate the need for human effort as both sending and receiving operators had to perform manual tasks to encode and decode signals).

It should be borne in mind that the invention of the telegraph, in 1837, was two years before Daguerre and Fox Talbot both announced their new discovery of 'photography', creating images directly from the visible world via the passive, mechanical way that light acts on film in a camera. A piece of chemically treated light-sensitive film is exposed to light (via a carefully controlled shutter mechanism and aperture) then developed to produce a negative, which is in turn used to produce a print. Itself a focus of much experimentation and over one hundred years of technological development (Hirsch 2000; Hirsch and Valentino 2001), the ability to create images through photography revolutionized the art world, our sense of history, and perhaps our sense of self: the ability to distribute photographic images via electricity would go on to revolutionize the news and publishing industries too.

Early Electronic Images: Facsimile Machines

The concept of transmitting pictures by electricity occurred to a few scientists at around the same time as the idea of the electric telegraph. In 1843, a young clockmaker from Scotland named Alexander Bain designed and patented a machine for sending drawings over the electric telegraph wire, refining his ideas to construct a working model in time for the London Fair of 1851 (McConnell et al. 1999). Based on revolving cylinders, the picture, made of non-conducting ink, was 'scanned in' by a metal needle which moved along the length of the cylinder (rather like a long playing record). Wherever the non-conducting ink was present, the current in the circuit between the transmitter and receiver was interrupted. The receiver, another cylinder, coloured the copy of the picture in by electrolytic action with a metal needle moving over a chemically treated sheet of paper, missing out the areas where the current had been interrupted and producing a copy of the image in negative. The image had passed from physical, to electrical, to physical. Bain's ideas were seen at the 1851 fair by the English physicist, Frederick Bakewell, who built prototypes of a transmitter and receiver. The Bain-Bakewell picture telegraph was never used in everyday practice – it was too far ahead of its time – but is technically important because it establishes the principle of optical transmission: that of scanning an input and reassembling an image for output.

Word of these technologies spread through the scientific community. An Italian, Giovanni Caselli, applied for an English patent in 1855 for his version of a machine for 'improvements in transmitting *fac-simile* writings and drawings by means of electric currents' (cited in McConnell et al. 1999, 15). Caselli established the first commercial facsimile service, between Paris and Lyon, in 1865. Reports of Caselli's 'Pantelegraph', as he called it, were so widespread that the Chinese emperor even sent representatives to Paris to assess how useful it was. Such facsimile machines are now commonly available, once called telefax, now more commonly called fax: making remote copies of a document by scanning the page being sent and producing electrical signals that represent it. The signals are transmitted from machine to machine via the telephone line and at the receiving end, signals are changed back into an image and printed.

By the mid-1860s, the developed world possessed the understanding and the means to enable an image to be scanned in, distributed and reproduced electronically. Photographic images were first sent by fax in the 1890s; the screening process used to print the pictures (still in use in newspapers today, printing the picture by a fine pattern of small dots, with larger dots representing dark areas and smaller ones representing lighter areas) provided the discreet units which enabled encoding: the size of the dots determining the shade of grey reproduced in the copy. However, these early means of transmission and duplication were certainly not digital: telegraphic signals are not binary because they also employ pauses between bursts of current that contribute to a message, meaning that signals are not strictly resolved into a numerical code. It is also worth noting that these systems had no capacity to process or store images, and the information that comprised the early fax transmissions was only in existence for a brief period between the sender and receiver. However, the concept of capturing and breaking down an image, sending, then reconstructing it elsewhere forms the basis of digital imaging technologies. This underlying concept remained the same as the technology which enabled transmission of data was developed: as well as the telegraph, the more sophisticated telephone system and its related networks was becoming more commonplace.

An easy way to break up an image into individual parts is to lay a grid over it and deconstruct it into discreet dots (or 'pixels', see pp. 35–37), separated into scan lines. If the size of the grid is known, and a numeric value is assigned to the colour in each square in the grid, a numeric, or digital, representation of an image has been produced which can be reconstructed elsewhere. The term 'raster' is used to describe such images, constituted from small definable units of colour. The word raster comes from Latin via German, meaning 'to rake', describing how the image is broken up into definable rows and sections of picture elements or pixels. (The term 'bitmap' replaced the word raster for these type of images later, once they were stored in digital computers, as the colour of each individual square is 'mapped' to a defined number of bits or memory, see pp. 8–9.)

In the late 1900s, technological advances meant automated light-sensitive scanning was available: the optical system which captured the images was dependent on analogue cathode ray tubes and photomultiplier outputs, which produced a more or less faithful electrical analogue of the variation of reflectance of the document surface according to whether it was light or dark at a given spot. By using such optical technology to analyse an image broken up into discreet sections or pixels, digital scanning and encoding of photographs was possible. This was established in 1920 with the Bartlane system, named after its British inventors, H.G. Bartholomew and M.L. MacFarlane:

> The picture to be sent was first printed as a screened image (as used in newspapers). It was then scanned [optically], and the size of each screen dot was assigned a code and an automatic tape perforator punched as a line of holes across a standard paper telegraph tape. The number of holes punched corresponded to the size of the dot on the image, ranging from all holes for large dots to one hole for small dots. The tape was then sent as at telegraph message on the standard Western Union automatic equipment and received as a duplicate tape that the receiving equipment converted into a photographic image (McConnell et al. 1999, 29).

Initially, each pixel could only be assigned one of five numerical values, relating to five shades of grey. By 1929 this had increased to allow 15 shades of grey to be captured and represented. Many early transatlantic news images appeared in newspapers after being delivered via this system: their slightly blocky nature can be easily identified. It is important to note that sending an image transatlantically cut down transmission time from a week (the time it took a ship to cross from the US to the UK) to a couple of hours. This is reflected in the increasing pace at which newspapers featured photographs of events on the other side of the Atlantic at that time.

By the 1930s, the transmission of images by digital fax was commonplace:

> with many major companies involved, including the Associated Press, AT&T, RCA, Western Union, and the *New York Times*. News organizations developed not only machines but also networks to distribute photographs to the plethora of magazines and newspapers that wanted them (Lipkin 2005, 122).

Yet although the digital fax converted images into digital signals by breaking them into refined units and expressing these units numerically:

> it was missing the vital elements of image processing and electric storage. The amount of data needed to store or process an image was simply too large for the computers of the time. The Associated Press's system of the 1930s was capable of sending an eight-by-ten-inch image at 170 lines per inch, with eight bits per pixel. (This means that each pixel could be described by eight binary digits, allowing 256 possible shades of gray.) A single eight-bit image this size would require 2,306,867 binary digits to describe it, an astronomically large number even for computers that would be developed twenty years in the future. The ENIAC (Electronic Numerical Integrator and Computer), [the first fully electronic computer, and] state of the art in 1949, used 18,000 vacuum tubes, filled a large room, consumed as much electric power as some small towns, and yet could only store twenty decimal numbers at a time. ENIAC was adequate for calculating gunnery tables, which was its intended purpose, but it was unthinkable that such a machine would be able to store and process images (ibid. 122).

Numerous large, cumbersome computing devices followed in the decades after, capable of doing mathematical equations faster than a human but able to do a fraction of what modern laptops (or even mobile phones) can do today. Access to computers was limited, and computer time was both expensive and scarce. Input to these machines was done by punchcard, which represented numbers or text by the presence or absence of holes in predefined positions on stiff paper, which could then be fed into the machine. These computers did not have a graphical interface; they did not have the technology to display images, and programs were fed in, at first by punch card and later by command line interfaces. Early printout devices were plotters: large basic machines which could not draw curves and so any output data was composed simply of lines. Processing and outputting digital images with a computer remained decades away.

Electronic Image Development

The first 'electronic' image was made by the mathematician and artist, Ben F. Laposky in 1950: an analogue wave pattern photographed from a cathode ray oscilloscope, and named Oscillon Number Four – Electron Abstraction. These 'Oscillons' were generated by using an analogue computer to control the output viewable on a scientific oscilloscope screen, in which an electron beam was moved from place to place in a pattern which traced out individual lines of an image and captured on high speed photographic film (see Laposky 1969 for more information). Much experimentation with analogue means of displaying signals via cathode ray technologies preceded the development of computer graphics. Investment at the time was also being made in television technologies, and techniques were invented which would enable live images from television to be stored onto tape. The stream was broken into 15 frames per second, and each frame divided by a grid into small units. Cathode ray tube optical sensors were used to capture light, shade and intensity values for each of these 'pixels', which were then converted into digital electrical impulses and stored on tape along with the associated sound data. The first broadcast quality video recorder, the VR–1000, invented by Charles P. Ginsburg and the Ampex Corporation, was available in 1956 (see Burns 1998 for an introduction). These developments indicate the growth in interest and understanding of the potentials which could lie in being able to manipulate and store image data digitally, and the attempt to produce and store image data. However, what was required to make digital images more usable was development in computing technologies which would allow these images to be manipulated.

The Digital Image and Computers

It would be over 35 years after the invention of the digital image that computers could be powerful enough to store or manipulate them. In 1957, Russell A. Kirsch and colleagues at the National Bureau of Standards in Gaithersburg, Maryland (Kirsch et al. 1957) constructed a simple mechanical drum scanner which they used to trace variations in intensity over the surfaces of photographs. The resulting signals were converted into arrays of 176 by 176 square binary digits, 'each binary digit representing the blackness of a unit square 0.25mm by 0.25mm in the picture' (ibid. 223) using the familiar photomultiplier tubes as sensors which would emit an analogue electric current equivalent to the amount of light that hit it. This data was then fed into a SEAC 1500 word binary computer which made various line drawings from the file information. Patterns of light and shade had finally become electronically processable digital information, and the resulting image 'had all the hallmarks of a modern digital photograph, being binary, digital, electric, bitmapped and stored' (Lipkin 2005, 123). Kirsch also suggested uses for image processing research, in developing character recognition software, or simulating the way in which the human visual system functions, stating that this was:

> a new type of research facility … which allows complex investigations to be made into the nature of pictorial information and into ways in which computers may be programmed to process such information with the same comparative ease that characterizes human processing of visual information (Kirsch et al. 1957, 228).

His impetus for constructing a scanner in the first place had been to provide data for the field of image processing: computers can only analyse data if it is in digital form, and his team wished to develop image-enhancement procedures and filters. Kirsch noted, of the first computer picture made from binary scans of a photograph of his baby son, 'With two superimposed binary scans, it was possible to approximate sufficient gray levels to make the image recognizable, though not satisfactory to grandparents' (Kirsch 1998, 9). Digital imaging using computer technology and image processing research had begun (but it should be noted that, 50 years on, computers still can not process and understand visual information as effectively as humans, see pp. 181–183).

The Digital Image and the Space Race

A major thrust in the development of digital imaging and the production of computer graphics came with the political and cultural events in 1960s America: vast sums of money were spent on new technological developments as a means of defence in the Cold War. The resulting 'space race' saw the establishment of the United States National Aeronautics and Space Administration (NASA) programme in 1958, partially in response to the Soviet Union's launch of the first artificial satellite. Research and development in the area of information, communication and computer technology grew exponentially in government funded academic and commercial research programmes during this period.

Advances in digital imaging technologies were many and varied. Analogue video signals, sent back from NASA's unmanned planetary Ranger spacecraft, were converted into digital format to be stored on tape, then enhanced using image processing routines, to remove spurious 'noise' received with the picture signal, and improve contrast in the photographs (Cargill Hall 1977). During the 1960s, while utilizing space probes to map the surface of the moon, developing protocols to enable human space flight and in preparation for the moon landings, NASA began to use digital technology in order to pass communication signals back to earth which were not distorted by the shielding effect exerted by the atmosphere on analogue radio waves (Noordung 1995). This required the development of new protocols to transmit and receive digital information. The development of the technology to enable space exploration also meant experimenting with the imaging technology required to record those explorations (for example, in the Gemini Project, see Grimwood 1963 for records of the experiments carried out in beaming digital images back to the earth): the television pictures beamed back from the moon landings were digital in format. Digital imaging was also necessary to embrace the spy potential of satellites, and governmental agencies, such as NASA, ploughed research resources into the development of image processing techniques to improve the quality of pictures transmitted back to earth. Digital imaging as a commercial research and product development field was truly established, with many external companies contributing: the term 'computer graphics' was coined in the early 1960s by computer scientists working at Boeing Corporation (Fetter 1964) to describe attempts at the synthesis and manipulation of digital visual content.

The Development of Personal Computing

Although there was growing interest in capturing, processing and outputting digital image information, user interaction with computers at this time was still accomplished through a 'command line interface'. Instructions to the computer were text, typed in via a keyboard, in often arcane, bizarre and perplexing notation. The most important development in relation to digital imaging, during the post-war period, was the creation of computing environments that allowed graphical information to be presented to the user, and manipulated, on screen: the production of 'computer graphics'. Research in human–computer interaction and user–friendliness, emanating from two laboratories funded by the Advanced Research Projects Agency's (ARPA) Information Processing Techniques Office in the 1960s, developed many of the features that have become all pervasive in personal computing environments today. A small human factors research group at the Stanford Research Institute, founded in 1963 by Doug Engelbart, began to develop what they termed the 'electronic office' – a system that would integrate text and pictures in a way that was then unprecedented. The modern computing environment owes much to the work of Engelbart: his best known invention was the mouse, developed in 1965. During the same period, David Evan's and Ivan Sutherland's large graphics research group at the University of Utah developed Sketchpad, the first computer program to store images and display them directly onto the screen, allowing the user to zoom in and out of image sections. Sketchpad involved drawing directly onto a cathode ray tube display with a 'light pen' and then modifying the geometrical possibilities with a keyboard. It is widely regarded as being a crucial breakthrough in both digital imaging technologies and human computer interaction (Darley 1990). These systems were then too expensive to be practical ('in the 1960s a fully equipped minicomputer occupied several square yards of floor space and cost up to $100,000' (Campbell-Kelly and Aspray 2004, 238)), and the cost of meeting these demands could be justified only for research purposes in a few universities and some large industrial research laboratories, but, by the end of the decade, the price of computer components was falling fast, enabling companies to exploit the ideas, which had been presented at various conferences and symposiums, commercially.

Strategic planners in Xerox had become concerned at the competition from Japanese photocopier manufacturers: perhaps it was time to diversify from their exclusive product? In order to drive research and development, Xerox established the Palo Alto Research Center (PARC) in 1969 to work on technology 'for the office of the future', which emerged as a network of desktop computers called the 'Alto'. The graphical user interface evolved through the design of this series: the Alto had a mouse, a bitmapped (i.e. raster rather than cathode ray tracing) graphical display capable of presenting two- or three-dimensional graphics and pointing mechanisms, and the 'desktop' had the now familiar icons, folders and drop-down menus which feature in today's computer systems. The Alto was unveiled at the National Computer Conference in Chicago in May 1981, although it remained too expensive to be commercially successful. This model was followed by the 'cheaper' Xerox Star (at $40,000 it was still priced higher than a year's salary), but this early computer influenced Steve Jobs and Steve Wozniak to produce the first Apple Macintosh computer and so paved the way for technical development of home and personal computing.

It is beyond the scope of this book to cover in detail the history of the development of the personal computer (see Campbell-Kelly and Aspray 2004; Swedin and Ferro 2005 for readable introductions), but it is useful to appreciate that falling costs of computer components and rising storage and processing capacities of computers, meant that access to computational power became more commonplace, allowing (and requiring) research and development to be carried out on the intricacies of picture-generating software and systems. Computing science researchers had to develop hardware and software technology, and data structures which:

> in some sense would mirror the barely realized but visually obvious relationships inherent in a two-dimensional picture. (In fact, the origin of much of today's data management theory can be traced to early work in computer graphics.) Algorithms for hidden-line removal, shading, and scan conversion were needed and generally proved far more complex than was first anticipated. Even as ostensibly simple a task as drawing a straight line segment or arc of a circle on a digitally oriented display turned out to require algorithms which were by no means trivial (Weibel 1984, 54).

Standards began to emerge for the format in which image data should be saved and stored (see Chapter 4), and techniques were developed to make image files smaller through a means of compression (see pp. 50–58), which made transmission and storage of images less computationally expensive. Additionally, advances in display technology meant there was a move away from displays which drew pictures on the face of a cathode ray tube (vector devices created pictures by drawing many straight line segments on a storage tube screen in 'random-scan' displays). Instead, raster technologies became more popular, displaying the screen in the same way that television sets do, painting the image in a fixed sequence, from left to right and top to bottom in a sequence of individual dots or pixels. The components to drive raster displays were becoming mass produced and therefore affordable, and:

> as the 1970s came to a close … Display memory got cheaper, making bit-mapped raster displays feasible. Rasters offered a host of benefits: high data content, flicker-free display, low-cost color and low-cost monitors. Some line quality was sacrificed, because the several-hundred-line-resolution pictures (memory was cheap, but not that cheap!) had the 'jaggies'. But for the first time, brilliantly colored, filled in graphics became affordable. Raster emerged as the clearly dominant technology by the end of the 1970s (Machover 1998, 4).

In the mid-1980s, expensive, high end computer systems not readily available to the general public could run one of the dedicated image manipulation packages which were becoming available (such as Scitex and Quarkxpress). Used to retouch or create sophisticated digital images and publishing layouts by newspapers, publishers, photographers and artists, these programs replaced manual, highly skilled, time-consuming procedures that had to be carried out by trained photographic technicians. Commercial database systems began to be developed which enabled storage and retrieval of image data (Tamura and Yokoya 1984). Artists experimented with the limits of this new technology in earnest, and the related field of computer graphics began to see the use of digitally created animations and scene manipulation in the film industry (Darley 1990). Meanwhile, home computers continued to develop and were powerful enough to deal with graphic formats by the end of the 1980s. These provided to the general public, among other things, an affordable means to store and display digital images and perform sophisticated image and graphic manipulation tasks using software such as Adobe Photoshop (launched in 1990). By the close of the twentieth century, most basic, affordable personal computing systems were able to handle standard full colour images, and were capable of running sophisticated photo-manipulation software that allowed digital manipulation which rivalled the accuracy and resolution of traditional photographic darkrooms.

The Network Environment

Alongside the development of technologies which would enable home computing to become available, engineers and computer scientists were also busy constructing networks which would allow computers to source and exchange information. The Internet's roots stem from the US's defence tactics in the Cold War at the end of the 1960s, where links were established between the available computers via the telephone network to establish data sharing between remote sites: if one site was destroyed, the other computers would hopefully still communicate and data could be preserved and moved around the network. The early ARPAnet system (the name stems from the Advance Research Projects Agency of the US defence programme) was used by the military – although histories of the development of the protocols which underpin the network would also seem to suggest that many computer scientists were undertaking research for enjoyment, to see if developing a large-scale network of networks, or the Internet, was possible (see Naughton 2000 for an entertaining and thorough introduction to the Internet's development). Non-military computers were allowed to connect to the network in the late 1970s, while Europe developed its own networked system which could also communicate with the US network. Gradually, a web of computer networks began to spread throughout the western world, predominantly funded by government agencies and used exclusively in research, until the first commercial companies began to operate on the Internet in the late 1980s. However, the Internet then was very different to the environment we are familiar with today: there were no standards for data representation or display, and it was difficult to know what exactly you were downloading when you requested a file or data set. There was no *lingua franca* to ensure data would look the same on different machines, and the slow network speeds and slow processing speeds of computers connected to the network, ensured that using the Internet remained quite a specialist endeavour.

This changed when a young researcher working at the CERN particle physics laboratory in Geneva had a dream about a way that the structure and format of textual documents could be retained for sharing over the network. Aware of work done at IBM about textual markup and representation, and the concept of hypertext – at the time a theoretical system that could allow textual information to be read in non-linear fashion, akin to the way the human brain connects related information sources – Tim Berners-Lee developed Hypertext Markup Language (HTML), a succinct, self-contained set of tags and rules (although based on the already existing Standard Generalized Markup Language) which would allow the format of text to be encoded into a simple ASCII text file. By Christmas Day 1990, he finished the first browser (software which could display HTML) and simply called it 'World Wide Web' (Berners-Lee 1999). Use of his system within the scientific community grew, establishing a network of servers on the Internet (computers which host and deliver digital information when it is requested) particularly to deal with World Wide Web traffic. HTML was proving to be an efficient and useful common means for information exchange via networked computing.

The World Wide Web browser was entirely text-based. The first web browser to incorporate images, Mosaic, took the functionality of World Wide Web and allowed images to be included in the main body of the browser window. Developed by a team of staff and students at the National Center for Supercomputing Applications at the University of Illinois at Urbana-Champaign, and launched in February 1993, Mosaic was incredibly popular. The ability to incorporate images into web pages increased both the web's usability and available information: digital images soon became intrinsic to web design, for use as logos, banners and backgrounds, as well as providing image-based content and subject matter for web pages. For those creating web pages, the ability to create and manipulate digital image data became a necessity as images were proving to be a powerful communicator in the Web domain.

Throughout the 1990s the physical Internet network, and the number of World Wide Web servers delivering information via this network, expanded dramatically with a corresponding exponential increase in users, creators and number of web pages. The Internet is becoming increasingly difficult to measure,[1] but it can be reasonably assumed that there are now more web pages than there are people on the planet. The Internet, and its subset the World Wide Web, is the perfect vehicle for the distribution of both professional and user created digital content: having a reliable and fast network environment which can act as a way to share, disseminate and view digital information has encouraged the creation of both digital versions of analogue material (through digitization) and digital born media. The role of the Internet in encouraging the uptake of digital image technology should not be under-estimated, and digital images of artefacts, objects, people and places are often the central focus of information available online.

Digital Image Capture Devices

But what of the peripheral devices which allow digital images to be created, such as scanners and digital cameras? Creating digital images requires an input which converts an analogue optical input into electrical signal. Creating raster digital images requires a sensor which can pick up the intensity (and nowadays colour) of light for each given pixel in the grid. Optical, automated light sensor technology had been available since the 1900s, and was used in the Bartlane and digital fax scanning systems. It is fair to say that very little has been written about the history and development of these early systems, which became relatively widespread (histories exist for early Optical Character Recognition systems dependent on such scanning technology, but these tend to concentrate on the 'reading' capacity of systems which were able to convert printed characters into another format, see

1 See www.news.netcraft.com for a monthly web server survey, measuring how many servers are active online, and www.internetworldstats.com for an attempt at providing statistics about Internet usage.

Schantz 1982 for a comprehensive history of attempts at automatically reading text which date back to 1809.) Early scanners were predominantly drum scanners, where the article was wrapped around a drum while a single cathode ray light sensor checked the brightness at a single spot becoming a chain of observations as the drum continually spun the image. However, as discussed above, there was no capacity to store these scans which were created to enable transmission of the image.

Scanners

Kirsch's drum scanning device, for inputting images into the computer, created the first device for inputting digital image data directly into a computer and several decisions made:

> in the construction of the first scanner have been enshrined in engineering practice ever since. Perhaps the most insidious was the decision to use square pixels. Simple engineering considerations as well as the limited memory capacity of SEAC dictated that the scanner represent images as rectangular arrays … No attempt was made to predicate the digitization protocol on the nature of the image. Every image was made to fit the Procrustean requirement of the scanner (Kirsch 1998, 10).

A larger scanner than the 176 by 176 pixel array (SEAC scanner) would be necessary if the computer was to have access to larger images. In 1964, R.T. Moore, M.C. Stark and L. Cahn at the National Bureau of Standards built a precision scanner that could accommodate a much larger image, built around a commercial lathe body offering dimensional precision of 1/200 inch and capturing 2.98 million pixels of information at one of eight levels of grey (Moore et al. 1964). They also wrote computer programs which could manipulate the information, save the image to magnetic tape and produce printouts. However, such scanners were bulky and expensive, and required specialist magnetic tape machines to save the information. Additionally, cathode ray sensor technologies were both expensive and difficult to maintain. IBM began selling these scanners commercially in 1968 (Datamation 1966). However, it was not until a more sophisticated, lighter, electronic device for sensing the light across a given area was created that scanner and camera technology would become more accessible, portable and widespread.

In 1969, two researchers at Bell Labs, George Smith and Willard Boyle, invented a device which used silicon's reaction to light to produce digital signals. Silicon is sensitive to visible light and also broad bands of the electromagnetic spectrum. When light hits silicon, the action of the photons on its surface causes it to release electrons in direct proportion to the amount of light received. Smith and Boyle developed a technique to transfer this electrical charge along the surface of a semiconductor, constructing a device which contained an array of linked light-sensitive sensors. The digital charge across the array is converted to a varying voltage, which can be sampled, digitized and stored in computer memory. By 1970

Bell's researchers were able to capture images with these simple Charge Coupled Devices, or CCDs. Several companies, including Fairchild Semiconductor, RCA and Texas Instruments soon began manufacturing CCDs. The first imaging CCD was produced by Fairchild in 1974 and had a format of 100 x 100 pixels, (giving a total of 10,000 pixels, or 0.01 megapixels). Component prices soon fell and these lightweight, small light-sensitive devices went on to change the course of imaging in disciplines ranging from astronomy to biotechnology, and the production of commercial digital imaging capture technology (see Janesick 2000 for a comprehensive introduction and history of CCDs and TASI 2006a for an accessible overview of the technology behind CCDs).

CCDs were first integrated into scanner technology in the early 1970s. Ray Kurzweil developed the notion of the flatbed, as opposed to drum, scanner: where the sensor could move across the paper, rather than having paper move around a drum with the scan head held fixed. Such an idea was dependent on the use of small, lightweight, light-sensitive devices and Kurzweil's flat-bed scanner used Fairfield 500 linear CCD arrays to scan a horizontal strip of page about 1.2 inches in height at a time, building up the complete image in the computer. This product became commercially available in 1975, although remained expensive and slow compared to today's flatbed scanners (Kurzweil 2007). In a now a familiar story, the falling cost of computer components led to further technological developments and products becoming available: Microtek launched a black and white, 300dpi (dots per inch), flatbed, sheet feed scanner in 1985; colour digital flatbed scanners were launched at the general market by Xerox and Kodak in 1991. The Twain standard for interfacing scanner software with computer hardware was released in early 1992, providing a standard set of function calls by which a computer could control the features of any brand of scanner attached to it. Flatbed scanners are now viewed as essential, affordable peripheral devices, and at the time of writing, basic entry level models were available for less than half the price of this book (although professional scanning systems still command a premium). Smaller, portable hand-held scanners and individual scanning pens, which can capture lines of text from printed material and incorporate them directly into word processing software, are also available. Most people who want to (in the developed world, anyway) can now have access to scanning technology, and it is relatively simple to create digital versions of analogue images (although standards and procedures for digitization projects exist to ensure that digital images are captured properly, see pp. 120–122).

Cameras

Early developments in capturing images electronically with a camera involved using technology similar to that which drove early digital video recorders: in 1986 Canon introduced its first fully integrated professional still video camera system (SVC). Slightly larger than a 35mm auto focus SLR camera, it used a floppy disk to record 50 low or 25 high resolution images, stored in conventional video format.

Followed by Nikon and Sony, these cameras provided a practical alternative to the use of silver-based photographic film and were favoured by the news media who wished to quickly transmit pictorial information: however they were still analogue, requiring conversion of the images via an image capture card if they were to be made available for computational manipulation or transmission. Image quality, based on the video formats, was also rather poor. Relatively costly and mainly for professional and industrial use, still video cameras were a precursor to digital cameras as we understand them: devices that can capture images directly in digital format and store them on memory cards or a computer disk.

The development of digital cameras was also dependent on the adoption of CCDs as a lightweight, light-sensitive device for image capture. The first recorded attempt at building a digital camera was by Steve Sasson, working as an engineer at Eastman Kodak, in December 1975. Sasson used the 100 x 100 pixel CCD array developed by Fairchild Semiconductor as its sensor. Around the size of a toaster, the camera weighed 8 pounds, recorded black and white images to a cassette tape and took 23 seconds to capture its first 0.01 megapixel image. The prototype camera was a technical exercise and not intended for production: CCDs were expensive, and high quality image capture devices require large CCD arrays which were not available at the time. However, Kodak's short-sightedness in not pursuing the commercial possibilities of this invention meant that other companies would be the first to develop digital image capture devices, and capture the resulting market that went with it (Dobbin 2005).

Early 'digital cameras' actually used scanning backs: a CCD array inserted into the traditional film camera in the place of film. This usually involved removing the back of the camera and replacing it with a bulky digital unit which held the CCD array, electronics and liquid crystal display for preview. These early hybrid models produced low quality images, as they were dependent on the sensitivity and size of the sensors, but throughout the 1990s the technology improved and by the end of the decade several manufacturers were producing these for individual camera models. The benefit of this approach is that high quality lenses can still be used for photographic capture; and scanning backs are still used today for professional digital photography when image quality is important, such as in the fashion industry or taking detailed pictures of manuscript material. These professional, expensive, scanbacks now incorporate large arrays of sensors: the Phase One P45 digital back, launched in 2006, is capable of capturing 39 megapixels of image data per shot (Phase One 2006). It is usually used with high performance Hasselblad cameras, which are renowned for their quality and have a very large sensor area, although such systems still cost upwards of $40,000 at the time of writing. Where digital imaging technology has had most uptake, however, is in the smaller, cheaper, consumer entry level, point and shoot cameras, which now account for the majority of the digital camera market.

The first all-digital cameras began to appear in the late 1980s. Designed for amateur point and click photography of friends, family and scenery, these usually have a direct viewfinder, with later models incorporated an LCD display on the back of the camera to display pictures. By 1991, inexpensive versions, often bundled with image processing software, were available: space shuttle astronauts began to carry digital cameras on their missions and use laptop computers for immediate image processing (Advanced Imaging Magazine 1991). Around the same time, a different type of sensor, the CMOS (Complementary Metal Oxide Semiconductor, which had been developed around the same time as CCDs but technical issues and cost prevented its widespread use) went into mainstream production. CMOS sensors operate in a slightly different manner than CCDs (see TASI 2006a for an overview) but nowadays have the benefit of having much lower fabrication costs for sensors capable of capturing more detail. As a result, the performance and functionality of entry level digital cameras rose, while lowering manufacturing costs and increased marketing initiatives resulted in prices to the consumer falling. By the mid-2000s, high quality, affordable digital cameras were readily available to the general public. At the time of writing, fully digital professional level digital SLR (Single Lens Reflex) cameras, which allow greater control over such variables as focus and exposure, are becoming available at a more affordable cost. Digital cameras are now viable replacements for film-based models, and recent advances in sensor technology promise to produce digital cameras with lower costs and superior resolution to photographic film.

Digital cameras are popular in both the professional and amateur environment for a variety of reasons: the instantaneous viewing of pictures taken (rather than waiting for hours or days for film processing); the lower cost of operating (unlike film cameras, which require film supplies and film processing; after purchasing the camera itself there is little continued outlay necessary to view pictures unless they are printed out); the ability to email pictures, or mount them on websites, with very little bother; the fact that images can be copied or printed repeatedly without degrading; the ability to take hundreds of pictures on one device without processing (unlike photographic film, which typically captures 24 or 36 images per roll); the ability to insert metadata into the file (see Chapter 7); the photographer having the choice regarding which pictures to print before paying for a whole set to be developed; the photographer having access to desktop-based manipulation and processing technologies (rather than have to rely on a remote laboratory); the reduced environmental impact of digital versus chemical film products (and their associated plastic packaging); and the shrinking size of devices (making them incredibly portable), including the integration of digital cameras into ubiquitous, lightweight mobile phone technologies.

In 1997, Philippe Kahn, driven by his desire to share photographs of his newborn daughter, developed technology that cobbled together his mobile phone and digital camera to allow him to send a digital photograph through a mobile phone (Maney 2007). A few years later, inexpensive mobile phones fitted with digital cameras could take photographs of the same quality as digital cameras that cost ten times that amount a decade before. In 2003, worldwide sales of film cameras (60 million units) and digital stand-alone cameras (35 million units) were almost matched by sales of mobile phones containing cameras (90 million units:

source Henning 2003). Infotrends, a leading market research and consulting firm for digital imaging technologies and markets, reported that sales of sub $1000 digital cameras reached 60 million worldwide in 2004, 78 million in 2005, and were expected to sell around 100 million units in 2006. They predict sales of over 100 million units a year to continue until 2010 (Infotrends 2005). There are portents that traditional film photography is now becoming a specialist hobby or profession: Eastman Kodak announced it had stopped selling traditional film cameras in the United States, Canada and Western Europe in 2004 (ZDNet 2004). Konica Minolta and Fuji Photo Film announced they had withdrawn from the traditional film and camera business in 2006, and many high street retailers no longer stock film cameras or photographic film supplies (Hoyle and Lewis 2006). As Lipkin (2005, 126) succinctly says, 'It is possible that a child born in the year 2000 will grow up with no experience of film cameras, just as a child born in the 1990s has no experience with vinyl albums.' The format of image information being produced by modern western society continues to change rapidly.

Camera, Computer and the Network

Towards the end of the twentieth century, a number of converging technologies encouraged the uptake of digital photography and digital imaging. The availability of desktop machines to view and manipulate images, the networked environment provided by the Internet for the sharing and dissemination of images, and the availability of cheap computational peripherals, such as scanners, digital cameras and mobile phones, all encouraged the production and use of digital images by both individuals and institutions. It was followed by a corresponding rise in user expectations regarding the quality and amount of digital image information that should be able to be produced by desktop machines or be available online.

Public bodies began to fund programs that would make digital information available to online users. Libraries, archives, museums and art galleries began to create digital representations of their collections for online use (the history and development of digitization programs and strategies, and the uptake of these technologies by the information sector, is covered more fully in Chapter 5). The creation of digital content by professional institutions was matched with an increased interest from the general user community in creating their own content. In mid-2003, the term 'Web 2.0' was coined to describe a growing online phenomenon of websites which were community driven, service-based, with high-level tools which also harnessed the collective intelligence of large groups of users (see O'Reilly 2005 for a comprehensive overview of the concepts which underlie 'Web 2.0'). Online storage and organization of personal digital image collections, often made available to the general public and made more searchable through the use of tagging and metadata (see Chapter 7), has been one of the success stories of Web 2.0. Online services such as Yahoo/Flickr; Google; Photobucket; MSN; and MySpace host hundreds of millions of photographs posted by millions of users (see Chapter 6). Photography has now become vastly more popular than it ever was and has been transformed from a personal to a community experience. An expanding service industry is growing alongside the user generated content, providing, for example, online services for ordering digital prints and facilities for digital photographers to sell or license their images for advertising purposes. Such industries are undermining traditional photography manufacturers and photo-stock agencies.

The pervasive nature of digital imaging technologies in the developed world has also led to recent changes in news coverage, as the general public can now capture an immediate and personal response to subjects and events that would traditionally be covered by news agencies, often before traditional media outlets are aware of the incident or able to despatch reporters. Within 24 hours of the 7 July 2005 bombings in London 'around 1,000 photos and 20 pieces of amateur video were sent in to the BBC News website, with many being featured on the site' (BBC 2005a). This footage can aid Police in their investigations and calls for the public to submit such eye-witness material are now common (BBC 2005b). In December 2005, when an oil depot exploded in Buncefield (Hertfordshire, UK), causing one of the largest fires within Europe since 1945, 6,500 images of the blaze were emailed to the BBC within hours (BBC 2005c). User generation of digital content is set to become ever more common, and more important, blurring the distinction between professional and amateur, democratizing news reporting, and providing historical and judicial evidence. Photographic and video evidence from mobile phones and digital cameras captured the events of the Virginia Tech college massacre by a gunman in April 2007, with a spokesperson for Sky News remarking that user generated content is 'another source, just as the diaries of infantrymen are a source for a historian studying Waterloo' (Robinson 2007). The maintenance and preservation of such digital material for future users, historians and investigators is the responsibility of the professionals within the media and information environment. Understanding the developing technologies is the first step to ascertaining how best to deal with this overflow of digital image information.

Conclusion

The history of digital imaging is rooted in the eighteenth and nineteenth centuries, but it is only in the last 10 to 15 years that it has existed as a practical technology due to developments in communications technology, increased access to cheaper and faster computers, and the lowering cost and improving performance of the peripherals which create digital images. The means to capture, process, display, disseminate and print photograph like digital images, which had hitherto been available in only a few specialist shops, now falls within the reach of a wide community of artists, photographers and information professionals, as well as the general public. The recent rapid uptake of digital imaging and the growing provision of services and online tools, means it appears to be, and functions as, a new medium, changing the information environment and creating new concerns for those working in the information professions.

Further Reading

There is very little cohesive writing that has been done on the history of digital imaging technology: aside from the very specialized histories on, say, fax or CCDs. Historical overviews are scattered between photographic and computing textbooks, often as footnotes or asides. Some recent photography books mention the history of digital images: Hirsch and Valentino, in their book *Photographic Possibilities, The Expressive Use of Ideas, Materials and Processes* (2001) present a useful and overarching overview of the history, application and techniques involved in both traditional and digital photography, giving a very readable and useful account of the capturing, storing and printing processes used with each medium. Lipkin (2005) explores the extent to which modern artists are utilizing digital images coupling works by well known contemporary artists with an analysis and history of the medium. Hamber (2006) details the development of commercially available digital imaging technology in a consideration of how digitization has been used by the commercial art world, while a chapter in the text of Rudolf (2006) describes the recent evolution of the technologies which underpin digital cameras. Other recent general histories of photography touch on recent digital developments: coverage of these will become more widespread as older editions are updated in the future.

An overview of the development of computing can be found in Ceruzzi (2003); Campbell-Kelly and Aspray (2004); and Swedin and Ferro (2005). Berners-Lee (1999) and Naughton (2000) are essential reading regarding the development of the Internet. Although these texts are all light on the history and development of digital images, it can be useful to appreciate the history and development in computing technologies which underpin recent changes in society and working practice.

Texts specifically regarding the use of digital images in the library and information environment are recommended in Chapter 5.

Chapter 3
Digital Image Fundamentals

> Pixel, noun: A mischievous, magical spirit associated with screen displays. The computer industry has frequently borrowed from mythology: witness the sprites in computer graphics, the demons in artificial intelligence, and the trolls in the marketing department (anonymous).[1]

To understand issues regarding the capture, use, delivery, storage and preservation of digital images, it is necessary to understand the fundamental aspects of how digital images function. Given that the majority of digital images created by the home or professional user are bitmaps (see Chapters 5 and 6), this chapter details the fundamental characteristics of bitmap images and the underlying principles which drive bitmap representation: the individual pixels within the grid; the colour information stored about each pixel (bit depth); the spacing of individual pixels (resolution); changing image size (interpolation); and issues regarding file size and the compression of bitmap information. It also highlights various issues of relevance to the information professional working with digital image data.

Pixels

Bitmapped digital images work by fooling the eye. Any image can be divided into a uniform grid, with each element in the grid assigned a colour. Like an individual tile in a mosaic or the squares in a chessboard, each individual picture element is a discreet unit which has a place and a colour within the larger image. The human eye-brain system is keen to resolve this back into a continuous tone image.[2] The grid becomes invisible when small enough, as the size of individual elements falls below the threshold of human vision. The image appears to have continuous tone as we perceive the image as a whole, rather than being made up of constituent building blocks, 'For most viewers, this occurs when there are fewer than 50 pixels per inch'

1 This commonly repeated quote is often attributed to Jeff Mayer (also known as 'Moriarty' in Usenet forums), but in a personal communication to the author he denied being the source.

2 The New Zealand artist, Maurice Bennett, has made a career out of constructing large-scale portraits of celebrities using slices of toasted bread: the differently coloured pieces of bread acting as the 'picture elements'. When seen from a distance, we can easily reconcile these into, say, images of Elvis or the Mona Lisa (see www.mauricebennett.co.nz/tportraits.htm).

(Lipkin 2005, 14), but this varies from individual to individual, and research has indicated that experts which deal with visual evidence may require many more pixels an inch to see a continuous image (Martinez and Hamber 1989). The smaller the individual elements of the grid used to represent an image, the more detail of the original image will be captured and the closer the representation will resemble the original.

The phrase 'picture element' has been used to describe the individual points in a bitmap image since it was introduced in an article about television in *Wireless World Magazine* in 1927 (Dinsdale 1927).[3] In his 2006 article, Richard Lyon traces how the phrase was picked up by computer scientists and those working on imaging technologies and applied in various ways throughout the 1950s and 1960s. A shortened version, *pel*, was proposed by engineers in 1964, but did not gain widespread acceptance. Instead, the abbreviation of the word picture to pix was adopted (a popular slang abbreviation used by various gossip columnists and Hollywood headline writers) and picture element became 'pixel' in an academic article in 1965. The term was picked up by various other computing scientists, appearing in reports from IBM, JPL and NASA in the late 1960s and early 1970s, and became entrenched in textbooks and teaching materials. 'Once *pixel* reached a critical recognition level with the help of the textbooks, it was widely adopted in the 1980s' (Lyon 2006, 7) and has since been universally used when referring to the smallest definable unit in a bitmapped image.

The term pixel is context sensitive, and can be used to discuss the way image information is stored and manipulated within a computer or how digital images are physically captured and displayed. We can talk mathematically regarding how individual pixels are stored: each pixel contains complete information about a particular point of an image, detailing the colour (hue, lightness and saturation) and place of the individual pixel within the grid. From a mathematical point of view, this array is merely a collection of numbers that may be transformed and manipulated in a wide variety of ways. Such an array is called a bitmap – a representation of the image data that parallels the manner in which it is stored in computer memory. Pixels can also be physical, representing the smallest constituent part of an image printed on a page, illuminated on a screen or the pixels in a photosensitive array in a capture device. CCD image sensors in digital cameras have a distinct number of pixels in individual rows which they use to sense light, converting light into electrical signals. It has become common to measure and compare the quality of digital cameras by how many pixels they have in their light-sensitive array (for example, an array of 2048 x 1536 pixels is 3,145,728 pixels in total, giving a

3 Previous to this the individual points in television or other electrically transmitted images had been called *Bildpunkte* (literally, 'picture points') in a German patent filed by Paul Nipkow in 1884, and in the first English language text written about television (Dinsdale 1926) referred to as 'a mosaic of selenium cells, a greater number of small parts, thousands of little squares, and a succession of little areas of varying brilliance' (Lyon 2006, 1).

camera described as 3.1 megapixels). For display purposes, pixels are the actual physical dots on an output device, each one taking up a small amount of surface space and being the smallest, independently programmable element on the display surface. For example, on a screen display, each pixel usually occupies a square region on the screen[4] and displays one colour at a time. Objects are drawn on the screen by making different pixels different colours: if the pixels are densely packed, the jagged, square edges of individual pixels are not noticeable. If the pixels themselves are visible, the image is said to be pixeled or bitmapped. Computer printers are also used to output images, dividing the image into a number of pixels to printout individual points onto paper.

Bitmap image pixels are generally square: most image formats, capture and output devices, use pixels of equal height and width (and the fact that these are distributed uniformly along an x and y axis explains why digital images are always rectangular). However, once the image data is stored in mathematical form, pixels do not have a fixed size: pixel size is variable depending on the size of the grid chosen to display or output them (often described in dots per inch). The number of pixels in a given area is described as the *resolution* of the image. The amount of colour information stored for each individual pixel is determined by *bit depth*.

Resolution

The word 'resolution', in relation to images and vision, was originally used to describe the effect of an optical instrument in making separate parts of a field of vision distinguishable by the human eye: for example, the magnification at which the stars of a nebula became visible through a telescope, or the magnification at which a microscope gave the ability to distinguish between separate objects on a slide (OED 1989b). From the 1960s, this became applied to digital images, and the ability to reproduce fine detail regarding the number of pixels, or samples, within a digital image. Since then it has been commonly used to denote the number of pixels which constitute the digital image.

Resolution is usually denoted by a measurement such as pixels, or points per inch (ppi: measuring the number of pixels in an image within a linear one-inch space), dots per inch (dpi: measuring the number of individual dots of ink a printer can produce) or lines per inch (lpi: used to denote how close together lines are in half-tone printing, the method commonly used in newspapers and magazines

---

4 Pixels are not necessarily always square. Many graphics applications and image processing operations assume that a certain pixel aspect ratio will be used in display, and that pixels are square, and most computer monitors have square pixels. However, pixels in some digital video formats are rectangular, or 'non-square', where a 100 pixel horizontal line is shorter than a 100 pixel vertical line: engineers wanted to make higher resolution television images without changing the number of scan lines on the display. Any rendering of a digital image onto this display must take this into account.

where images are represented by a series of dots of different size and density). The terms are often used interchangeably when talking about image resolution, dots per inch being the most common, and conventionally understood to cover different media (although points per inch being the most accurate, since raster images are composed of pixels). The reason for using the Imperial inch rather than the Metric centimetre as a unit of measurement is due to the fact that most of the early development of imaging technologies was carried out in the US, where Imperial measurements are still in use.

Pixels, points or dots per inch is a convenient measure to use when describing and comparing digital image resolution. If a digital image is three-inches wide, and the total number of pixels across it is 900, the resolution of the picture is 300 pixels per inch (900 divided by 3) usually expressed as 300ppi, or 300dpi. Because pixels in digital imaging technologies are square, there will always be the same number of pixels horizontally as vertically in each individual inch. If you take a square inch of the 300dpi digital image, you will find 300 rows of pixels, with each row containing 300 pixels, giving 90,000 pixels in total in that square inch (300 by 300). It is much more convenient to discuss, and easier for humans to visualize, 300dpi, rather than 90,000 pixels per square inch, even though they refer to the same thing.

For cameras, resolution is stated differently. Rather than the number of pixels in an inch, the resolution given is usually the maximum resolution a digital sensor at the back of the camera can achieve, normally expressed as the absolute number of pixels in the grid, rounded up to one decimal place. For example, a grid of 3072 by 2048 pixels in a sensor gives a total of 6.29 million pixels, or 6.3 megapixels (MP). Megapixels are the standard unit used by manufacturers when quoting the camera's highest resolution. This is not pixels per inch, then, it is pixels per image (and the camera manufacturer has no idea or interest of how large or small a physical picture taken with their camera will be). This different use of the word resolution can lead to confusion: for consistency, in this book, resolution will mean the number of pixels per inch in a digital image.

Interpolation

The topic of resolution can be confusing because it isn't fixed and immutable. If you change the size of a digital image, without changing the number of pixels within it, you change its resolution. The computer only has the number of pixels stored in the file to work with, recording the colour of each pixel contained within the grid. Pixels do not have any intrinsic size: the size is determined by how many pixels are contained within the grid, and the size of the grid is stored within the image format (see p. 65). If the grid is resized (in an image manipulation program) without also increasing or decreasing the number of pixels, the resolution of the image changes. For example, if you have a 900 by 900 pixel image, and the image is three-inches wide, then the resolution is 300dpi (900/3). Each square inch contains 300 x 300 = 90,000 pixels. If you resize the image to six inches wide, without increasing the number of pixels, the 900 by 900 pixel image now has a resolution of 150dpi as the 900 pixels are stretched over 6 inches instead of 3 (900/6= 150). Each square inch contains 150 *x* 150 = 22,500 pixels. If you resize the image to sixty inches wide, the 900 by 900 pixel image has a resolution of 15dpi, and each square would only have 225 pixels. Likewise, if the size of the image is decreased without changing the number of pixels within the image, the resolution of the image, per inch, increases. Computers will allow manipulation of digital images to any size that is wanted: however, if a digital image is meant to look like a continuous tone image, rather than a grid of coloured squares, the resolution has to remain above a certain threshold to fool the human eye.

Interpolation is the term given to the mathematical creation of missing data. Interpolation techniques are often used to create new pixels to insert into, or choose which pixels to delete from, a resized image, in order to maintain image resolution and ensure that the image does not become pixelated. Interpolation is also sometimes referred to as resampling, or 'up sampling' and 'down sampling', to describe the process of changing the number of pixels in the image. Many programs can scale images using this process to ensure that images appear to be the right size: word processing packages allow interpolation on the fly, many web browsers scale images to ensure they can be viewed within the browser body, and most operating systems scale wallpaper images so that they fit on the screen properly.

Reducing the image size and discarding pixel information is relatively straightforward – the computer systematically goes through a file and discards some of the information stored, although the process is still computationally expensive. Adding pixels to an existing image is slightly more complicated, especially when colours are involved. There are many ways in which the new values of new pixels can be calculated: one simple method is pixel replication where one pixel at the lower resolution is made into multiple pixels in the higher resolution image. Another technique would be to generate a new pixel by using the average colour of the value of the two pixels on either side of the one required. These simplistic approaches typically cause visible disruption in the resulting image, which may appear fuzzy (i.e. a sharp divide between black and white will yield a row of grey pixels). More sophisticated, complex software algorithms have been developed to calculate the values of new pixels in relation to their neighbours, assigning values to the new pixels based on ones which are already there, but essentially interpolation algorithms cannot add meaningful detail to an image, providing an approximation of pixel value which may or may not look appropriate depending on the image involved.

When an image is increased in size by interpolation, then, lots of new information is inserted into it which was not part of the original image. Likewise, if the image is decreased in size, original information will be discarded. This raises questions of verisimilitude and authenticity, particularly if the image is to be used as a primary source for research purposes (see pp. 194–198). When increasing or decreasing image size (or manipulating digital images in any way whatsoever), it is good practice to keep a backup (or copy) of the original file. When a large image file is needed (for printing, for example), made-up pixels may be better than nothing, but caution should be placed on using images for research purposes which have been manipulated in such a manner by a computer.

Given that resolution indicates the number of pixels in a digital image, with each pixel sampling light and colour values at its given point, it is easy to understand that the more pixels per inch – the higher the resolution – of an image, the higher the quality of the image will be. The more pixels that there are in an image, the greater detail it will contain. This is determined not by the quantity of pixels overall, but the size and quality of those pixels: for example, an image of a medieval manuscript scanned at 600dpi in full colour will contain many more samples per inch, and much more colour information than an image of the same manuscript scanned at 72dpi in black and white, making it a better representation of the original.

However, the more pixels contained within an image, the larger its file size will be (see pp. 49–50): image quality is exchanged for speed and hard drive space, as larger files take longer to disseminate, display and process. At the moment, it would be uneconomical to store everything at high resolution (and full colour). However, if the resolution is too low, the pictures will look visibly disrupted, and the image will be a poor likeness of the object or scene that it attempts to represent. Those dealing with digital images have to make choices regarding what would be an appropriate resolution to capture, and store, digital image data, to make sure they are doing so efficiently, while capturing enough information to ensure the image is useful.

What Resolution Should Be Used?

The resolution chosen when scanning a picture, or producing a derivative from a larger image file, will depend on the image's purpose. When producing an image for use in desktop publishing, for example, it may be possible to establish the exact measurements of the image required, and the resolution required by the printer to ensure professional print quality. Likewise, the manufacturers of individual printers, or professional print companies, may provide guidelines regarding which resolution will give the best results using their products. However, it is often not known what purpose a digital image will be put to. There are various rules of thumb which exist regarding resolution, and it can be useful to understand the basic reasoning behind these. However, with archival rare and fragile material, it is an established procedure to scan 'once for all purposes': taking one high resolution image from which other smaller images can be derived, to ensure that the original source material is subjected to as little handling and light exposure as possible. Those creating digital image representations of objects can either choose the optimum resolution for imaging an individual object, or to follow one of the many guides to good practice, or sets of guidelines, which have established benchmarks and recommended (among other things) suitable resolutions to use for capturing, delivering and storing digital images in the LIS sector.

The common choices made regarding resolution are closely linked to display and printing technology, hence the need to refer to measurements of points per inch (scanning sampling and display technologies), dots per inch and lines per inch (printing technologies). When a digital image is rendered – prepared for screen or outputting to a printer, the number of pixels which are available for display or printing may not match the number of pixels in the image file. If preparing images, particularly for these output mechanisms, it can be useful to use resolutions which are suited to them.

Monitors tend to display images somewhere between 72 and 100ppi, depending on the type and quality of the display (with top range models currently available with 200ppi displays). This is quite a low resolution, but the points of coloured light blend together to the human eye, giving a smooth, attractive image. Because of the nature of the way the human eye works, fewer pixels are needed when backlit to give a continuous tone image, as the brightness of the light smoothes out some detail. Over the years the total number of pixels contained in PC monitors has increased dramatically. In the early 1990s, 640 *x* 480 (307,200) pixels was standard, but nowadays, 1024 *x* 768, or 1280 *x* 1024[5] pixels are the most common, with higher resolutions, such as 1600 *x* 1200 becoming more popular (W3Schools 2007b). If you get close enough to the screen, individual pixels can be made out (and they exist numerically) but, in general, at arms length, it is difficult to discern individual pixels on today's screens. As a result, if preparing images primarily to be displayed on screen (such as those featured in a web page), the resolution of the display mechanism is adequate: 72 to 100ppi. It is worth noting that if a much higher resolution image is viewed on screen, the screen is only capable of displaying at its 'native' resolution, and so images are 'down sampled' using interpolation, and displayed at a size relative to the screen resolution (to see all the image information contained within the file, the size of the on-screen image would have to be increased). If an image with a lower resolution than the monitor is displayed, it is visibly pixelated, with the constituent pixels discernible.

Printed images require a lot more pixels than those designed for display on screen: again, this is down to the way the human eye works. When an image is outputted, the computer can only use dots of ink or toner, hence dpi. Remove the seductive glow of the monitor and the image can be seen more clearly with reflected daylight, with rough edges or pixelation much more noticeable to the naked eye. To match the sharpness of a conventional photograph, it is necessary to print at around 300dpi. Most inkjet printers (where a printhead is cranked back and forth across a paper, forcing ink through fine nozzles as it goes) are capable of between 300 and 1200 dots per inch. The higher the original resolution of the

5 Computer monitors tend to have a 4:3 aspect ratio, although recently, monitors with 16:9 and 16:10 have become popular to accommodate widescreen film formatting.

image, the bigger the picture will print without showing the pixels: the higher the number of dots per inch printed, the higher the quality of the resulting print.

When attempting to print an image developed for a screen display, printers will construct an image with many more pixels: inserting new pixels into the existing image via interpolation (and so reducing image usefulness and quality. Allowing users free access to low resolution images is one way of preventing the production of counterfeit or pirate goods from a digital image: low resolution images will not be of high enough quality to use for commercial printing). When producing digital images for print it is useful to know the output resolution of the device being used, and the technique that will be used for printing. Test prints should be used to examine the quality and accuracy of sample output from digital image printers.

An alternative printing technique is screening. Traditionally this was done by laying a transparent half-tone screen made up of a dot pattern over the film before exposing it, reducing the continuous tone image to a series of differently sized dots that could be printed, with text, using a single ink colour. The higher the number of lines per inch (lpi) of dots the printer is capable of producing, the smoother the image looks. Most images are screened using an imagesetter: a high quality printer that can output at resolutions of typically 1200 to 4800lpi. Printing in this manner is used in the publishing industry to produce lithographic plates, although this has been largely superseded by a technique called 'computer to plate' which allows digital images to be output directly onto a printing plate. Again, it is useful to know the technique which will be used for printing and the resolution required to suit the technology.

However, when capturing a digital image of an object for use by others, where you have little control over how the image will be used, it is wiser to create one high resolution scan which can be the basis of other derived images of varying resolution, and kept for archival purposes. What resolution should that scan be – or what useful limits are there for scanning in high resolution images? The 'optimum' resolution can be selected for each individual object: deciding what part of the image is important, and making sure this is visible in the digital representation:

> Selection of the optimum resolution starts with a determination of what is the smallest meaningful element that must be legible in the end product. When dealing with textual materials, this determination is relatively easy: find the smallest letter, numeral, diacritic, or symbol that must be clearly distinguished. In printed books the smallest textual element is often the superscript footnote numbers or letters with diacritics; with handwritten documents there is a great deal of variation. It is much more difficult to determine what the smallest meaningful element in a photograph or artwork is. In part it depends on who will use the scanned image and in what way. A non-specialist may look at a landscape photograph casually, while a geologist may need to be able to distinguish the stratigraphy of the cliff in the background (Image Quality Working Group of ArchivesCom 1997).

Needless to say, it can be time-consuming to go through the process of selecting the optimum resolution for every document in a collection which is to be digitized. It is also difficult to judge how images will be used by a user, and which 'meaningful element' is indeed meaningful.

A much more advisable approach, when digitizing a large-scale collection, is to refer to digitization guidelines, which present a carefully detailed best practice approach to the image capture of different media, taking into consideration the different ways resulting images may be used. These standards have evolved over time (see pp. 120–122) but are now relatively stable, although different institutions still recommend different resolutions for similar purposes. The Library of Congress suggests that a minimum of 300ppi should be used to capture images of printed text, music, manuscripts, photographs and graphic arts, with higher ppi being used to capture image detail where further processing may be possible, such as 400ppi for images of text for analysis in Optical Character Recognition programs, or 400ppi for the recognition of artifactual features in music scores or manuscripts. For rare books, or manuscripts, 600ppi should be used as a minimum and for images which will be used for reproduction, the maximum resolution the capture device is capable of should be used (Library of Congress 2007, 11). As a general rule of thumb, 300ppi is recommended for images which will improve access, 400 to 600ppi is necessary for the purposes of reproduction or research on artifactual features. Thumbnail and other smaller-scale images (such as those suitable for online delivery) can be derived from these large master files. The recommendations also cover colour (see pp. 185–191).

Other institutions producing digitization guidelines vary slightly from these resolution recommendations, such as those produced by the US National Archives and Records Administration (NARA 2004, 51). A table comparing various institutional guidelines is available from the Cornell University Library Digital Imaging Tutorial (2002b), indicating the differences expressed in different guidelines: most are meant to be informative, not prescriptive. When creating digital image surrogates from objects, knowledge of the material to be digitized, institutional requirements for use of any digital images created, and up to date consultation of a range of imaging guidelines should inform practitioners of the current recommendations in the sector regarding appropriate resolution to be used for image capture and delivery.

What Resolution Will Overtake Film?

At what resolution does – or will – digital photography capture the same amount of information as film? This is a common and understandable question – but it is rather open-ended. Film captures image data at the molecular level (the predominant light-sensitive materials used today are minute silver halide, silver bromide and silver iodide crystals suspended in an emulsion), so the level of detail is high, but film comes in a variety of sensitivities (measured by ISO/ASA, the scale for measuring film speed as defined by the International Organization for Standardization (1987)): the detail differs from speed to speed, with more sensitive film being grainier, as the larger, more light-sensitive crystals in the film become visible to the naked eye. This means you have to know what type of film you are comparing digital images with to ensure a fair comparison.

The sharpness of a photographic system can also be affected by any component of the system (such as lens, film, scanner, enlarging lens, etc., which can be mathematically modelled by a Modulator Transfer Function, see Koren (2001)), so to undertake a fair comparison, the sharpness of both systems taking the photograph must be the same.

To further confuse the issue, the size of individual pixels in digital camera sensors differs from camera model to model, and it is generally considered that bigger pixels in a sensor are better pixels, as they produce more signal and less noise, therefore, the make, size and type of the camera sensor must be taken into account. If a comparison is undertaken of a picture taken by cheap, point and shoot digital camera with small 6MP sensor (which tend to have sensors with pixels 4–5 microns in size), and a professional D-SLR camera with a large 6MP sensor (with pixels 9 microns in size), the SLR picture would be of visibly higher quality. Additionally, some newer models of D-SLR have sensors which can be set to be more sensitive to light, just as you can use different speeds of film in a traditional film camera (with standards, again, provided by the International Organization for Standardization (2006)): however, the higher the ISO selected on a D-SLR, the more noise becomes apparent in the image.

A study of scanned images by Clark (2001) has shown that if the sharpness of the systems is identical, it would take about 12 megapixels for a digital camera to equal 35mm photographs shot with fine grain modern film. However, the noise (from a digital camera) or grain (from film) affects the overall quality and plays an important role. It has been suggested that digital photographs taken by digital cameras with large sensors, such as most professional level D-SLRs, equal 35mm photos shot with fine grain modern film at only 6 megapixels (Hecker 2007). Cheaper, point and shoot digital cameras tend to have smaller sensors, and so generate a lot of noise: the quality of their pictures in comparison to film is poor, even if their sensors have a large number of pixels.

It should also be noted, though, that digital sensors treat colour differently from analogue film (see pp. 185–191) and so differences will be present in how colour will be represented between a digital and traditional print image of the same object or scene. As a result, the question of when digital photography will replace film should be tempered by the notion that the two technologies function in different manners – and although one can be an alternative to the other, they each bring various characteristics to the medium which cannot be replicated or replaced.

Bit Depth

The term bit depth, or colour depth, refers to the number of bits which are used to represent the colour of each individual pixel within a bitmapped graphic. The amount of colour information stored for each pixel is dependent on the number of bits available: the greater the number of bits assigned to each pixel (for example 1, 4, 8, 16, 24, 32 or 48) the greater the number of colours and tones the image can contain, and the display can attempt to reproduce. However, the more colour information captured and stored, the higher the resulting file size. The play-off between storage and dissemination costs, usability and usefulness means choices have to be made regarding the optimum bit depth to capture and store an image.

1-Bit Bitonal

The simplest, and least computationally expensive bit depth, is 1-bit. An individual bit can be in two states, 0 or 1, and so there can only be two colours in a 1-bit image: $2^1 = 2$. The colour of each individual pixel can be described as 0 or 1: black or white. This simple colour representation is often referred to as a binary tone, or bitonal, image.

Early computer graphics displays, until the early 1980s, were only capable of displaying one colour against the screen's background, and these monochrome, or bitonal, representations would generally glow green or amber against the screen's background. However, since graphics technology has improved, the use of bitonal images has become limited, as the black-or-white nature of the image limits the range of tone and detail it can represent. It may be suitable, in some cases, to capture clearly printed text in a 1-bit bitonal image, but the current archival recommendation is that black and white material be captured in greyscale to ensure that the tonal-range of the original is represented (Library of Congress 2007).

4-Bit Colour

When colour comes in to play, more information is needed to capture the information and so a higher bit depth is needed. An early development in using colour in computer systems was 4-bit colour, which allows 16 possible colours per pixel (four individual pixels, each capable of being in one of two states: giving 2^4 different combinations, which equals 16). This became the Video Graphics Array (VGA) display standard for early PC monitors. However, the range of representation is extremely limited, and there is little use for 4-bit colour in modern computational systems.

8-Bit Colour

8-bit colour allows 256 different colour combinations ($2^8 = 256$). Although this is an extremely limited range of colours, 8-bit colour images are capable of producing reasonably natural looking colour reproduction. 8-bit colour is the simplest colour profile available in modern computer systems (and the minimum Super Video Graphic Array standard for monitors, although most are capable of displaying more colours than this). The 8-bits can either directly describe the red, green and blue channels (3 bits for red, 3 bits for green and 2 bits for blue), or, more commonly, describe a selected colour palette of the 256 most important colours within a 24-bit colour image, acting as a form of compression by only saving those 256 colours, and discarding the remaining colour information. However, images captured in 8-bit colour have a limited ability for major corrections, transformations and repurposing, because manipulating the file may cause certain colours to dropout of the image entirely, due to the limited number of shades available. Additionally, because the range of colours is so limited, although an image may look natural, the fidelity of the colours when compared to the original object or scene is poor. For accurate colour representation, much more colour information needs to be captured or stored to ensure the veracity of the image, which means a higher bit depth is required. Most modern graphics hardware is capable of displaying much more than 8-bit colour, and so this bit depth is outmoded.

8-Bit Greyscale

8-bit greyscale allows 256 possible different shades ranging from black to white ($2^8 = 256$ different combinations, 0 is normally black, 255 usually pure white). Greyscale images are distinct from black and white (bitonal) images, as they also capture many shades between black and white, and the range of tone and detail they can capture is much higher, providing a natural and detailed image to the human eye. Less information is necessary to store a greyscale image than an accurate colour representation, and so greyscale is a popular choice when the inclusion of colour is not imperative to an image. As a result, 8-bit greyscale is the standard for capturing non-colour images and representations of documents.

16-Bit Colour

16-bit colour, often called 'high colour' on PC systems, or 'thousands of colours' on Macintosh systems, is capable of representing 65,536 different colours (2^{16}). 5 bits are dedicated to the red and blue channels, and 6 bits dedicated to green, given that the human eye is more responsive to different shades of green. 16-bit colour can match the effective shading and density range of photographic originals and is sufficient to provide life-like colours to the human eye, although we are capable of distinguishing more colours than this (measuring the amount of colour information the human eye is capable of discerning is no easy task, but it is estimated that we can see around two million different shades, see Pointer and Attridge 1998). Therefore, greater colour detail than is available in 16-bit colour is advised for archival images. Although 16-bit colour is still used in certain systems and programs, it is not advocated for image capture and storage under current guidelines.

24-Bit Colour

24-bit colour, often referred to as 'true colour', on PC systems, or 'millions of colours' on Macintosh systems, is capable of capturing a spectrum of colour samples beyond the range of human colour perception. In the 24-bit image, each pixel is represented with 8 bits devoted to red, 8 bits devoted to green and 8 bits devoted to blue. Each of the red, green and blue channels can have a value between 0 and 255, which means the possible permutations available in 24-bit colour is 256 x 256 x 256: 16,777,216 possible colours, technically many more than the human eye can distinguish. However, although there are over 16 million different permutations, it is still possible to see areas in 24-bit digital images where this is not enough to avoid visual disruption to the continuous tone image. If there are 256 shades of blue, this may not be enough to capture the nuances of an image which mostly contains blue: the human eye may still distinguish 'colour ramps' (also known as 'colour banding' or 'posterization') in areas where one of those shades of blue switches to another.

24-bit colour display is the highest bit depth available on affordable monitors at present. As a result, for archival quality colour images and future proofing against technological development which may rely on large amounts of colour information being available, 24-bit colour is recommended. Surrogates derived from 24-bit archival masters have greater colour fidelity, and are less likely to suffer from 'artefacts' (see p. 52). However, such flexibility does result in a storage penalty: file sizes are large, and to avoid the associated costs of storage, delivery and manipulation of large amounts of unnecessary data, colour capture of materials where colour is not an imperative feature (such as black and white manuscripts, newspapers, etc.) is to be avoided.

32-Bit Colour

32-bit colour is actually 24-bit true colour, with an additional 8-bit 'alpha-channel' used for additional control, information and special effects, such as transparency. If no transparency information is needed, the value of the additional 8 bits is set to zero, and these are used as padding: many modern computers process data internally in units of 32 bits, so speed can be optimized if this amount is used for each individual pixel, even though this makes file sizes larger. For production of archival master images, transparency (or other special effects) data should not be necessary, and therefore 24-bit colour is adequate.

48-Bit Colour

Given the limits of modern computer monitor displays, the advantages of capturing any image using a bit depth larger than 24-bit colour may not be obvious. However, some professional quality image manipulation software allows 48-bit colour, where sixteen bits are devoted to each of the red, green and blue channels, giving

65,536 shades of each channel, resulting in a colour model capable of describing 281 trillion colours (PhotoShop allows basic manipulation of 48-bit colour images at present, but many facilities are not available without converting to a lower bit depth). Storing images in 48-bit colour is still relatively rare, although TIFF is capable of storing this amount of colour information. Many capture devices, such as scanners and professional digital SLRs, are capable of capturing information in 48-bit colour, allowing smoother and more accurate representations of transitions in both highlight and shadow areas of the image, and rendering differences in light and shade accurately, but such images tend to be converted to 24-bit colour after acquisition. There has been a move towards using 48-bit colour for archival purposes: the primary purpose of doing so would be to preserve as much of the original data as possible, retaining the additional precision of the capture device, preserving the greatest possible detail for future use, and avoiding issues of colour banding in continuous tone images. Technology continues to be developed which is capable of capturing and displaying high-levels of colour information efficiently.[6] However, the file sizes generated when dealing with 48-bit colour are prohibitively large and, at present, 48-bit colour remains beyond the recommended limits for colour information capture.

Converting Bit Depth

Images captured in one bit depth can be converted to another: for example, 48-bit images can be resampled as 24-bit, but this involves discarding colour information which cannot be regained. Obviously, conversion of a lower bit depth to a higher bit depth, such as greyscale to colour, will require inventing colour information not contained within the original file, and this is not recommended beyond creative endeavours. Mathematical models have been developed to allow conversion from one bit depth to another: for example, converting a colour image to 8-bit greyscale is not a simple translation task, due to the relative sensitivity of the normal human eye to each of the primary colours (humans are much more sensitive to shades of green and much less sensitive to shades of blue). As a result, different percentages must be adjusted between red, green and blue to ensure the range of values across the greyscale image functions in the same way as we see the range of colours in the original colour image.

The ability of monitors and printers to accurately represent higher bit depths is limited. It is frequently the case that the colours defined by the pixel values stored in a file differ from those that can be displayed by the output device (the gamut, or complete subset of colours that a device is capable of outputting, can be very different from the range of values listed in a digital image file). A

6 Such as High Dynamic Range Imaging (HDRI), which allow a greater range of values between light and dark areas to be captured, through the use of floating point notation. Although currently in its infancy for commercial applications, this is in common use in cinematic production.

rendering application must translate between those in the file and those available. Quantization can reduce the number of colours in the source data to match the number available on the destination device, but it can cause unacceptable changes in appearance, such as banding, and introducing new colours not present in the source data. Another technique, dithering, places different coloured pixels next to one another to fool the human eye into seeing a colour not available on the device. Dithering is useful for printing, but can make image editing on screen difficult.

What Bit Depth Should Be Used?

8-bit greyscale is the current recommendation for capturing and representing printed text (such as books with illustrations, pamphlets, typed pages and newspapers), music (such as sheet music, annotated scores and music manuscripts), manuscript materials (such as handwritten manuscripts and typewritten copies) and photographs and graphic arts where colour is not an important attribute in the document (Library of Congress 2007, 11–12). There is little point in capturing or storing colour information when it does not bring any additional information to the representation, and merely serves to increase the size of the file.

Colour should be captured and stored in a digital representation of an object when it is an important attribute of the original, which gives additional information and which would be missing if an image was presented to the user in greyscale. It is currently recommended that items such as maps, colour photographs, manuscript, music or printed material which features colour, should be captured and stored using 24-bit colour. Additionally, if recognition of artifactual features is important, such as condition, or the images are being produced for research on artifactual features, then 24-bit colour should be used to ensure all detail possible is captured. 24-bit colour is often necessary when producing representations to be used in reproduction or printing (Library of Congress 2007, 11).

Image Size

There are various different ways to describe image size: the size of the file in kilobytes (usually referred to as 'file size'), the size of the image in pixels (more commonly referred to as 'pixel dimensions') and the size of the resulting image when printed. It is important to know that 'image size' can refer to any one of these, and to determine exactly what is meant when the term is used.

It should be understandable that as the width, height and bit depth of an image increases, the computational resources required to process the image increase in an exponential fashion. The file size of an image – the amount of space it takes up in computer memory – can be calculated by the formula:

$$\text{Image Height } x \text{ Image Width } x \text{ Dots per Inch}^2 \; x \text{ Bit Depth}$$

That is, calculate the total number of individual pixels in an image, and multiply that figure by the amount of colour information stored per pixel, giving the total amount of information in bits needed to store the pixel information within the file. To convert that figure into bytes, it needs to be divided by eight, as 8 bits = 1 byte. There will be additional information necessary too which describes the file, contained within the file header (see p. 65), but the pixel information comprises the main part of any image file.

As an example, a standard 4- by 6-inch photograph, captured at 72 dots per inch, in 8-bit greyscale, will need a data stream of 124,416 bytes, or 124 kilobytes, to describe the pixel information (4 x 6 x 72 x 72 x 8, /8). That same 4 by 6 photograph, captured at 72 dots per inch at 24-bit colour (4 x 6 x 72 x 72 x 24, /8), requires 373,248 bytes, or 373 kilobytes (kb) of memory. Increase the capture resolution to the recommendation of 300dpi, then the file size increases exponentially as the total number of pixels increases (4 x 6 x 300 x 300 x 24, /8): 6,480,000 bytes; or 6,480kb; or 6.48 Mb (megabytes). If we want to capture at archival resolution for reproduction, 600dpi, the file size grows exponentially again (4 x 6 x 600 x 600 x 24, /8): 25,920,000 bytes; or 25,920kb; or almost 26 Mb. It is easy to see how increasing the resolution and bit depth of an image drastically changes the file size, and that dealing with a large collection of such large files may become both computationally and financially problematic.

Compression

Images captured in high enough quality to be of use (whether high resolution, colour information, or both) can have very large file sizes, due to the amount of information stored for each individual pixel within the data stream. The time and resources required to store, process and transmit large files can be problematic: the amount of memory taken up by large images, or required to process large images, on a system can limit certain applications, and large images are not suitable for exchanging via the Internet. Data compression techniques solve this problem by reducing the physical size of a block of information, by reducing the number of bytes required to represent the data set, and thus reducing the amount of memory required to store a particular data set. This allows a larger number of images to be stored on a given medium, or increases the amount of data that can be sent over a communications channel (such as the Internet) in a given period.

It is important to understand that compression algorithms do not ‘squeeze’ or ‘squash’ data: instead the pixel information within the data stream is rewritten, so that an image represented in one form can be converted to another form that requires fewer bits, making the representation as efficient as possible:

> Compression algorithms are often described as squeezing, squashing, crunching, or imploding data, but these are not very accurate descriptions of what is actually happening. Although the major use of compression is to make data use less disk space,

> compression does not actually physically cram the data into a smaller size package in any meaningful sense … Instead, compression algorithms are used to re-encode data into a different, more compact representation, conveying the same information. In other words, fewer words are used to convey the same meaning, without actually saying the same thing (Murray and van Ryper 1996, 155).

There are a variety of approaches which can be taken to re-represent the bit stream of an image file: some are designed to store the pixel information efficiently (which is important when sharing and exchanging images via the Internet), while others store images accurately (important for maintaining the veracity of image data). Each approach imposes different design criteria and constraints, and depends on whether loss of data is acceptable or can be discerned by the human eye, or whether it is more important to maintain all information available in the original image for future use than to worry about storage and transmission costs.

In the early stages of computing technologies, disk space was expensive and scarce, and it was necessary to compress all image files. Nowadays, with the plummeting costs of media and hardware, and alternative methods of distribution and storage (such as online services), it is less pressing to compress every image file. However, compression is still routinely used for storing large volumes of original data, but it should be noted that there is a trade off: when files are compressed, they need to be decompressed before use, often increasing access time to the data when it is required.

Types of Compression – Lossless and Lossy

There are two major types of compression – lossless and lossy – which are terms used to describe the relationship of the original data to the compressed version of the file. With lossless compression, an image decompressed and viewed will be identical to its state before being compressed. Lossy compression, on the other hand, eliminates some information in the compression process and the original data cannot be reconstructed from the compressed file. Neither approach is better than the other, as they have different benefits and drawbacks, and the approach chosen will be determined by the purpose of the required image.

Lossless compression techniques ensure that no information is discarded and that the original information can be reconstructed into a bit-by-bit identical representation of the source file. Depending on the type of image the technique is applied to, lossless compression techniques can typically reduce the size of images by up to 50 per cent. Given that the original file can be reconstructed entirely, the compressed version is a mathematically efficient representation, and no factors of human perception play a role in developing or validating lossless algorithms. However, although a 50 per cent reduction in file size may sound impressive, depending on the size of the original file, the resulting compressed file may still be very large and not suitable for, say, dissemination via a network. However, lossless compression does provide efficient storage where it is imperative that all information stored in an image is preserved for future use.

Lossy compression techniques discard information from an image. The resulting image differs from its pre-compressed state: it may be close to the original, but an exact representation will never be able to be recreated. The perceptually based techniques work by eliminating data which is not visible to the human eye:

> the human eye is insensitive to certain elements of images, so the loss of some image information can be tolerated … lossy techniques depend on human visual sensitivity for their success (Watson 1994, 2).

All lossy compression techniques result in some loss of data and therefore reduce the quality of an image but can achieve dramatic storage savings, giving greater compression than lossless methods. The techniques range from the simple to the elaborate, and the level of compression can be adjusted on a case by case basis so that most data can be discarded while changing as little of the visible detail in an image as possible. However, overdoing lossy compression can result in unintended visual effects, or 'artefacts' becoming obvious in images, where information is deleted and inserted awkwardly into the resulting representation. Lossy compression methods should not be used where the quality and integrity of the resulting image is important, such as in archival copies of digital images.

How Compression Works

Compression takes advantage of patterns within image data, to find an equivalent representation which occupies less space. Graphical information has many qualities and can commonly have features which are redundant (not important to the image and removing them would produce an image which, to all intents and purposes, looks the same to the human visual system); predictable (patterns often emerge, or blocks of similar colour are present which can be more simply expressed); or unnecessary (for example, expressing more variations in colour than the human eye can actually see). Compression algorithms work in two different approaches: either they abbreviate repeated information or they eliminate information that we would find difficult to, or cannot, see.

The abbreviation of repeated data can be accomplished by transformation: where a pattern or order in the data set is exploited and expressed in a different, more compact form, reducing redundant information and transforming the original data set into an equivalent data set that is in some way smaller. The technical term for this is 'mapping': patterns in the original data are mapped to codes for the patterns in the transformed data. Additionally, abbreviation can be accomplished by minimizing the total number of bits required to represent the entire data stream by re-encoding the data more efficiently.

The act of compression through eliminating information is often referred to as 'reduced precision': the precision of individual data values within a data set are reduced, which means the number of binary digits (bits) required to represent each item is also reduced and so the resulting data stream is smaller than before. Known quirks of the human visual system are often exploited to reduce types of data which are not easily detectable by the human eye, so file sizes can be reduced without affecting the visual quality of the image or making changes which are not easily detectable. For example, often the colours sampled in a digital image are more precise than the human eye can distinguish, as we are more primed to identify changes in light and tone than colour:

> The human eye does not demand the same resolution for the colour information in an image that it requires for intensity information. The data representing high colour resolution can often be discarded. Decades ago, artists exploited this fact and offered 'tinted' photographs, in which colour had been applied with a brush (low resolution) over a black-and-white photo (a high-resolution intensity map). Today, colour … compression schemes often employ the same principle (Kay and Levine 1995, 21).

See Watson (1994) for an overview of the principles behind developing algorithms for compression which work by replicating the function of the human eye–brain system.

Data which has not been compressed is known as 'unencoded data' or 'raw data'. The part of the computer program which performs compression is known as the compressor, or encoder: 'encoded data' or 'compressed data' describes the data after it has been compressed. A decompressor, or decoder, uses knowledge of the compression algorithm to take a compressed data set as input, and output the original data set (or as close an approximation to the original data set as possible, if lossy compression was used).

The success of different compression techniques is often expressed as a compression ratio: the ratio of uncompressed data to compressed data. The second number is typically expressed as 1. For example, 10:1 means 10 bytes of the original data are represented by one byte in the compressed data. Larger compression ratios imply more successful compression and smaller resulting data sets: 10:1 is five times more efficient than a compression ratio of 2:1. High compression is generally deemed to be ratios of 20:1, even higher ratios are possible and useful. Often low compression ratios are satisfactory, but higher compression ratios can be required for dissemination and distribution of image data.

However, not all images respond to compression in the same manner. The effectiveness of compression techniques depend on the type of data they are applied to, and vary from individual image to individual image. The more ordered the data, the more the order can be exploited, and redundant information contained within the data stream can be removed. Completely random data streams cannot be compressed: they will often become larger when the algorithms attempt to re-encode the data stream! Additionally, the effectiveness of different compression techniques must be judged on a case by case basis: depending on colour and light information stored within an individual image, some will respond better than others to compression and achieve a high compression ratio without any visible deterioration in quality. Others will require a lower compression ratio to be of any real use: the maximum useful compression ratio per image can only be determined through trial and error.

Common Compression Techniques

A conceptual basis of the algorithms used for compression is essential for those who are manipulating image files. The most common compression techniques in use today are Run Length Encoding (RLE); Huffman; Lempel-Ziv-Welch (LZW); and Discrete Cosine Transfer (DCT). Although others exist (and continue to be invented, refined and developed, see Nelson 1995; Pu 2005; and Salomon 2007), the common file formats (see Chapter 4) utilize at least one of these techniques: some using a combination of two or three to ensure the most efficient compression of information as possible.

Run Length Encoding (RLE) Run Length Encoding (RLE) is one of the simplest compression techniques available, being a pattern recognition scheme that searches for the repetition of identical data values in a list. Consecutive pixels in the data stream that have the same value are encoded using a run length (the number of time it occurs) and a pair value (the data value that occurs more than once). For example, the string:

abbbbbbbbbbbbbbbbbbcddddddddd

Is replaced by

1a18b1c9d

That is a much shorter way to represent the same information. (In effect, instead of saying, 'here is a red pixel, here is a red pixel, here is a red pixel', the algorithm says, 'here are three identical red pixels'.) This is lossless compression, because no information is lost, it is just stored more efficiently than before. (For further examples, and an explanation of RLE, and other compression schemes, see Kay and Levine 1995, 11–16.)

RLE is suitable for compressing any type of data, but the content of the data will affect the compression ratio achieved. Some data sets (especially those with large areas of constant shade or hue) can be highly compressed by run length encoding: RLE works well with long strings of repeated values, so is effective for images that have many repeated values with a limited colour range, such as cartoons, logos or black and white images of text, and compression ratios of between 2:1 and 5:1 are typical in these cases.

However, in busy or complex colour images, such as photographs or images of paintings, large runs of contiguous data are rare, as the complexity of the image is expressed via a large number of very different colours, which seldom appear in consecutive bytes with the same value. For these type of images, run length encoding will actually produce a larger file and give 'negative compression' (if the image contains no consecutive bytes with the same value, but individual values one after the other, the run length encoding algorithm expresses the original data as one pixel of this, and one pixel of that, and one pixel of this, increasing the size of the resulting file).

RLE is simple to implement and quick to execute, and despite its limitations can be a useful lossless compression method. As a result, it is supported by most bitmap file formats, including BMP, JPEG and TIFF.

Huffman Encoding Huffman Encoding, named after its inventor David Huffman (Huffman 1952), is a dictionary-based compression scheme which minimizes the number of bits needed to represent a data set. If a sequence of values is repeated more than once in a data stream, then this sequence can be exploited to compress the data. A unique code can be assigned to the repeated sequence and then stored in a dictionary (or 'codebook') containing pixel value sequences that have already been encountered. The compressed stream contains codes that represent entries in the dictionary. The dictionary is transmitted within the file to allow the information to be read and decompressed.

The beauty of the Huffman approach is that, rather than using a fixed number of bits to represent values (such as 8 bits per pixel), variable length codes are used. The most frequently used sequences are assigned the shortest code in the dictionary, and the least frequently used values are assigned the longest code. During compression, when these sequences occur in the uncompressed data they are replaced by a code that references the sequences in the dictionary. The longer the dictionary sequences, and the more frequently they are repeated in the uncompressed data, the greater the compression and file size decreases. (See Miano 1999, 61 75 for a full exploration of Huffman encoding).

Huffman encoding is lossless: in effect, it produces minimal code, or the best that is possible when re-encoding a data set without discarding any information. Huffman codes typically produce compression ratios of 2:1, but the amount of compression is data set dependent, again depending on repetition in the data for its effectiveness. However, due to the complexity of the dictionary creation and referencing, it is relatively slow to process for both compression and decompression. Nevertheless, it has proved very popular, has attracted a large amount of research interest, and has been adopted in many file formats such as PNG, JPEG and MPEG.

Lempel-Ziv-Welch (LZW) Encoding LZW encoding is an efficient, popular, and commonly used, method of compressing image data, stemming from a whole body of research into efficient lossless compression. In 1977, Abraham Lempel and Jakob Ziv created the first of what is now known as the LZ family of substitutional compression algorithms (Ziv and Lempel 1977). Further research refined the algorithms for effective compression of binary data (Ziv and Lempel 1978). In 1984, while working for the technology consulting firm Unisys, Terry Welch modified the compression algorithm for implementation in high performance computing (at the time: the processing power of high performance computers then was equitable to the desktop computers of today, Welch 1984). The LZW compression technique was created, and has been adopted widely ever since, as an efficient general compression scheme capable of working on almost any type of data.

LZW is another dictionary-based compression scheme, similar to Huffman encoding, where sequences of values in the data stream which repeat more than once are exploited to compress the data. A dictionary of these is compiled and maintained, and the pixel data stream is compressed by replacing strings of data with short codes which represent entries in the dictionary. However, unlike Huffman encoding, LZW does not use variable length dictionary codes, but fixed length codes. Also, LZW does not need to construct a table of codes in advance of recoding the data: it builds a more effective table of codes as it goes along, making it very adaptive. Additionally, the data is encoded in such a way that the dictionary does not need to be transmitted as part of the file: the decoder can reconstruct it dynamically from the image data itself while receiving the data. This makes compression efficient, while being lossless: the compression algorithm re-encodes the data in a more efficient formation without discarding any information at all, allowing the original image to be reconstructed after decompression. Compression and decompression is also reasonably fast.

LZW works well on a variety of data, but, as with all compression algorithms, the compression ratio achievable by LZW is data dependent. Simple, bitmap line drawings or images with block colour, such as logos, can be compressed at 16:1 or higher, as there will be large expanses of identical colour which can be effectively stored. However, no compression can often be achieved on some complex data sets, such as photographs or noisy, high content images, as there is little repetition of information within the file.

LZW is used in GIF and also in TIFF formats as a means of lossless compression. However, LZW has been plagued with legal issues. LZW was patented on 10 December 1985 by the Sperry Corporation, who now own Unisys, owners of the original patent on the algorithm. On 22 December 1994, CompuServe Information Service announced that it had entered into a license agreement with Unisys for the use of the LZW method in their GIF file format, causing anger and panic in the graphics and online community, who had believed the GIF file format was in the public domain. Variations of the LZW compression algorithm still remain under patent by Unisys, requiring developers *writing* applications which compress using this method to pay license fees (decompression is not covered under the original patent). PNG has avoided these legal issues by using variations on the original LZ algorithm which are not under any patent restrictions.

Discrete Cosine Transfer (DCT) Encoding In comparison to the lossless run length encoding or dictionary-based compression schemes, lossy compression algorithms discard information which is deemed unnecessary in an image. Discrete Cosine Transfer (DCT) is the name given to the generic range of operations which attempt to reduce the size of individual values within a data set, encoding the smaller values with fewer binary digits and so compressing the data stream. The underlying scheme is relatively complex, but can produce higher compression ratios than lossless compression.

Sections of bitmapped images often contain data values that are close in value to each other from one pixel to the next (for example, a section of sky in a digital image of a painting may appear as pixels of many similar, but slightly different, shades of blue). Instead of storing the actual data values for each pixel, DCT calculates the difference between these values across various small sections of the image, called blocks, using a mathematical operation called the cosine function. The human eye tends to ignore high frequency (rapid) changes in colour across small areas, being more concerned with changes in light intensity, and DCT exploits this characteristic by discarding rapid changing in colours across blocks in the image. Individual pixels no longer exist: they are represented by a series of patterns which describe how the pixel values vary. The calculation is complex (see Rao and Yip 1990), and fairly computationally expensive, but the resulting representation can look very similar to the original image while the size of the file is much reduced. However, given that information has been discarded, the original image cannot be recreated from the original data set: DCT is efficient, but lossy.

DCT is the basis of JPEG compression (see pp. 76–79), developed to provide an efficient way to compress photographic information, and efficiently cope with the type of complex image data that other lossless compression schemes have little success with.

Combination of Compression Approaches Some formats (such as JPEG file format) combine two or more methods to achieve compression ratios larger than any one scheme is capable of producing itself. This usually starts with transformation (transforming the data set from one representation to another), then precision reduction (where unnecessary information is discarded) and efficient encoding of the final data set (where the resulting data set is represented in a more efficient manner). For example, the JPEG file format uses a combination of Huffman encoding, DCT, and, finally, RLE to ensure that the resulting data set is represented as efficiently as possible. Other file formats, such as TIFF, allow you to choose whether or not you wish to compress the file, and whether to use lossless or lossy compression.

Compression Issues

Compression is a useful and common method to increase the number of images it is possible to store on a device. It is important to stress that lossy compression of image information is unsuitable for long-term storage of image data, as original information will be lost forever. Given that lossy compression works by exploiting quirks in the human visual system, it is difficult to ascertain how images have been changed when applying those techniques, and every loss and change to the original data erodes data quality and research usefulness (there has been much discussion about this in the library and archive sector, see Dale 1999). Archival digital images should only be stored with lossless compression, if any at all:

> Compression is mainly an issue for transferring data over networks. Image compression in an archival environment must be evaluated carefully. At present, most institutions store master files uncompressed. Instead of adapting the files to fit current limitations associated with bandwidth and viewing devices, the digital masters remain information-rich, ready to be migrated when new, perhaps better, file formats or compression schemes become available. Visually lossless compression might be used for certain types of originals, such as documents, where legibility is the main issue (Frey 2000).

The nature of compression techniques available within popular file formats have, to a large extent, determined which file formats are suitable for long-term archival storage of image information: the focus of the following chapter.

Of course, the use of compression is not limited to image files: all types of digital files have the potential to be compressed, with specific schemes being developed for different media. Generic utilities that 'zip' groups of files into compressed 'archives', such as PKZIP (www.pkware.com/software-pkzip) and WinZip (www.winzip.com) are often used to save storage space or to facilitate transmission of large groups of file across a network. The same issues apply for long-term storage of all digital media: only lossless compression schemes are suitable to ensure that all information is available for future use. Most generic ZIP utilities use lossless compression algorithms (with many using the deflate compression algorithm, see PKWare Inc 2007, section 10), but this should be checked before relying on such proprietary, non-standardized programs to provide effective and efficient encoding of digital information in the long term.

Further Reading

There is a plethora of introductory information available regarding the fundamental aspects of digital images. General guides to various multimedia issues, formats and tools can be useful, such as that found in Li and Drew (2004). Additionally, introductory texts to digital cameras can often provide examples and explanatory text: Lojkine (2001) is a useful and readable introduction to digital images; although getting a little dusty, the basics are all explained in easily understandable text with good examples throughout.

For texts written primarily for the library, archive, cultural and heritage audience, Besser and Trant (1995) and its updated version (Besser 2003) cover fundamental features such as bit depth and resolution, with relevant examples provided. Giani (2006) specifically deals with problems which occur when using interpolation to resize images, and the impact this may have on images for use by memory institutions. Other texts produced regarding digitization in the cultural and heritage sector tend to focus more on the many management, curatorial, infrastructural and institutional issues faced by digitization projects (Kenny and Rieger 2000; Lee 2002; Hughes 2004) rather than concentrating on the digital images produced themselves (which is something this book seeks to address). Nevertheless, they are very useful for their intended purpose and place imaging issues in context, if lacking on the technical detail regarding digital images.

One of the best places to find further information about digital images is online. Cornell University Library's 'Moving Theory into Practice: Digital Imaging Tutorial' (2002b) is a popular and useful introduction, which concentrates on the practicalities of digital imaging, important issues and technical details. There is also a bibliography of additional, related reading. The Technical Advisory Service for Images (www.tasi.ac.uk) has various online resources which explain the technical underpinnings of digital imaging: in particular, *The Digital Image* (TASI 2006d) is an informative introduction and they have a comprehensive and up to date bibliography on all aspects of digital imaging available on the website.

For those who really want to get into the technical underpinning of digital imaging technology, *The Digital Image* by Ron Graham (2nd edn 2005) is the definitive reference book, addressing the fundamental physics, mathematics and perceptual phenomena behind digital images, covering optics, electronics, photography and semiconductor technology, and providing numerous examples of digital imaging applications. The book also covers how digital imaging technology functions, giving the reader an understanding of how digital cameras and scanners capture images, although it is a fairly technical read. Likewise, texts such as the *Mathematics of Digital Images: Creation, Compression, Restoration, Recognition* (Hoggar 2006) contain an in-depth exegesis of the types of algorithms introduced in this chapter, as do Nelson (1995); Pu (2005); and Salomon (2007), but may be more of interest to those with a mathematical background. Instead, for introductory but thorough explanations to compression, texts on file formats usually contain readable explorations of the different approaches, such as those found in Brown and Shepherd (1995); Kay and Levine (1995); Murray and van Ryper (1996); and Miano (1999). An introduction to the principles behind digital camera technology, written specifically for the cultural and heritage audience, can be found in Rudolf (2006).

Chapter 4
Image File Formats

> *Graphics file formats are immortal.* Like it or not, data files from the dawn of the computer age are still with us, and they're going to be around for a long time to come. Even when the way we think about data itself changes (as it inevitably will), hundreds of millions of files will still be out there in backup storage. We'll always need a way to read, understand, and display them (Murray and van Ryper 1996, xv).

If you should open a bitmap image file in a textual editor to read through its contents, it is difficult to perceive the information as an image. The image data itself generally consists of a list of values of the colours of individual pixels, and associated instructions for computing applications regarding how this data should be displayed. To ensure that image data can be stored, accessed, shared and rendered on a computer screen or output device as a visible image, the information must be structured to some known, defined specification or 'file format'. Image formats can be viewed as files that store any type of persistent graphical data (as opposed to text, spreadsheet or numerical information) that is intended for eventual rendering and display. The values and instructions contained within an image file allow computers to paint a representation onto the output device for the human eye to see, provided that the image data is stored in a known way according to a format specification, and that the application developer has included instructions in the program which will allow it to process data in that format.

There are now over one hundred image formats in existence, and that number continues to grow. Some formats rely on particular software and hardware, working best with the systems they were designed for. Some formats are used for specific purposes, such as the storing of program icons on specific operating systems or industry specific formats, such as those used for efficient rendering in computer games. Not all image formats can be read by all viewers or computer programs, but some are designed specifically for cross-platform use.

A cultural and heritage digitization project will mostly work on creating two-dimensional representations of artefacts and documents, or *bitmap* graphics (see pp. 8–9): data files or structures representing a generally rectangular form of points of colour called pixels, where the image is built-up in a mosaic like fashion from many coloured squares. File formats generally implement either vector graphics or bitmaps, but rarely utilize both. For this reason, this chapter concentrates on the file formats of bitmap graphics: the common, two-dimensional image formats generated by a digital camera or scanner.

This chapter gives an overview of issues surrounding image file formats and introduces how bitmap digital image data is created, stored and rendered by computing systems. An imaging and digitization project will generally use commonly available bitmap formats to facilitate interoperability and information exchange of digital image data. The most popular image formats that an information professional may come across are discussed in detail (GIF, PNG, JPEG and TIFF), detailing their history, development, application and the underlying computational techniques which they utilize to store the image data. GIF and JPEG files are commonly used to save images which need to be compressed in order to be delivered easily across a network, such as the Internet. The PNG format is becoming more popular for this purpose. TIFF files are generally upheld as the current archival standard for long-term storage of high quality digital image data. An overview is also provided of a selection of other image formats which may also be encountered (RAW, EXIF, BMP, PICT, PSD, Kodak Photo CD and PDF).

Graphics file formats can be complex: the original specification of each format can often span one or more volumes. This section cannot provide a complete reference to each format mentioned, but does provide sufficient information to understand the main concepts behind each format and references for those who wish to know more about particular implementation issues. The overview provided for each format should inform those working with image files in a digitization project: in understanding how file formats work and how best they can be appropriated, those undertaking a digitization project will be better placed to preserve the integrity of their image-based data.

What is an Image Format?

A format describes the way data is stored, to allow others to access and view the information contained within the data file. Data must be represented in some physical way to be stored and transmitted, and the goal of file formats is to ensure that data is stored according to a predictable set of rules, which will allow device–independence of information, as it can be shared or accessed on other systems, which access the data according to the predictable nature of its storage. A graphics format describes the way that the data that describes an image is stored.

The development of various image file formats evolved from the need to store, organize and retrieve graphics data in efficient and logical ways, with the general intention for display, manipulation or transmission of the image data. Image file formats describe how pixel data are stored in the file, and different formats organize data in different ways, compress data using a variety of schemes, and encode and represent image data using various approaches.

Why are there so many different graphical data formats and why are they so often incompatible with each other? As more graphics applications were created (see Chapter 2), the ability to save pictures for later manipulation or display became increasingly important. Different applications use different types of data in different ways to satisfy different user needs. First, each type of data requires its own format and there are many different types of data: bitmap and vector data are used and stored differently, so file formats for each are required. Second, in the absence of widely accepted standards, companies developing hardware or software for use with image data tend to develop proprietary formats which best suit their platforms and applications, and the documentation and licensing that would enable the use of these formats is often restricted to prevent usage beyond the developer's control. Finally, a wide range of design principles are employed when developing a file format: the design of a data format is based, in part, on available memory, processing speed and the circuitry components of hardware systems targeted to use the data, but also functionality and user requirements. Graphical data sets tend to be large, and as a result, programs that manipulate and display image data tend to require large amounts of available processing power. The format may be designed to increase the speed of data access and to process image data as quickly as possible or to retain and store large amounts of high quality, accurate image data where speed or computational cost is not important. Alternatively, the format can be designed to compress the data into as small a file as possible for delivery via a network. Additionally, data formats must meet the specific needs of a broad range of diverse applications, hardware and users, while also keeping up to date with advances occurring in technology. A format captures the state of a technology and freezes it in time, while the technology that the format is based on usually continues to advance. New formats, and standards, are constantly required to keep up with technological development. This will result in a broad spectrum of graphical data formats that can be confusing to both the expert and average user alike, from:

> the early 1980s, official standards groups began to create common graphics subroutine libraries, and then graphics files, to encourage portability of files and code amongst different applications and different hardware. In the 1990s, color, animation, and desktop … applications [were] employing new colour capabilities and better compression techniques. The result is a graphics 'Tower of Babel' with dozens of different formats in use by hundreds of different programs (Kay and Levine 1995, xvii).

Formats must be documented: the data is structured according to specific conventions, which should be recorded in specification documents written and maintained by the format creators, who may be commercial companies, standards committees or lone developers. As a result, documentation for graphics file formats comes from many places (and not all documentation is up to date or well written). The formats which become popular are generally those which are well documented, and make their documentation available in the public domain, allowing developers to easily integrate the format into their applications.

Some formats become official standards, being formally ratified by a recognized organization or an official governing body through a time-consuming and costly process of proposal evaluation, documentation and election. (Organizations which ratify standards include the International Organization for Standardization (ISO); the International Electrotechnical Commission (IEC); the International

Telecommunications Union (ITU); and the American National Standards Institute (ANSI).) Some formats are *de facto* standards, being a product or specification developed by a company or individual, but adopted and used by entire industries with large marketplace acceptance. These are common in computer technologies: sheer numbers of users can make a format a standard, with other vendors feeling obliged to support the format in order for their product to stay competitive in the marketplace. Due to the number of users involved, there is an argument that proposes that only good products will ever become *de facto* standards, but the disadvantage of any *de facto* proprietary standard is that the authoring organization can modify it at will, without consulting the user community. See Brown and Shepherd (1995, 38–55) for a comprehensive overview of the mechanisms which generate both official and *de facto* standards for image data.

How Do Image Formats Work?

Although there are many different image file formats, most work in a broadly similar way. Most typical data sets consist of a linear list of data values, commonly referred to as a data stream. The entire data stream makes up the file. The difference between individual image file formats lies in the details: what type of data is stored, if it is compressed and how it is encoded. Data can be encoded in either binary information or in symbolic form, such as in ASCII: binary coding is generally used for bitmap data and symbolic form is generally used for vector data.

The order of the data values within the binary stream is important for many applications: graphical hardware devices are designed to operate on data streams organized in particular ways. Each individual part of the data stream will have a certain amount of information (in bits or bytes, known as a 'field') devoted to it, or have particular identifiers (known as tags) to indicate the start and end of that particular section of the file. A typical structure of an image data stream may be: File Signature, Image Header, perhaps a Colour Palette, then the individual pixel colour data and finally a File Closing Marker. Some file formats may also occasionally allow File Footers.

The main function of a File Signature is to serve as an identifier, declaring which file format is being used to order the subsequent data. Most data streams include information that describes them within themselves – metadata – which can be used to identify and interpret the data stream correctly. At the start of a file is often a signature and version number: a tag consisting of a unique set of bytes that distinguishes a data stream from all other possible data streams, declaring to the computer system what format the data is stored in. For example, if you open up a GIF image in a textual editor, you will see that the file always begins 'GIF87a' or 'GIF89a', depending on which version of GIF is being used. This signature allows software systems to automatically identify a data stream and send it to the appropriate software interpreter. Not all file formats contain an identification tag, relying on a file name suffix for their identification (you can generally deduce the format of an image file from the three letters that appear at the end of the filename after the dot), but this is a poor approach as the name can be accidentally changed by the user.

The image header which follows usually contains a certain amount of technical information which describes the image, such as pixel dimensions, image height and width, bit depth used to store the colour information, the number of lines of pixels in the image, a file version number and a 'flag' which will indicate whether compression is used and which scheme for compression has been used if more than one is allowed. The content of image headers is not standard among different file formats and different numbers of bytes are devoted to each field depending on the format in question, but typically these consist of a set of fixed fields, with those which are required being specified in the format documentation.

A colour palette can be used within some bitmap image formats to store colour information effectively. A colour palette is used to map individual pixel data to RGB colour values within the image. A colour palette is specific to each individual image, providing a 'lookup table' or 'colour map', which defines a limited range of colour intensity values, which appear in the image. The pixel data stores indexes to a value in the colour palette for each individual pixel, rather than stating lengthier RGB colour values for each pixel, so it can be an effective way to compress image data (if the limited number of colours which can be stored in the colour palette allow a good representation of the image to be reconstructed). Colour palettes are generated from each individual image from looking up the spread of colours across an image. If all the colours in a 24-bit image of, say, a sunset are collected and counted to see how many pixels belong to each of these colours, a graph called a histogram can be produced, showing how much red, green or blue, and all the variations in-between, are present within the image. A few important clusters of colour information usually appear, showing which of the colours are most important: in a picture of a sunset, we would expect more reds. Mathematical algorithms to 'split and merge' this information can produce, from a 24-bit image, the 256 colours necessary to best resolve the image into, or even the two best colours to represent an image in the case of a logo or button (this is the technique used for GIF images, see pp. 69–72). Colour palettes are only available in some formats, others only support direct or 'true colour' (where colour values are stored only as direct intensities of RGB in the pixel data). Some formats support both colour lookup tables and true colour, giving the user the choice of which way they wish to store the colour information, and some allow the user the choice of how many colours they wish to include in the palette. The image file can store in the file header information as to which 8-bit values for red, green and blue correspond to each index.

The major part of a data stream for an image will contain graphical data, where each individual pixel's colour information is stored. For a bitmap data set, the colour of individual pixels (whether that is true colour or pointing to a value in a colour palette) and the location of individual pixels within the grid needs to be specified.

The location of individual pixels in the grid is generally not explicitly stated, as it is usually inferred from their order in the data stream: most bitmap data sets define a rectangular volume specified by width and height in pixels, and the pixels in the data stream are placed into the grid in the order defined by the format, one after another, in horizontal rows referred to as 'scan lines'. The most commonly used pixel order stores each row from left to right and stores the rows from top to bottom (which is the same way most bitmap devices display digital data, and for printers to print the top of an image and proceed down the page), although some formats allow a variety of orderings of pixel data. Because the position of a data point in the image file determines what pixel this data point represents, the data points (which are bits) are said to be 'mapped' to the image: hence the name, 'bitmap'.

An alternative common way to store and display pixel data is using 'interlacing'. Scan lines are displayed in a predefined order (which may look random to the user), providing a quick overview of the image data while gradually and progressively filling in the fine details on subsequent passes: a low resolution display which fades into full resolution. This is a potentially very useful feature, usually used for online delivery, which allows a user to discern the content of the image before it has displayed in its entirety, allowing them to stop the transmission of the image if they determine that the data is not wanted, saving them time (and sometimes money). The GIF format provides a good example of how interlacing works: defining an optional interlaced ordering that requires four passes to process all of the scan lines of a bitmap data stream. The first pass displays one-eighth of the image scan lines, painting every eighth row onto the output device. The second pass through the image contains another one-eighth of the scan lines, starting at the fourth row and then painting every eighth. The third pass starts with the second row and paints every fourth, and the last pass starts on the first row and contains the remaining scan lines, which is every second scan line in the image. If the user terminates the transmission of the image before the last pass, they have avoided the need to download or access 50 per cent of the image data.

If the order of the pixels on the output device can be determined by their order in the file, only colour information is needed to be stored for each pixel, with a predefined amount of information (in bytes) devoted in the data stream to store the colour value of each individual pixel: the 'bit depth' (see pp. 44–49). It is this set of colour data which will make up the majority of a bitmap image file. This chunk of colour data is the part of the file which can be compressed to make the file size smaller (see pp. 50–58 regarding how different types of compression work).

An end of file marker (EOF), terminator or 'trailer' marks the end of the data stream and so the end of the file. Some file formats can also contain a footer, which can provide information in addition to the header. This is mainly used when the file format is upgraded to accommodate new types of information and when it is not convenient to change the header. Storing additional information in the footer can be a useful way to maintain backward compatibility with previous versions of the format.

Each individual file format can have other fields added to this basic outline of how image data tends to be stored. Additions include giving the image creator the possibility of storing additional metadata within the file itself, such as TIFF, which allows textual information about the image file to be stored within each file itself. In the case of GIF, the file format allows animations to be produced by providing the ability to save more than one individual image in each file.

A graphics format file reader is responsible for opening and reading a file, determining its validity according to the specification and interpreting the information contained within it. Writing an image file is the inverse of reading – writers may send data directly to an output device or may create image files and store data according to the specification chosen by the user.

Format Conversion

File formats can be converted from one to another. This can be useful if the organization of the data stream is incompatible with the requirements of a particular device or application, or if the original format is not one suited for, say, online delivery or interoperability. However, restructuring and conversion of a data stream requires computational memory, and often some amount of computational manipulation. (If there are insufficient computational resources to restructure the data, the data stream will be unusable.) The process of the conversion of data from one format to another format ranges from the trivial to the impossible, depending on the formats in question. It is beyond the scope of this chapter to discuss every detail involved with every possible conversion, but, in general, the conversion of one bitmap format to another is generally straightforward, although this may still entail detailed conversion programs that require large amounts of processing power and memory. Conversion from bitmap to vector and vice versa is generally problematic.

The conversion of image data depends on the quality of the software components (readers and writers) which generate and interpret the formats, and the quality of the original image data available for conversion. A range of image manipulation programs, such as Photoshop, the Gimp and Paint Shop Pro, make the conversion process relatively straightforward, but not every format can be converted to every other format. In some cases conversion of one format to another may lower image quality, especially when compression algorithms are used (see pp. 50–58). Lossless-to-lossless conversion (for example, PNG to GIF) can be performed without quality loss. However, lossless-to-lossy (TIFF to JPEG) or lossy-to-lossy conversion will result in visible image quality loss, dependent upon the degree of compression used.

Bitmap formats are generally converted into another bitmap format, one pixel value at a time. The file headers and the data contained within the bitmap file may vary considerably between formats but this information can be added or discarded at the discretion of the software in order to make the best conversion possible. Computationally intensive conversions generally involve rearrangement of the pixel colour data (a colour palette may have to be added or removed, or the conversion between one colour model to another may be necessary (see pp. 185–191). Converting interlaced data presents a problem when converting an interlaced image into another format: a scan line table must be created to write out the scan lines in their proper, non-interlaced order, and this can take time to process.

Unsuccessful bitmap conversions can occur when translating a file written in a format with a lot of colour information to one which stores less colour information (for example, converting 24-bit colour into 8-bit data). Colour information will be lost and, if a colour palette is used, it may not support the storage of enough data to reproduce the image accurately. Usually, some image processing operations (such as quantization or dithering) are used to increase the appearance quality of the converted image (this is also the case when resizing an image, see pp. 38–40). However, in such cases, the converted image will appear different from the original, which can be a concern where the veracity of image data is important, such as in the provision of images of manuscripts or other primary historical sources which will be used for research (see pp. 194–198).

Corrupt Image Files

Occasionally, image files will become corrupt. This will become apparent when no image displays, or shifted or broken parts of the image appear, or the colours displayed appear in a strange way. The causes for this vary and can be difficult to ascertain. The display environments may not be properly configured, the file format may not be supported by the display program (or a variation or version of the file format may not be supported by the display program), the display program may be incorrectly interpreting the file or the file data itself may have become corrupt. File formats may become corrupt in a manner of ways (for example, a buggy, poorly designed program writing the files; a bad write of the data to the storage medium; faulty processing of the data in an application; or even a poorly designed file format which leaves room for application developers to interpret the specification in various ways). Unfortunately, most formats do not provide any real error checking, making it even more important to retain multiple copies of a master image file in a standard format to ensure future access to the data.

Individual Graphics Formats

Information professionals will generally come across a few bitmap image formats that are readily used in the online environment and for the digitization of cultural and heritage material. The following section provides in-depth information about these commonly used formats. GIF was one of the first image formats to gain widespread acceptance, and is still in use today for the provision of online image material, although the format has some problems in displaying continuous tone images, such as photographs. PNG was designed to supersede GIF, but is still not widely adopted beyond the computer and engineering communities. JPEG was designed to deal with the effective storage of photographic images, to overcome the shortcomings in the approach taken by GIF, and is the most commonly used image graphics format at present for both online delivery and as the output format for digital cameras, although there is confusion about the implementation of the JPEG specification. TIFF has been the recommended archival storage format for digital images for the past decade, and is becoming increasingly popular as more and more digital cameras can output images in this format. These formats are described here in detail, giving their historical and developmental background, as well as a technical overview, to elucidate the features that have made them popular, and the issues that may be encountered while appropriating them.

GIF: CompuServe Graphics Interchange Format

Graphics Interchange Format (.GIF) was developed and introduced in 1987 by CompuServe,[1] who wished to provide a coloured image format for cross-platform exchange that would use compression effectively, resulting in smaller file sizes that would be faster to transmit via the Internet. (At the time, connection speeds to the Internet were phenomenally slow compared to today's standards.) Created as an image communications protocol for interoperability and the interchange and viewing of image data stored on local or remote systems, GIF is not associated with any particular software application, but many applications can convert to and from GIF. GIF was the first image format to become universally accepted and, with the integration of GIF images into web pages, made possible by the Mosaic browser in 1993, quickly became the *de facto* format for displaying online images in the early days of the World Wide Web.

The original format was called GIF 87a (CompuServe Incorporated 1987) and along with GIF's efficient use of compression and its interoperability became popular as (although the format was copyrighted) the documentation was 'made available for use in computer software without royalties or licensing restrictions' (ibid. 1), allowing and encouraging other software developers to display and create GIF graphics within their programs.

GIF 87a was revised in 1989 (CompuServe Incorporated 1990) to provide GIF 89a, which provided two new features. One colour in the image can be defined as 'transparent', meaning the background of a web page or document would shine through those defined parts, allowing users to generate images which seem to be freed from the rectangular nature of bitmaps. Second, GIF 89a supports simple animation by allowing multiple images to be displayed with a simple control over

1 CompuServe Information Services were the first major commercial online service in the United States who offered email facilities from 1979 and dominated online access in the US during the late 1980s and early 1990s before their acquisition by AOL in 1998 (CompuServe Incorporated 2006).

delay time. When the images are changed rapidly, the human eye perceives them as continuous motion rather than individual frames and the image appears to be animated (rather like a flick book). However, there can be problems in trying to display these animations on different viewers: there is no official standard that describes how multi-image GIFs should be displayed and many image viewers will just display the first image in a GIF file. Web browsers will tend to display each image in sequence as rapidly as they can if no control regarding the amount of time between the individual frames is specified. Because of these problems, many applications still continue to produce only GIF 87a files for backward compatibility.

GIF is often trumpeted as using lossless data compression – which it does, provided that there are only 256 distinct colours in the image. This is a much misunderstood point. Images up to 24-bit colour can be stored as GIF, but the format converts the colour information for each pixel into a palette or 'colour lookup table', most used colours first, with a maximum coverage of 256 RGB colours. Each individual pixel is assigned one of the 256 values in the table, for display when the image is rendered. The means of compressing this individual pixel data in the GIF format may indeed be lossless but the format has already discarded much colour information that may have been available in the original image, so care must be taken when saving an image as a GIF if colour values are important.

The 256 image colour limitation seemed reasonable at the time of GIF's creation because few people could afford the hardware to display more. However, this limitation makes GIF unsuitable for use with photographic images which mostly depend on many different colours. Instead, it is suited to logos, buttons, cartoons, diagrams or trademarks with a specific limited colour palette: the colour palette in GIF can be reduced to a minimum of two exact colours, which can be useful when reproducing logos, flags or other image types which have areas of defined colour.

The file format itself is a straightforward bitmap, following the basic image format model of having a signature at the start of the file ('GIF 87a' or 'GIF 89a') followed by header information giving image width and height, and the global colour palette information. The actual bitmap pixel data then follows: the colour value for each pixel is given by scan line and pixel, and this information is then compressed using the LZW compression scheme before being stored. If there is only one image in the GIF file, the GIF terminator then indicates the end of the file. Unlike all of the other formats mentioned in this text, GIF allows multiple images to be stored in a single file, although the vast majority of GIF images only contain a single image. (If more than one image file is being stored in the GIF for animation purposes, the further information about height and size, local colour map and bitmap data for each individual image in the file is included before the file terminator. GIF 89a also stores further information regarding the speed of display of these images.)

Users can choose the order in which pixel data is stored in the image file. It is possible to store GIFs as interlaced images: which, rather than being painted onto the screen in the default manner from the top left pixel to the bottom right, pixel by pixel and row by row, uses a gradual successive display of pixels in widely spaced rows. This provides the end user with a full, gradually resolving and clearing, overview of the appearing image, which can be helpful in deciding whether to wait for the full image to download. GIF uses a 'four pass interlacing scheme', as mentioned above.

The pixel information in GIF is the part of the file which is compressed before storage, using the Lempel–Ziv–Welch (LZW) lossless algorithm (see pp. 55–56), modified slightly to use the line grouping of pixels effectively. LZW is most efficient when compressing recurring sequences of data, such as blocks of the same colour in an image, and the use of this compression algorithm is another reason why GIF is so effective in dealing with images with limited colour palettes, achieving high levels of compression and small file sizes when dealing with images with large areas of the same colour. GIF also performs well with images that have sharp detail or transitions, such as diagrams and maps, which other compression formats (such as JPEG) may struggle with. For this reason, and the limited 256 colour palette, GIF is best suited to images with a few distinctive, defined colours such as logos, banners, buttons and diagrams.

GIF was originally 'designed to support current and future image technology' (CompuServe Incorporated 1987, 3). Unlike other major graphics formats, no enhancements to GIF are under way. 'This, coupled with inherent limitations compared to other formats, has made it essentially dead' (Miano 1999, 188). However, the popularity of the format continues with its widespread use on the World Wide Web: it was the most widely used image format online until the late 1990s when JPEG replaced GIF for photographic images because of its better compression and greater colour depth, but GIF remains popular for buttons and banners, and no other image format has provided a convenient mechanism to deliver small animations online. GIF has its detractors, though: not because of the effectiveness of the format, but because of its legal status.

By the early 1990s, GIF had rapidly become the most popular format for the delivery of image files via the Internet. However, CompuServe did not know that the LZW format used for compression in GIF was governed by a patent that was owned by the Unisys Corporation[2] (Sperry Corporation 1983). (The writer of the original specification had filed for a patent, which was granted to his employer, and CompuServe never checked to see if LZW was patented when it issued the GIF specification.) In December 1994, when Unisys became aware that the newly-popular GIF file format used LZW compression, they announced that they would be seeking royalties on their patent; all commercial programs capable of

2 Unisys is a multi-billion pound corporation providing Information Technology services and consultancy, such as server technologies, developing IT infrastructure and outsourcing; see www.unisys.com/index.htm for more information.

producing GIF files would be required to pay a license fee to Unisys (the patent did not cover decompression of the algorithm, so image-viewers capable of only displaying GIF files were not required to pay a license fee). In 1999 this charge was extended to free and non-commercial software capable of creating GIFs. Because the file format had become a *de facto* standard and was so widespread, most companies producing these programs had little choice but to pay, and this caused great confusion and consternation among programmers (Battilana 2004). Although the patent has now expired, variants on it were also registered, and it remains the case that most commercial applications that create GIF files have a GIF/LZW license from Unisys. However, individuals or institutions creating GIF files with any licensed program do not need to worry about acquiring a separate license:

> People realized, upon closer examination, that it is not illegal to own, transmit, or receive GIF files (provided that no unlicensed compression and/or decompression of the files occur). It was, in fact, the implementation of the LZW algorithm that was under licensing restriction (Murray and van Ryper 1996, 176).

Given the now expired state of the original patent, this should not be of real concern to those creating digital images (but variations on the patent still remain under patent). Nevertheless, there are repeated calls to 'Burn All Gifs' (http://burnallgifs.org/archives/) and replace them with non-patented file format and network protocols (such as PNG, which was developed in response to this licensing issue). GIF has so far retained its popularity over PNG, but this may change in the future as PNG becomes better supported and more popular (although PNG does not support animation).

Most images created in a digitization project, or taken by digital camera, will require greater facilities for dealing with the range and complexity of colour in photographic images than GIF provides. However, it remains a useful, simple and compact format for logos and buttons which are to be used online.

PNG: Portable Network Graphics

Portable Network Graphics (.PNG, pronounced 'ping') is a system independent bitmap image format meant to supersede and exceed the GIF standard and provide a format for interchange of image data via the Internet. The motivation for a new standard was the patent held by Unisys and CompuServe on the LZW compression method used in the GIF format (see pp. 55–56): when Unisys began demanding license fees from programmers writing software that could produce GIF images it became impossible to use it in certain products, such as free software or shareware. JPEG quickly replaced GIF for photographic images – being more successful in dealing with them anyway – but JPEG does not deal well with images that have large blocks of a single colour, often giving whole areas of a single colour many shades approximating that colour (see pp. 78–79). A well designed, developed and documented file format in the public domain was necessary as an alternative to the GIF format.

The PNG Development Group, a committee organized by Thomas Boutell (a software programmer and evangelist for open source, well written, open standards), was started within days of Unisys's 1994 announcement that they would demand licences for GIF usage. Development of the PNG standard proceeded swiftly. Several drafts were issued to the public, with the final version of PNG 1.0 released on the 1 October 1996, just over a year and a half after the project had begun. Whereas many formats are created by one or two programmers without much thought for future developments, the twenty-five authors named on the first PNG specification (Boutell 1996) were all interested implementers, and the comprehensive nature of the format has given PNG the reputation for being 'one of the most complete, well-thought-out and well-written file format specifications' (Murray and van Ryper 1996, 702). Its position as an alternative to GIF, and the stance of the committee against GIF, is stated in the unofficial recursive derivation of the name PNG: 'PNGs Not GIF' (Murray and van Ryper 1996, 701).

The design goals of the PNG Development Group were to create a simple, easy to implement, portable format, which was freely available and unencumbered by the licensing fees and patent disputes which had overshadowed the usefulness of GIF (Murray and van Ryper 1996, 701). Indeed, PNG was designed to at least meet or exceed the capabilities of GIF. To that end PNG and GIF share various features, such as lossless image data compression, index mapped images capable of up to 256 colours, interlaced display, transparency, being independent from both hardware and operating systems, and being a format designed specifically to be suited to sharing and displaying images via the Internet (for example, there is no facility in these formats for preparing images with the colour spaces necessary for printing).

PNG improves on various GIF features: aside from the patent issues regarding data compression, its technical implantation is often viewed as being superior to GIF. It has a faster progressive display function, described by those in the community as 'a majorly gnarly two-dimensional interlacing scheme' (Roelofs 2007b). Instead of a progressive display based on widely separated rows, which is the approach taken by most interlacing schemes such as that implemented with GIF, PNG progressively displays pixels in a two-dimensional fashion, a few at a time, over seven passes through each 8 x 8 block of an image. Because the pixels in the gradually displayed image appear in a more dispersed pattern, the human eye can discern a typical PNG image after only 20 to 30 per cent of the image data has been displayed (as opposed to 50 per cent or more needed with the GIF scheme) (Murray and van Ryper 1996, 702) which can be a very useful feature allowing users to ascertain whether or not they wish to wait for an image downloading or not. A full explanation and demonstration of this feature can be found in Roelofs (2007c).

There are a number of features found in PNG but not GIF: PNG supports true colour images up to 48-bits per pixel, where GIF supports 24-bit RGB, and

PNG also supports greyscale (to 16-bits per pixel), an 'alpha channel' that is a means of controlling transparency information and gamma correction information for correct display of colour images (see p. 187). PNG also includes a means for data stream corruption detection and a facility for storing user-defined data such as text within the image format, which are both missing from the GIF specification. Additionally, a standard toolkit is freely available for developers wishing to implement PNG readers and writers, and a standard benchmarked test set of images is also available for testing any applications developed to read PNG images (both are available from www.libpng.org/pub/png/).

PNG is therefore superior to GIF in all aspects expect one sole major feature not found in PNG: GIF is capable of storing multiple images, and, when these are shown at a fast frame rate, these generate animation sequences. (There is a move to extend the PNG specification to create a 'PNG-like Image Format Supporting Multiple Images, Animation and Transparent JPEG' called MNG, Multiple-image Network Graphics, but this is still under development (Roelofs 2007a).)

The PNG file itself is organized into a sequence of blocks referred to as 'chunks'. Chunks can be defined by three sources – the most important being the PNG standard, which details the compulsory chunks the file must contain. Two other sources point to PNG's relationship with the development community: 'Registered Public Chunk Types' can be submitted by developers for consideration for addition to the standard, if they think they have provided something useful, and 'Private Chunks' can be defined by specific applications (but these may not be able to be read in other applications). Each chunk has a unique name and contains an independent block of data conforming to a specifically defined structure.

The four standard chunks which appear in a PNG file are called 'critical chunks' and consist of: the header chunk (there must be only one, appearing as the first chunk, which contains basic information about the image data); the palette chunk (stored colour map data associated with the image data, if a colour palette has been used with the image); the image data chunk (containing the actual pixel values); and the image trailer chunk (which denotes the end of the file). Other optional chunks can be used for special purposes, such as the Image Gamma chunk that stores the original gamma value of the image, allowing correction of display in subsequent viewings, although these optional chunks may not be available in all PNG readers and writers (Roelofs 1999).

The information in the image data chunk is always stored in a lossless compressed format, using a technique called the Deflate compression method which is related to the LZW method but is not subject to any patent claims or licensing agreements:

> the algorithm, called a 'sliding window' method, has a buffer (32K in our case) that is logically passed over the input stream. Output is based on patterns found in that window, which are then Huffman-coded for further compression. This method (without the Huffman pass) was first described by Lempel and Ziv in 1977, but not patented. In 1978, they described a different method of collecting patterns in text that was

> simpler and almost as powerful. Terry Welch (now with Unisys) described a particular straightforward way to implement their LZ78 idea – the dreaded LZW patent (Crocker 1995, 38).

The Deflate algorithm (originally designed by Philip Katz for the PKZIP utility, see PKWare 2007, section 10) is well documented, freely available (and fast) and is a major reason why PNG is recommended over GIF as the format for delivering graphics via the Internet.

It is advocated by many in the Web development community that PNG should now be used instead of GIF for images where JPEG is not a suitable alternative (usually in the case of non-photographic images). However, although the PNG format is very stable, is supported by most applications and is now supported by most web browsers, it has been slow to replace GIF as the main online image format for graphics and logos. This has been mostly due to lack of complete support from the major browsers:

> While most browsers supported PNG images natively since the late 1990s – the 'Big Two' (Netscape and Internet Explorer [MSIE]) having finally caught up in late 1997 (early 2000 for MSIE on the Macintosh) – the *level* of support was downright pathetic until 2001 or so and didn't achieve 'ubiquitous goodness' until … the release of MSIE 7.0 in October 2006 … And even the newest version still has multiple bugs. Meanwhile, most other browsers … have had excellent PNG support for years … What will it take to move the Browsers support rating firmly into the 'Excellent' category? Leaving aside the issue of Windows users' migration to browsers with good PNG support (e.g., Firefox, MSIE 7, or Opera) – which may take another year or two – Microsoft needs to fix MSIE (Roelofs 2006).

It is not that Microsoft Internet Explorer 6 does not recognize the PNG format, but that it cannot display certain aspects of it (related to the different types of transparency possible with PNG and the gamma support) which could result in some images only being partially displayed, or not at all. At the time of writing (April 2007), MSIE 6 remains the most popular browser used to access web pages, with approximately 40 per cent of those online using it as their browser of choice (W3Schools 2007a). There is no doubt that PNG is superior to GIF as an image format for displaying graphics online, but it will not succeed GIF as the common online format for buttons, icons and graphics until the browser that most web surfers are using can be guaranteed to display every PNG image without significant problems. As a result, at the moment PNG is useful for images which have no transparency information and projects should be encouraged to use PNG for these images. For the moment, the old *de facto* standard GIF still would seem to offer better interoperability (although this will change as users eventually migrate to MSIE 7 and beyond).

JPEG: Joint Photographic Experts Group, JPEG Specification, JFIF Format and JPEG2000

JPEG refers to a standards organization, a method of file compression, and more commonly, a file format. JPEG2000 is a different file format. This can cause confusion, as the relationship between the bodies, standards, formats and implementation is not often made clear.

In 1982, the ISO formed the Photographic Experts Group (PEG) to research methods of transmitting multimedia such as still images, text, music and video via digital communications networks, and to produce a set of industry standards regarding how these media could be efficiently stored and disseminated. Independently of this, in 1986, a group at the Comité Consultatif International Téléphonique et Télégraphique (CCITT: an organization responsible for setting communication standards, now known as the International Telecommunications Union Telecommunications Standardization Sector, www.itu.int/ITU-T/) began to research efficient methods of compressing colour and greyscale image data for facsimile transmission. It was noted that this was very similar to the work being carried out by PEG, so the two groups combined forces forming a committee that began to work towards a 'joint' single standard in 1987, naming themselves the Joint Photographic Experts Group (www.jpeg.org).

The JPEG standard developed by the committee, which took its name from the committee, is actually a lossy compression method which was published in 1992 (CCITT 1992) and approved by ISO in 1994. However, this standard does not define an image file format. It says nothing about what an application needs to do in order to create images that can be exchanged among different applications, or how colours should be represented, but deals only with how component values are stored and describes an effective method of compressing image data which has a variety of colour information, such as that found in photographs. JPEG is the most important, and most used, current standard for image compression and is used in a variety of file formats, including TIFF.

As the JPEG standard does not actually describe an image file format, a further research group not associated with the JPEG ISO committee, the Independent JPEG Group (www.ijg.org), took the JPEG compression standard, filled in the gaps and developed a format that would allow the creation and exchange of single files compressed with the JPEG method (Hamilton 1992). This file format, JPEG File Interchange Format (JFIF), is generally what people mean when they refer to JPEG images and has become the dominant format for the storage of digital and digitized photographic images. A file saved as .jpeg or .jpg is in the JFIF format.

To confuse matters further, the Joint Photographic Experts Group released a different specification, JPEG2000, to describe a new standard capable of lossless compression that will exceed the capabilities of the JFIF format (JPEG2000 files end with .JPC or .J2K). This format is the focus of much interest, although has yet to have widespread support in web browsers and applications.

To understand the genesis and implementation of JPEG images, it is therefore important to understand the background to the standard, the implementation of the standard as JFIF, and further development of the JPEG group's work in JPEG2000.

The JPEG Standard Why is the JPEG compression method so effective, and popular? Previously available image formats, such as GIF, use compression methods that do a poor job of compressing 'real world' subjects, such as photographs. Photographs contain hundreds of thousands of colours and rarely any repetition. The JPEG standard was produced specifically to define a method which could compress this continuous tone image data (with a pixel depth from 6 up to 24-bits) effectively.

To do this, it takes advantage of the human eye–brain system's inability to see extremely fine detail. The human eye is much less sensitive to changes in colour than it is to brightness: an acceptable image can be reconstructed using many fewer colour samples than light samples. (For example, think of tinted sepia photographs: a wash of pink colour over the variegated light values in a face is enough to make a portrait look almost realistic, when skin tone colour is actually much more complex. We perceive the light variance rather than noticing the sameness in colour.) JPEG compression takes advantage of this: discarding colour information which the human eye does not readily see, and compressing the resulting data stream, to generate images of a smaller file size that can often look indistinguishable from the original, or 'visually lossless'.[3]

There are four general steps used in JPEG encoding that carry out the compression process: sampling, Discrete Cosine Transform, quantization and Huffman Coding. First, colour information in JPEG is decimated by being partially dropped or averaged across an area. In this sampling process, pixel data is converted from an RGB colour space to the YC_rC_b colour space (see p. 188) and colour difference values are sampled at half the resolution of the luminance (light) values, discarding a lot of colour information. A Discrete Cosine Transfer is then used to ascertain how fast the colour intensities vary across 8 pixel blocks, called data units, and a new image is formed by grouping together the average weights of the areas where there are a lot of colour changes (known as high frequency areas). The DCT is the heart of JPEG compression: converting the bitmap data into rate of change information. The human eye prefers slow changes in colour rather than fast ones, so weights that correspond to slow changes are favoured, and fast changes in colour frequency can be discarded, as the low frequency data is the one which is important for reconstructing an image. Small changes in colour values are evened

3 Watson's 1994 edited volume *Digital Images and Human Vision* contains in-depth discussion about the role of replicating the human brain system's approach to vision in order to compress digital images effectively: in particular, the paper by Klein (1994, 81) discusses JPEG's approach as being 'remarkably similar to the representation actually used by the visual system'.

out. A compression algorithm is then used in the quantization step which discards unnecessary information further (values are divided by some large integer and truncated). The user is allowed to choose how large a denominator to use in the compression, and so chooses how much information to discard: this is presented to the user as a desired level of quality, with an estimate of how much the file size will also change. The division and truncation steps can discard almost half of the colour information while retaining an image which remains a close approximation to the original: making this step the 'lossy' stage in JPEG compression (a lossless mode exists but is rarely used). Finally, Order and Run Length Encoding is then used to eliminate repetition in the data, and Huffman encoding takes advantage of the more frequently occurring values to make the new data take up as small amount of memory as possible. The resulting image is compressed greatly from the original, but has lost much of its colour information permanently.

Decompression of a JPEG image reverses the above steps: the quantized results are decompressed and a reverse DCT is used to reconstruct the image. However, the low-order colour information which was lost in the quantization is no longer available and is replaced by a sequence of zeroes. The colour information is lost and the original image cannot be reconstructed fully.

The JPEG lossy compression algorithm can achieve the greatest compression of any bitmap format in common use. Dramatic compression ratios of up to 20:1 or even 25:1 are possible without any noticeable degradation in image quality, depending on the picture being compressed. This means that a 1Mb bitmap file can be successfully compressed to 50Kb using JPEG compression, with the contents still visible and useful. Higher compression ratios are possible, but will result in image files that have noticeable differences from the original, inserting abrupt colour changes, and other erroneous data known as 'artefacts'.

Most implementations of the algorithm allow users to choose between compression ratios of differing quality. Highest Quality (using a compression ratio of 2:1, with no perceivable data loss), Excellent (12:1, lossy, but indistinguishable from the original with the human eye), Good (32:1, very lossy, but satisfactory for many applications), Low (100:1, discarding a large proportion of image data, producing very small file sizes, but images with recognizable image inaccuracies, or 'artefacts'). Successful compression with JPEG is a matter of experimentation and preference, and is both data dependent and image quality dependent. It is important for the creator to establish priorities: are they trying to deliver the smallest possible file size or one where particular details are still recognisable? If detail is important, the smallest level of recognizable detail required should be visible in the compressed image. The only way to achieve this is through trial and error.

JPEG compression (and decompression) is computationally intensive and can be slow, but the outstanding compression possible generally outweighs the processing power required. However, it does not fit every compression need, as it is not successful with all images. Large areas of a single colour will not compress well and neither will images with a small number of colours or those which contain sharp edges: 'artefacts' will be introduced into such images, making them worse in appearance. (GIF is a useful alternative for compressing images with the characteristics which do not suit JPEG compression). Additionally, given the lossy nature of JPEG compression, any image which has been compressed using this method should not to be used as an archive copy.

JPEG compression is a useful tool for reducing the file size of large photographic image files without any visible change in appearance, and so has become a very popular method for creating image files of a suitable size for data exchange and interchange. The creators of JPEG envisioned a multitude of commercial applications for JPEG technology, but it has mostly benefited 'a consumer public made hungry by the marketing promises of imaging and multimedia technologies' (Murray and van Ryper 1996, 191). The JPEG standard (CCITT 1992) which carries out the compression is fairly complex: it is actually a suite of 29 distinct encoding processes, defining a number of related image compression techniques, some of which are owned and patented by different companies (such as IBM, AT&T and Mitsubishi). The exact requirements for some parts of the licensing are unclear, so many of these routines are never used in graphics and imaging applications. It is possible that any given JPEG compliant decoder will not accept all variations of the JPEG standard, although in practice this is seldom the case. It is also interesting to note that very little of the JPEG standard is in common use – the standard simply defines too many ways to do the same thing – and so it is not worth implementing every part of it in every program. Most common implementations use the parts of the specification that are not subject to any licensing or patent restrictions.

To make the compression tools described in the JPEG standard more available, it was necessary to create a file format based on the JPEG standard, which would encapsulate the methods described, and allow files containing JPEG encoded data to be exchanged between otherwise incompatible systems and applications: resulting in the JPEG File Interchange Format. Most point and click digital cameras (and many professional ones) use JPEG compression (and output a JFIF file), rather than delivering the RAW data stream from the camera sensor.

JPEG JFIF File Format After the publication of the JPEG standard, a number of commercial applications began using the compression algorithms. It became obvious that a file format was necessary which could store JPEG encoded data and define it as a file format. The JPEG File Interchange Format (JFIF) was established on 1 March 1991 in a meeting convened by the software engineer Eric Hamilton at C-Cube Microsystems,[4] which involved representatives from many other commercial computing companies. The most recent version, 1.02, was published

4 C-Cube Microsystems was an award winning Californian Company, specializing in image compression and digital video applications. Founded in 1988, the company diverged into many different imaging areas, and was bought by LSI Corporation, a leading networking and storage company dealing with digital media, in 2001.

in 1992 (Hamilton 1992), and the format has remained fixed ever since (although it has had some recent additions in the Exif format, see pp. 89–90). JFIF has grown in popularity and is the dominant file format for digital photographic images in graphics and image manipulation programs, image display and interchange online, and the default output generated by most point and click digital cameras. For all practical purposes, something which is referred to as a 'JPEG' file is actually a 'JPEG file in the JFIF format'. Despite its widespread use, JPEG JFIF is a *de facto* standard, rather than one ratified by a standards authority.

The JFIF format defines the facilities missing from the JPEG standard to allow it to function as a file format. The format itself is basically a JPEG data stream with a few restrictions and an identifying marker. It provides a signature and header for identifying JPEG files, notes the colour space used (24-bit RGB, YC_rC_b or Greyscale), notes the pixel resolution and height and width of the image, which allows it to be displayed independently, and allows the facility to include a compressed thumbnail of the image in the file.

As for storing the order of pixel data: in most image formats, the entire pixel data is stored in one contiguous region in the file, but in the JPEG specification, each pass through the image for one or more components is stored in a distinct block called a scan. The original JPEG standard had four compression modes of this pixel data: sequential (encoded from top to bottom in a single scan); progressive (akin to interlacing, components are encoded in multiple scans intended to be displayed as they are encoded, rougher to finer versions, for use in image downloads); hierarchical (similar to progressive, but implemented in a much more complex way, which means it is much more computationally expensive and is seldom used) and lossless (which preserves the exact original image, but there has never been any compelling reason to use JPEG for uncompressed images and for all practical purposes, this is obsolete). 'Baseline Sequential' is the basis of the majority of JPEG implementations and JFIF supports baseline sequential pixel ordering and also progressive JPEG encoding, which works in a similar way to interlacing, presenting a hazy view of an entire image that gradually resolves into a crisp whole after progressive scans are displayed. This feature was not supported by web browsers until the latter half of the 1990s, but is now widely supported, and it is popular to save JFIF compressed in progressive mode.

JFIF does have some drawbacks: its lossy nature means it is unsuitable for generating an archive copy of an image, or for intermediate storage when repeatedly editing an image. It is very useful for generating copies of images for display online, and the lossy nature of its format can also be used as a means to prevent piracy: small images provided to users in JFIF format are seldom of high enough quality to be used in professional printing outputs.

JFIF is a popular output format for digital cameras, allowing a short shoot to print time, and the smaller file sizes allow a greater number of images to be stored on a digital camera than would be possible if using a non-compressed format. However, the compression used in JFIF means that some data has already been discarded by the digital camera before outputting the image to the user. Additionally, long or high-ISO exposures shot with JPEG can generate noisy images due to the characteristics of JPEG compression. Cameras which shoot in JPEG often allow different qualities of JPEG to be generated (FINE and BASIC): it is better to use JPEG-FINE if you wish to shoot in JPEG to ensure as much detail is retained as possible, as it produces the highest quality JPEG output (Rouse 2005, Chapter 3). In general, for high quality archival images, it is better to shoot in lossless TIFF format, and then generate JPEG derivatives for image display and exchange from the TIFF archival master file.

As far as its use in the LIS sector, JPEG JFIF is popular as an 'access image' format: the format presented to the user on a web page or CD-ROM, generated by the project as a digital derivative from the archival TIFF file. Although not a suitable format for storing an archive image due to its lossy nature and inability to store any metadata within the file itself, its popularity and success at compressing photographic digital information means it has been recommended as the access image format since the earliest discussions regarding digitization guidelines in the library, archive, cultural and heritage communities (Besser and Trant 1995; Canadian Heritage Information Network 1996; Reilly and Frey 1996). It is recommended that access JPEG images have a resolution of between 72 to 200 dots per inch, have a pixel array that comfortably fits on a screen (800–3000 pixels along the longest dimension), use 24-bit RGB and medium to high quality compression to ensure the image generated retains useful details (California Digital Library 2007).

JPEG 2000 For many years, libraries and archives have used the TIFF and JPEG standards to store digital images and make them available to users. Yet the versions used of these technology standards are relatively old, in computational terms, and do not take advantages of new advances in computing science and image processing. In the 1990s, the Joint Photographic Experts Group continued its work on effective image compression, looking to develop a new and entirely separate specification to supersede the original JPEG compression algorithm (which uses Discrete Cosine Transformation), with a new image format which would use wavelet transformation as its means of compression. Wavelet transformation is a relatively new concept in mathematics, used to divide a given function into different frequency components (an overview and introduction can be found in Cassereau (1994) and Polikar (2001), but the mathematical detail can be daunting), offering an efficient means to compress image information in either a lossy or lossless manner. In December 2000, Part 1 of the new standard was ratified by the JPEG committee (2000), and was named after the committee and the date of this agreement: JPEG2000. It should be noted that although this is an open standard, the standard is not patent free, and also has to be purchased to be accessed.

JPEG2000 has little in common with the original JPEG specification, or the JPEG JFIF file format: it is a completely distinct entity. JPEG2000 files can be identified with the .jp2 or .jpx suffixes.

The JPEG2000 standard has a long list of features, including:

> state of the art low bit-rate compression performance; progressive transmission by quality, resolution, component, or spatial locality; lossy and lossless compression facilities, random (spatial) access to the bitstream; pan and zoom (with decompression of only a subset of the compressed data); compressed domain processing (i.e. rotation and cropping) … (Marcellin et al. 2000, 523).

The list of advanced features far exceeds those of other available bitmap image formats and includes various facilities that are attractive to those looking for long-term image storage: sophisticated lossy and lossless compression facilities, resilience to corruption due to data redundancy, and a facility for on-the-fly conversion of derivatives to any size. Additionally:

> JPEG 2000 allows a wide range of uses and can support a wide range of formats and multiple resolutions. It can also offer both lossy and lossless compression modes. Most importantly it is a flexible file format which allows metadata to be built in to the file, a vital element of the digital preservation process. However, the standard is not yet widely in use and there is as yet no native support for it in internet browsers. More investigation and practical implementations of the standard are yet to be seen but it could be used as a potential archival standard (Digital Preservation Coalition 2007).

The LIS and heritage sectors are starting to seriously consider JPEG2000 as an archival format. Pilot projects are being carried out to ascertain its usefulness (Misic et al. 2002; Politou et al. 2004; Zellman 2006) and forums for discussion, both on and offline, are appearing (for example, http://j2karclib.info, and Digital Preservation Coalition 2007). However, at present, JPEG2000 remains difficult to implement, with a limited choice of software currently available that will support JPEG2000 within existing IT structures (Puglia and Rhodes 2007). Problems with patents and licensing within the specification have meant it is being adopted cautiously, if at all. The JPEG committee continues to work on the specifications that underpin the format, and it may be the case that this format supersedes TIFF as the digital image archive format, but only once the development community trusts that the open standard is free from licensing issues, and JPEG2000 becomes supported, viewable and usable in commonly available, popular applications.

TIFF: Tagged Image File Format

Tagged Image File Format (.TIFF, .tiff or .tif) is one of the most useful formats for the capture, storage and exchange of high quality digital image data. Since the early 1990s it has been embraced as an archival digital image format by the library and archive community, and is now also in common use as an output format from professional level digital cameras.

Originally developed by the Aldus Corporation[5] in the 1980s as an attempt to provide a standard format for storing and exchanging black and white images created by scanners and desktop publishing applications, TIFF was enthusiastically adopted by the desktop publishing industry and its related applications, and its popularity spread to all types of imaging and document storage. Different versions of TIFF were produced (1.0 in 1986, 4.0 in 1997 which added support for uncompressed RGB colour images, 5.0 in 1988 which allowed colour palettes to be used and support for LZW compression, and finally 6.0 in June 1992, which added support for CMYK and YC_rC_b colour spaces and JPEG compression methods). It has not had a major update since version 6.0 in June 1992, although several technical notes have been published with minor extensions to the format (there are persistent rumours that a new TIFF version is forthcoming, but version 6.0 remains the most current, to date). Although the specification was copyrighted by Aldus, later supported by CompuServe and Microsoft, and is still owned by Aldus (now absorbed into the Adobe Corporation) the documentation is publicly available (Adobe 1992), making TIFF 6.0 a *de facto* standard for digital images.

What are the reasons for TIFF's popularity? At a time where other formats make image data compact and compressed for online delivery and exchange, the aim of TIFF is to retain and preserve as much image data as possible, making it useful for the storage of high quality digital master files. Independent from any computer architecture, operating system or hardware, TIFF's portability means it is the standard file format used in most paint, imaging and desktop publishing programs, or to exchange detailed outputs from these programs between different machines and platforms or for long-term storage of high quality image data.

The format itself is reasonably compact, is well documented, is designed to be extensible and provides many features that a programmer might need in a file format: as a result, it resists obsolescence and remains one of the best choices of bitmap formats for data exchange and storage.

TIFF handles black and white, greyscale and colour images and so is ideal for most storage needs: it can store colour information as either 1-bit, greyscale, 8-bit, 24-bit RGB, 48-bit colour depth (with a 16-bit field each for Red, Green and Blue) or a 64k colour palette. The format can also deal with opacity and transparency.

TIFF allows for the inclusion of unlimited amounts of information regarding the image, such as locally used metadata. Some TIFF 6.0 file headers are administrative and can be used to record technical information, for example, ImageWidth, ImageLength, Compression, StripOffsets, RowsPerStrip, StripByteCounts, Xresolution, Yresolution, Resolution Unit and BitsPerSample. Some of the file headers are more descriptive and can be used to record elements

5 The Aldus Corporation (named after the fifteenth century Venetian printer Aldus Manutius) was a computer software company, founded in the 1980s, gaining success with its PageMaker software for the Apple Macintosh, which is often credited in establishing the desktop publishing industry for home computing. Aldus merged with Adobe in September 1994.

essential for identifying the file, for example, project ID, institution, collection, year of publication, title, author and image sequence number. These fields can be useful for capturing the technical, administrative and archival details of a digital image within the file itself, meaning the image content cannot be separated from this basic metadata (although this basic metadata does not meet archival standards, see p. 173).

TIFF was originally a lossless format and can store uncompressed image data (up to a maximum of 4 gigabytes per image). Archival TIFF images should always be stored uncompressed, to ensure that all image information available is retained so that the maximum quality of information is available for future consultation. As various incarnations of TIFF appeared, support for numerous compression schemes to compress the pixel data within the TIFF increased, and the format now supports the biggest range of compression algorithms of any bitmap image format: TIFF 4.0 supported RLE and CITT T.4 and T.6 compression, TIFF 5.0 added LZW (which requires a license fee), TIFF 6.0 added JPEG. (However, as TIFF is not as user-controllable as other formats such as JPEG, using JPEG compression within TIFF does not really provide any advantages over using JPEG JFIF itself. TIFF also came under criticism for the way it implemented JPEG compression in TIFF 6.0 (see 'Problems with TIFF 6.0 JPEG', Murray and van Ryper 1996, 903-5), as the specification is ambiguous and contradictory. As a result, the TIFF 6.0 JPEG specification was not widely implemented). It is also possible to use an unsupported compression scheme in a TIFF file by adding the needed user-defined tags, should this be required by developers, although this will cause problems in reading files in programs that do not support that compression scheme.

TIFF's popularity in the library and archive sector is also due to the fact that TIFF meets most requirements for a 'durable digital object' (that is it has been used by a large community over a long period of time, is a file format which is published and freely available, is supported by a wide range of applications, supports uncompressed image data, has facilities for preservation of metadata, and enables 'full information capture' with no data being lost because of the format (van Horik 2005, 126)).

However, although the format does have wide support from both the LIS and professional photography community, TIFF does present a few problems to the user and developer. These include the large size of TIFF images, but more seriously, the structure and extensible nature of the format, which can be beneficial, but can also cause complications in sharing and exchanging data between applications.

The detailed image data within the TIFF file format results in large file sizes, often in the tens of megabytes. TIFF files cannot be displayed on the Web because they tend to be too large for online delivery (a deliberate choice by the developers of browsers: it makes much more sense to convert the image to a Web-friendly format such as JPEG instead, retaining the TIFF master file locally for future needs, or providing a link to the TIFF file which can be downloaded for local use). The large file sizes also mean any digital cameras shooting in the TIFF format must have large amounts of memory available for storage. This is a minor drawback given the benefits of being able to access detailed image information in the long term – but the costs of storing many large images resulting from a digitization project should not be overlooked.

TIFF has a reputation for being complicated, due to the rather unusual structure of the file format, and its versatile and extensible nature. The file format contains a rudimentary header, which is the only part of the file that has a fixed position, storing much of its data in a series of tags called Image File Directories, which are fixed neither in size or position, but are linked by a series of file values. This can be confusing for those writing applications that read in and output TIFF files, unless they have a thorough understanding of how the file format works, and this misunderstanding is often the source of programs not being able to read or write specific instances of TIFF files. Additionally, the extensible nature of TIFF files means that developers can add their own additional information, tags and options to the specification, allowing them to customize the TIFF format to fit any peculiar data storage needs. This can lead to confusion and a failure to correctly interpret tag data is another source of errors in reading TIFF files (TIFF has been described as being a 'write-only' format):

> TIFF has garnered a reputation for power and flexibility, but it is considered complicated and mysterious as well … Because TIFF is so extensible and has many capabilities beyond all other image file formats, this format is probably the most confusing format to understand and use (Murray and van Ryper 1996, 881).

Developers working with TIFF can add 'extensions' to the basic format, a catch all 'other' category whose number and complexity are legion: including the specification of advanced colour handling features, such as CMYK and YC_rC_b, and defining exactly which compression scheme is in use, such as JPEG or LZW encoding. TIFF creators must communicate exactly regarding which extensions they are using, and how they are to be used: there is such a wide variety of TIFF implementations that many applications can read certain types of TIFF but not others. Vendors can also register proprietary, private, undisclosed data field formats with Aldus Developer's Desk, to host some particular data in the file format, in some particular way. Some vendors claim TIFF compatibility while actually maintaining a closed format and this complex file/format specification is another common source of TIFF failure between applications.

To get around this problem, Revision 6.0 of the TIFF standard specifies certain 'baseline' capabilities, encouraging programmers to support a basic level of capability for all TIFF 6.0 software, which has improved TIFF's value for inter-application exchange. The baseline specification defines what tags are important to read, whether tags are required or optional, what type of image data is stored, and provides a minimum set of tags which must be present in a TIFF image (for example, ImageWidth, ImageLength and BitsPerSample). All TIFF 6.0 readers and writers must handle the baseline set of data fields. Optional baseline fields include opacity information. The TIFF reader may ignore or process optional fields, but they must not cause the reader to malfunction: for example, a baseline TIFF reader must continue to process basic image data, even if it does not have the ability to process opacity information.

Any TIFF file including tags which are not present in the baseline specification is said to be 'extended'. Extended TIFF 6.0 files should be avoided for archival image masters: it is important to use a format which is documented, can be read without recourse to specific technology and is known to be interoperable. In that case, archival standard TIFF should be baseline.

TIFF has been recommended as an archival format since the early days of image digitization projects, appearing as a recommendation in reports from projects trying to ascertain best practice in the brave new digital world, such as the Oversized Color Images Project at Columbia University (Cartolano et al. 1995), and the scoping study carried out to ascertain *Requirements and Options for the Digitization of the Illustration Collections of the National Museum of Natural History* (D'Amato and Klopfenstein 1996). More than a decade later, TIFF remains the format of choice for long-term storage of digital image masters (Library of Congress 2007):

> From the currently available formats, TIFF is the one that can be considered most 'archival'. It is a versatile, platform-independent and open file format and it is being used in most digitising projects as the format of choice for the digital masters (Frey 2000).

To retain as much image data as possible, the archival image data should be uncompressed and avoid the use of extension tags:

> In principle, the TIFF specification meets the criteria to act as the standard for the creation of digital durable surrogates, but features that obstruct durability, such as data compression and inclusion of non-standard private tags, should not be used (van Horik 2005, 130).

Institutions have a choice regarding the amount of colour information which should be captured in the TIFF file, this is dependent on the type of document being digitized:

- Grayscale TIFF files are produced where color content does not exist or is not deemed significant. Books, manuscripts and sheet music fall into this category.
- Fine quality grayscale or color TIFF image files are produced where color information exists in the content, or where the artifactual value is extremely important. Rare books, maps, and photographs are within this category.
- Rarely, bitonal TIFF files may be accepted when representation of the document content is the sole requirement. This consideration is generally the result of external Relationships (Library of Congress 2007, 2).

Recommendations for capture resolution also vary depending on the materials to be digitized (see pp. 40–43; and Library of Congress 2007, 11), but start at a minimum of 300dpi up to 600dpi, depending on the level of detail required.

Used with care, TIFF is a powerful and popular format, and is likely to remain the archival standard for some time.

Other Formats in Brief

As stated above, there are more than a hundred image file formats. Those working in the information profession will tend to come across the main formats discussed above, but may also be aware of other formats which are popularized by the digital photographic industry (such as RAW and EXIF), favoured by common operating systems (BMP and PICT) or programs (PSD), are legacy formats which were previously commonly used in digitization projects (Kodak Photo CD), or are becoming increasingly popular for the online exchange of information (PDF). These formats are more briefly discussed, for reference, below.

RAW

RAW data is actual, uncompressed, binary image data, captured directly from the sensor of a camera. No header or colour palette information is captured and the RAW information is nothing more than a series of pixel values starting from the upper-left pixel and continuing downward, with up to 48-bits of colour being stored for each pixel. Digital cameras usually convert and process the RAW data into output file formats such TIFF or JPEG, but this facility can be disabled to give access to the dynamically superior RAW data which has not had generic colour, smoothing and sharpening conversion algorithms applied to it, allowing the image editor greater control of how the data is manipulated.

RAW files need to be converted to allow manipulation and further processing by a stand-alone program or feature in an image editor, which allow users to take the unprocessed RAW data directly from the camera's sensor and convert it into a usable image file that loses none of the quality of the image captured. The unprocessed binary nature of the data means RAW is often viewed as a 'digital negative', as files may be processed and converted many times without damaging the underlying data, and the photographer has to process and convert the files post-capture on their computer in the 'digital darkroom'.

RAW is becoming increasingly popular with professional photographers working with digital media. In a survey published in 2006, most professional photographers preferred to deal with image data in RAW format (Jones and Specht 2006, 15). The reason for its popularity is the advantage delivered by preserving the maximum amount of original image data captured by the digital censor, avoiding the in-camera RAW to TIFF or JPEG processing which uses predefined settings not available to the user. Preservation of all available image data in the RAW format gives the digital image editor greater flexibility over technical settings such as white balance, exposure, tonal range and colour range; greater quality and creative control over the digital image; and allows the user to choose the way in which image data is manipulated rather than relying on the in-built camera settings. However, the large amount of image data captured in the RAW format results in large file sizes per image, reducing in-camera performance, and there can be drawbacks in having to process each image before it can be used as this introduces post-processing time. A comprehensive introduction to RAW and how it may be used can be found in Andrews et al. (2006): although there is much written there about how wonderful RAW manipulation can be, and little consideration to how using it may impact on a large-scale imaging project.

There is a prediction that the RAW format will provide 'an archival image format that could potentially rival the usefulness and longevity of film' (Strunk 2006). However, in the short period of time that digital photography manufacturers have produced commercially available cameras, the RAW format has constantly evolved from brand to brand, and even within a particular brand as their technology develops, leading to the existence of over 200 RAW formats that store image and camera setting data in different ways, sometimes even encrypting information to prevent access to the data unless opened and manipulated by proprietary tools sold by the manufacturer. RAW data can masquerade under a number of different names (RAW, CCD-RAW and NEF), and poor, opaque documentation often accompanies each implementation of the RAW format, which leads to worries that:

> as manufacturers lose interest in their discontinued products, and drop support for them, the true impact of all of these 'dialects' will be felt. Photographers will find their older images inaccessible, as future software versions lose support for older cameras. In the worst cases, entire brands may disappear (Strunk 2006).

As a result, there has been a growing concern regarding the lack of one standard for storage of and access to RAW data. In February 2005, Adobe released a specification for a non-proprietary file format for saving RAW data, called The Digital Negative Format (DNG), putting it forward as a candidate for a common RAW standard to be adopted by both software and camera manufacturers (Adobe 2007a). However, other advocates of open source documentation of digital camera RAW files who formed a working party, OpenRAW (www.openraw.org), criticize the DNG format and have called for an open consortium to define a standard (Nixon 2006).

Until an open RAW format is adopted across the digital imaging industry, RAW image data is problematic for use in libraries, archives, museums and the cultural and heritage industry: archives need a more stable and long-term format. However, it is feasible (and acceptable) to capture data in the RAW format and output an archival TIFF file from the resulting RAW data, if advanced control over image data is necessary: 'If RAW files are archived, care must be taken to also archive all software necessary to open them and migrate to an open standard such as TIFF'

(TASI 2006b). It is doubtful whether, when capturing RAW and converting to TIFF instead of capturing directly to TIFF, the extra time introduced in the production of every archival TIFF image is worthwhile. The literature regarding use of the RAW format in digitization projects is scant, and it is not known of any projects who are actively using RAW data capture and processing at time of publication, but this may change in the future if it is found useful or necessary to use the superior tonal range of RAW for certain types of archival material.

Exif: Exchangeable Image File Format

Exif, Exchangeable Image File Format, is an image format designed for digital cameras which aims to provide a standard for storing interchange information about image files. Originally developed in 1995, its current version (2.2) was published in 2002 by the Japan Electronics and Information Technology Industries Association (JEITA 2002), but although it is in widespread use by manufacturers and is becoming the default image format in most commercially available digital cameras, it is yet to become an official standard.

The specification uses the existing JPEG or TIFF Rev. 6.0 file formats, with the addition of specific metadata tags (many more than are available in the standard TIFF specification) that capture information about the camera and picture taking conditions, such as camera make and model, ISO, focusing distance, flash, exposure, light sources, white balance and type of scene. Such data can be stored and used for possible colour correction in printing and display or used to keep records of where, when and how an image was created. Other Exif additions to the JPEG and TIFF standard include the generation of a thumbnail for viewing on the LCD screen of a digital camera, which can also be viewed later in image management programs.

Most digital cameras produced nowadays capture Exif data and embed it within the resulting JPEG or TIFF file (the files are said to be an 'Exif flavour of JPEG or TIFF', and are outputted as .JPG or .TIF in the normal manner). Some RAW formats also now embed Exif-type data in their structure, as it has become increasingly popular to embed information in an image file regarding its provenance.

Due to the complexity of the Exif file structure, dependence on existing specifications, and introduction of different tags and structures by manufacturers, difficulties with opening and processing Exif flavour JPEG or TIFF files are common, especially when attempting to open Exif flavour files with older software packages. However, most current image storage and manipulation tools can access the Exif metadata, many will maintain this data when writing to a modified file, and given the ubiquity of the inclusion of Exif metadata in JPEG and TIFF files being outputted from digital cameras, Exif flavour images are now becoming a *de facto* standard.

Exif data is not an alternative to providing proper archival metadata about an image's creation and content. Given that the Exif metadata resides within the file, users are not easily able to search large collections of images if this metadata is not made available elsewhere to allow textual searching. Moreover, although the Exif metadata captures various information about the image creation, it does not meet archival standards for image metadata (see p. 173).

Additionally, when delivering images to end users, care should be taken to avoid the inclusion of confidential, compromising or embarrassing information which could still be stored in the original Exif information in a TIFF or JPEG file. There are many examples of images available online where people have cropped or manipulated an image file for acceptable use, but the thumbnail of the original image, still embedded in the file structure and publicly viewable, may be less than savoury. It is possible that this may cause various legal and moral issues, and institutions should be aware that this embedded information may still exist in manipulated image files.

BMP: Microsoft Images Bitmap

Microsoft Images Bitmap (.BMP), a proprietary format owned by the Microsoft Corporation,[6] is the native image file format for the Microsoft Windows operating system, intended for basic display and storage of bitmap images in the Windows environment. It is a simple but fairly unsophisticated and poorly documented bitmap format allowing basic compression and as a result it is well supported by Microsoft applications but poorly regarded elsewhere (although files can be accessed on non-Windows machines): 'This format is used for Windows wallpaper. It isn't much good for anything else because the files tend to be very large' (Lojkine 2001, 35).

Over the years there have been several different and incompatible versions of the windows BMP format. The original format, created for Windows 1.0 (in 1985) and now defunct, was very simple, being designed to support the most popular graphics cards at the time, with a fixed colour palette and no facility for data compression. In Windows 2.0 (1987), support for a programmable colour palette and basic compression was added, allowing user definable colour data to be stored. Since Windows 3.0 (1990), the BMP format has been fairly stable, although further versions and revisions have resulted in changes to the format, which can lead to compatibility problems when dealing with older image files. Each new version has added new information into the file header, but no field was included in the file

6 The Microsoft Corporation is the largest software company in the world. Founded in 1976, Microsoft rapidly became the leading company in personal computing: developing, manufacturing and licensing a wide range of PC software, including the Windows operating system, and applications which can be used within it, such as the Office suite. These products have near ubiquity in the marketplace, but there are concerns from the development community regarding Microsoft products, including various security and implementation issues.

header to easily indicate the version, requiring some analysis of the file contents to determine the internal format of the data (see Murray and van Ryper 1996, 584).

BMP has many different modes, supporting images with 1, 4, 8, 16, 24 or 32 bits of colour information per pixel (although BMP files using 16 and 32 bits per pixel are rare). BMP also supports simple run length encoding (see pp. 54–55) compression for 4 and 8 bits per pixel. This means that the compression in BMP is only of use with large blocks of identical colours, making it limited in value. It is actually rare for Windows BMP files to be compressed at all: most BMP files are stored uncompressed, meaning they tend to be very large.

Technical documentation about BMP can be found in Microsoft (1993) and Swan (1993). Due to its proprietary, basic and non-stable nature, inefficient data storage and large file sizes, this format is not recommended for use in digital imaging projects.

PICT: Apple Macintosh QuickDraw/PICT file

The PICT (.PCT, .PICT, .PIC) is a proprietary file format which was introduced with the original Apple Macintosh computer in 1984 as its native metafile format. As a metafile, it is a hybrid format that can store multiple types of information, including bitmap, vector and type data, and is primarily used to exchange graphical information between various Macintosh applications.

Copyrighted and owned by Apple Inc,[7] PICT is associated with applications of the Apple Macintosh operating system, and is one of the best supported formats on that platform, becoming a *de facto* standard despite limitations in compression facilities and colour management. However, with the operating system change to Mac OS X (in 2001) it was replaced by Portable Document Format (PDF) as Apple's native metafile format. As a result, the PICT file format is now viewed as obsolete and has little to offer memory institutions carrying out digital imaging projects. Technical legacy information is still available from Apple Inc (1996).

PSD: Adobe Photoshop Bitmap File

Adobe PhotoShop (www.adobe.com/products/photoshop/family/) is the fullest featured, most highly respected and most commonly used commercial graphics editor and image processing package for the home computing and publishing market. PSD (.PSD) is the native, commercial, proprietary bitmap format owned

7 Apple Computer Incorporated (founded in 1977, but known as Apple Incorporated since 2007) is an international hardware and software company, producing many consumer goods and closely related software products, such as the Macintosh line of personal computers, and the iPod. With its counter-cultural roots, and attention to aesthetic and functional design, Apple is a brand which has a distinct reputation and devoted consumer following.

by Adobe[8] and used by the Photoshop program, and is the only format which retains all the editing power of PhotoShop.

PSD is designed for preserving image detail, not for efficient file size, being able to store the image as a set of individual layers which can be manipulated independently, incorporating text as part of the image file, and dealing with a variety of masks and blend modes regarding how each layer may be displayed. There is good support for different colour storage schemes (and Photoshop has good facilities for converting between a large range of colour spaces and different file types).

PSD files are generally uncompressed, or can use run length encoding (see pp. 54–55) as a basic means of compressing the image data, meaning images are lossless in the PSD format. This was chosen to optimize the speed of reading and writing the files while manipulating images in Photoshop, but results in large file sizes. The lack of superior compression schemes and resulting size of the file has hindered this otherwise flexible format from becoming one useful for general purpose interchange. When work on the PSD image is complete, Photoshop can generate a version of the image in another format (although other formats will not retain the detail: for example, the layers structure of the original PSD file will be lost).

Given the wide distribution and popularity of Adobe Photoshop, PSD can be described as an industry standard and image data is often left in that format for data interchange in the publishing industry. Many other graphics and desktop publishing tools can open PSD files. However, as it is an application specific format it is changeable and will continue to change as new versions of Photoshop become available. No real documentation regarding the format is available from Adobe. Although Photoshop is a useful, popular and well respected application, and one which any serious digitization project will invest in, the PSD format should be viewed as a temporary working format unsuitable for long term storage, but from which archival format images can be generated.

Kodak Photo CD

In 1992, the Eastman Kodak Company launched the first major consumer product for digital camera images: Kodak Photo CD. Although photographic film remained the medium for image capture, the Photo CD system allowed photofinishers to convert the processed film into digital form, returning to the customer negatives, prints and a CD-ROM which contained multiple copies of each image, scanned in at several different resolutions. The images could be displayed on television screens using a Kodak Photo CD player. Kodak Photo CD is actually the name of the complete CD-ROM-based storage and retrieval system (the Kodak PCD

---

8 Adobe Systems is a computer software company, founded in 1982, which specializes in desktop publishing software. Adobe Photoshop has dominated the image-manipulation software market since its launch in 1989.

Imaging Workstation (PIW), consisting of a film scanner, data manager, colour monitor, CD writer, thermal printer, CD-ROM XA drive and bespoke proprietary system software), but the term Photo CD is also used to describe the proprietary file format, also known as Kodak Image Pac, associated with the system.

Technical detail regarding Photo CD is scant and it is very difficult to describe the Image Pac format in any detail. What is common knowledge are the resolutions of the image scans (Kodak 2003a). Multiple versions of each image are provided in an arrangement called 'pyramid encoding', with 6 different resolutions being provided (or 7 in Photo CD Pro) in the 'Image Pac'. Images are derived from the highest resolution scan. Interestingly, given that the Photo CD was developed for viewing on a television screen, Kodak pegged their format to the standard resolution of television or computer monitor displays at the time: the 'Base' of 768 x 512 pixels. The smallest resolution available, Base/64, gave a thumbnail of 96 x 64 pixels, with a slightly larger thumbnail, Base/16, at 192 x 128 pixels also available. Base/4 gave a larger image at 384 x 256 pixels, which enabled base images which needed to be rotated to be displayed on the screen. Base itself, 768 x 512, filled the TV screen or monitor. Larger resolutions were also provided to give more detail: 4 Base was 1536 x 1024 pixels, the resolution for High Definition Television. The 16 Base, at 2048 x 3072, was the highest resolution on a *Photo CD* Master Disc, with a further optional level, 64 Base, at 4096 x 6144, available only to those paying a premium for the Photo CD Pro Master Disc. It is worthwhile noting that the larger files, 16 Base and 64 Base, if dealing with a transparency which would be used to generate a standard 6 inch by 4 inch photographic image, would be equitable to respective scanning resolutions of 512 and 1024 dots per inch for the 6 inch by 4 inch photograph, thus making those larger Photo CD images high enough resolution to still be well within, or above, archival resolution parameters today.

As for other technical information, Kodak has been reluctant to describe the proprietary, lossy 'subbard encoding scheme' they called PhotoYCC which they used to compress the file information: 'Briefly, the image is converted to a luminance-chrominance (luma-chroma) storage metric called PhotoYCC. The chroma information (CC) is then subsampled because there is less need for color detail information since almost all of the detail is retained by the luma channel (Y)' (Kodak 2003b). There are some white papers that are not readily available to the general public, such as Eastman Kodak Company (1994). Several choices regarding colour were available, 256 level greyscale, a user defined colour palette, 24-bit YCC (Kodak's own proprietary colour format which provides data in a format compatible with certain Kodak printers, although not much is known about this) and 24-bit RGB. The most popular among users was 24-bit RGB, and most software developers who wrote software which could deal with Kodak Photo CD released tools which used the format in the RGB colour space (Kodak released development kits which allowed the use of Photo CD images in common image processing packages in the later 1990s).

Although Photo CD was a proprietary system, linked to specific scanning technology that was only available through Kodak representatives, Photo CD was a cost effective and popular option for the digitization of cultural and heritage material in the early 1990s (Besser and Trant 1995, 21; Sandore and Dunkelberger 1996; Kenney and Rieger 1998). The system was designed and optimized to scan in 35mm film, but was capable of scanning transparencies or slides from 35mm to 120mm. Many cultural and educational institutions had previously invested in the creation of slide or transparency collections, and these could be used as surrogates for digitization, leveraging on previous investments (Kenney and Rieger 1998). Where images were not available, documents and artefacts could be photographed, with the resulting slides or transparencies used as both the source for digitization and an archival format to record the object. Additionally, institutions often contracted a vendor to do the scanning (and/or photography) off site. Photo CD became the obvious solution to many projects, providing a comprehensive digitization package at reasonable rates (although projects had little control over the variables used in imaging their holdings compared to in-house digitization studios).

An early database of digitization projects (The Clearinghouse of Image Databases, (http://elearn.arizona.edu/imagelib/) which seems to have been populated between 1994 and 2002) hosts technical information regarding early digitization projects. Many of these used Kodak Photo CD, including Artscan and Australian Contemporary Textiles (both at the Australian National University, Institute of the Arts, Canberra School of Art, www.anu.edu.au/ITA/AusArts/www/library/artscan.html); the ImageBase project at the Fine Arts Museums of San Francisco (www.thinker.org/fam/about/imagebase/); and the Thomas Jefferson University Archives Documentary Image Library (http://jeffline.tju.edu/SML/archives/). Other digitization projects to use Photo CD in their early stages include the Scottish Cultural Resources and Access Network (www.scran.ac.uk/, technical details available in TASI 2002a); and the HELIX (Higher Education Library for Image eXchange) project (details available in TASI 2002b). In 1995, there was a pilot project at the University of Illinois Library 'to test the feasibility of operating a production imaging workstation in a library setting, and to collaborate with Kodak to determine the best methods for capturing archival, high-quality images from film and through the use of a digital camera' (Sandore and Dunkelberger 1996), which gave a favourable report to the technology, describing it as 'a very convenient and effective means of capturing images' and commending 'the speed and accessibility of service, the quality of the Photo CD images, and the personalized nature of the service' (ibid.). For an overview of how Photo CD has been used in the digitization programme of the Victoria and Albert Museum, see Stevenson (2006, 72–75).

Photo CD was a transitional technology designed as an adjunct to the core product of the Kodak company to protect the film business, rather than establishing a long-term share of the multimedia market. The dual digital and analogue nature of the product meant it was very popular until consumer-level digital cameras and imaging technologies became widely and cheaply available (see Chapter 2). The library and archive sector also began to recommend non-proprietary formats for long-term digital image storage, such as TIFF (see pp. 82–87), and so Photo CD gradually fell out of favour. Kodak withdrew Photo CD services through its dealerships in 2004, and Kodak no longer offers technical support for the format. Most of the technical legacy documentation regarding the data format has disappeared from the website (Kodak 2007), however, drivers and software are still available for download, and the Photo CD file format can be easily opened in Adobe PhotoShop (and other Adobe products) for conversion to other more desirable file types.

In 1998, it was recommended in an overview of Library of Congress technical specifications for digitization that:

> Archives wishing to produce collections that are interoperable … [with others and] who plan to use Photo CD technology should either determine how direct access to those images may be provided to WWW users or plan to reprocess the Image Pac images to produce GIF and JFIF/JPEG images for WWW access (Fleischhauer 1998).

Nowadays, institutions that have existing Kodak Photo CD Image Pac collections should look to convert these into archival formats while this is still easy to accomplish.

PDF: Portable Document Format

PDF, Portable Document Format, is not a bitmap image file format but a format commonly used for document interchange which can have bitmap images included within the file. It is worth mentioning here due to its popularity and to misconceptions about its nature: PDFs often appear to be an image of a text, when in reality they are based on a set of vector instructions which generate a visual representation of text as an output, and may contain images embedded within these instructions.

PDFs have their background in Postscript, an important language for typesetting developed by Adobe Systems in 1984 (Adobe 2004), which was a versatile, all purpose language for describing the layout of text, vector graphics and bitmap images on print or page displays. This became a *de facto* industry standard for communicating graphics information between applications and hardware devices, such as between processors and printers.

PDF was developed to supersede the earlier implementations of Postscript for document interchange, and launched by Adobe with the Acrobat reader in 1993 (Adobe 2007b). Like Postscript, it is vector, rather than pixel-based: the ASCII text underlying PDF is a set of instructions that, when executed, creates a data stream that, in turn, generates an on-screen image of a document. PDF was designed predominantly for vector representation, so is good for effectively storing language data, but given that images such as photographs are poorly served by vector representation, the format was designed to allow incorporation of common bitmap image formats within the file: Windows bitmap (.bmp); GIF (.gif); JPEG (.jpg)' PICT (.pct, .pict); PNG (.png); TIFF (.tif); and two now superseded formats still included in the specification for backwards compatibility: PCX (.pcx, the format for a program called PC Paintbrush, popular in the early 1990s) and RLE (.rle, a simple run length encoded bitmap image format originally designed to be easy to encode and decode, in use in the mid-1990s) (Adobe 2007c). PDF uses different compression algorithms to effectively store the document data, using JPEG compression for any bitmap image content incorporated into the file (Adobe 2006).

PDF has become an increasingly popular means for sharing documents via email and the Internet. This is partly due to Adobe making the Adobe Reader program, which can read PDFs, freely available, recently making documentation for the creation of PDFs available (Adobe 2006) and allowing major word processing packages, such as Microsoft Word, to output to the PDF format. In January 2007, 'Adobe announced its intent to release the full Portable Document Format (PDF) 1.7 specification to AIIM, the Enterprise Content Management Association, for the purpose of publication by the International Organization for Standardization (ISO)' (Adobe 2007b): the first step towards making PDF a formal standard for document data interchange. (An archival format of PDF, based on PDF 1.4, had already resulted in the PDF/A ISO specification in 2005, see NDIIP 2007a.) Naturally, the nature of compression and storage of image files embedded within the document make it an unsuitable medium for the exchange of images if they are required to be of any real quality, or accessed on their own. Stand-alone image files, in archival formats, are still a necessity to maintain information quality. PDF is becoming an increasingly mature and attractive format for delivery of document information, but there are concerns regarding the long-term availability of PDFs: there are compatibility issues with different versions of the format, and the reading of PDFs in the future is dependent on the correct version of the program which can read them being available.

Choosing a Format: Imaging Guidelines

What image format should an institution choose to store its digital image data in? The 'best thing about standards is that there are so many to choose from' (Gill and Miller 2002), and:

> Choosing a particular format for a given application generally involves several interdependent considerations, including quality; flexibility, computation, storage, or transmission efficiency; and support by existing programs (Kay and Levine 1995, 33).

The suitability of a format for a given purpose is best determined by knowing its original purpose and how it is implemented – the purpose of this chapter. There has been much debate on the qualities necessary for choosing file formats for the library and information sector (Frey 2000; TASI 2006b; NDIIP 2007b). Nowadays, however, many concerns about whether an individual institution is making the right technical choices have been allayed by the issuing of standard guidelines for digitization projects, which recommend both preservation and delivery formats:

> the choice of file format is diverse, offering advantages and disadvantages that make them better suited to a specific environment. When digitising images a standards-based and best practice approach should be taken, using images that are appropriate to the medium they are used within. For disseminating the work to others, a multi-tier approach is necessary, to enable the storing of a preservation and dissemination copy (UKOLN 2006).

This 'standards-based and best practice approach' ensures that projects will be certain that their digital images will be accessible and useful to researchers, in both the long and short term. However, 'technology and institutional standards change too rapidly for a single set of standards to be applicable' (Hughes 2004, 199). The need for technical digitization guidelines was highlighted by early projects in the LIS sector (Besser and Trant 1994; Cartolano et al. 1995; Canadian Heritage Information Network 1996) and these guidelines have gradually evolved as the technologies change. For example, Kodak Photo CD was recommended in the late to mid-1990s (Image Quality Working Group of ArchivesCom 1997; Kenney and Rieger 1998) and was still being recommended as an archival file format in 2001 (Harvard University Library 2001), although just three years later Kodak withdrew support for the underlying technology. By 1995, TIFF was emerging as the alternative suggested long-term master format (Cartolano et al. 1995), gathering support (Canadian Heritage Information Network 1996; D'Amato and Klopfenstein 1996; Image Quality Working Group of ArchivesCom 1997), gaining institutional recommendation (Fleischhauer 1998) and in widespread use by 1999 (California Digital Library 1999).

TIFF remains the current archival image format standard today, with recommendations that thumbnail and/or preview versions of the image are prepared in different sizes to give users choice, and that these versions of the images be saved and made accessible to users in one of the popular formats for online delivery such as JPEG or PNG. Given that technologies, standards and recommendations are constantly changing, the best place to find up to date recommendations regarding image file formats for digitization projects is from the online documentation provided by trusted and well known institutions, such as the frequently updated *Library of Congress Technical Standards for Digital Conversion of Text and Graphic Materials* (Library of Congress 2007); those produced by national bodies such as the US National Archives and Records Association (NARA 2004); those produced by University Libraries, such as *Best Practice Guidelines for Digital Collections at the University of Maryland Libraries* (Carignan et al. 2007); the guides available at the California Digital Library (www.cdlib.org); the standards advocated by the Digital Library Federation (www.diglib.org); guides to good practice and resources produced by the Arts and Humanities Data Service (www.ahds.ac.uk); and those created and pointed to by the UK's Digital Curation Centre (www.dcc.ac.uk); and resources produced by the Technical Advisory Service for Images (www.tasi.ac.uk), for example, *Choosing a file format* (TASI 2006c). Most guides and recommendations are meant to be informative rather than prescriptive.

Further Reading

There are numerous books available on image file formats, which include overview chapters on computer graphics concepts and basic terminology, examples of how different formats are computationally implemented and much technical information regarding the specifications, such as Brown and Shepherd (1995); Kay and Levine (1995); Murray and van Ryper (1996); and Miano (1999). These were generally written for graphics and applications programmers, but have also been used extensively by illustrators and photographers, and have provided much of the source information for this chapter. However, these are becoming rather dated (for example, Kay and Levine do not mention PICT or RAW as they had not been invented when their book was written).

Nowadays, up to date information is best found online (although care must be taken that it is provided by trusted sources). The 'Digital Formats' website, developed by the Library of Congress, provides information about digital content formats. An initial offering was placed online in 2004 and expanded and updated analyses and resources have been added regularly since (www.digitalpreservation.gov/formats/). The National Archives, UK, are also developing an online registry of technical information regarding data file formats and their supporting software products, called PRONOM (www.nationalarchives.gov.uk/pronom/).

The website (www.fileformat.info) also provides useful, up to date information regarding all manner of file formats, including image formats. Murray and van Ryper's 1996 textbook *Encyclopedia of Graphics File Formats* was recently made available online there and contains much information which is still relevant today (www.fileformat.info/mirror/egff/index.htm).

Pointers to recommendations and guidelines for choosing an image file format for a digitization project can be found in pp. 96–98, above.

Chapter 5
Digital Images and Memory Institutions

> Prior to digitisation, the retrieving and re-filing of the prints consumed staff time. Batches of prints to be re-filed hung round on trolleys like patients in a busy A&E Department. The sight of a pink print request form approaching the Local Studies counter caused the heart to sink – it foretold at least half an hour wrestling with ancient filing cabinets, not to mention the wait for the notorious Central Library lift. And what could be more dispiriting, for staff and customer, to discover that the prints selected from the card index were not what were wanted at all? The idea of digitising the Print Collection was very attractive. It would reduce the wear and tear on the original prints and transform public access by allowing customers to browse the whole collection (Moorhouse 2004, 62).

The information, culture and heritage sectors were quick to embrace imaging technologies as they became available, primarily to facilitate access to items in collections by providing them in electronic format. Producing digital image versions of holdings through 'digitization' has become an industry in itself, and there has been much effort devoted to producing guides to best practice for undertaking the digitization of library and archive material.

This chapter focuses on the history and the developing role of digitization, in particular the production of digital image representations and surrogates, within memory institutions such as libraries, archives, museums and art galleries. An overview of the institutional adoption of digitization is given, highlighting issues of cost, purpose, longevity and use, and a round-up of sources for guidelines and standards is provided. The recent interest from and investment by commercial information providers is juxtaposed with institutional concerns and current issues regarding use and usefulness, the appropriation of new and emerging Internet technologies, and the role of amateur digitization enthusiasts is explored. Advanced imaging techniques used in the sector for the creation, analysis and dissemination of digital image-based material are also discussed. The chapter finishes with recommended readings regarding the role of digitization and digital media in the library and information sectors, which are essential for those considering a digitization project themselves.

Why Do Institutions Digitize? Reasons for Digitization

Digitization, 'the conversion of an analog signal or code into a digital signal or code' (Lee 2002, 3) is now commonplace in most memory institutions as digital representations of cultural and historical documents, artefacts and images are created and delivered to users, generally online. Most digitization projects start with the digital imaging of materials, as the majority of items being digitized are documents, photographs, artworks or objects which require a digital image to be taken of them before anything more sophisticated can be achieved computationally. If the goal is to produce electronic text (the LIS sector has a long tradition of microfilming of documents, and an obvious adoption of digital technology was to produce electronic text) the creation of digital images is a necessary first step before Optical Character Recognition software can be used to convert the image of the text into processable type. Copies of digital images are also used as the basis for 'keying in' or typing in a text, rather than distributing or handling fragile or rare documentary material to create electronic texts. As a result, the creation of digital images is by far the most popular type of digitization (although is not the only type, as the digital capture of moving images and three-dimensional imaging is also becoming more popular. However, digitizing sound, film and objects in 3D is more computationally expensive and requires more investment than the creation of two-dimensional digital images, and is therefore less appropriate for the digitization of static objects, which can usually be carried out simply and quickly using standard photographic techniques). As the creation of digital images is often the primary aim of digitization:

> anything that is accessible to photography can be digitised. The digitisation processes are numerous, and include:
>
> - image scanning
> - microfilming and then scanning the microfilm
> - photography followed by scanning of the photographic surrogates
> - re-recording video and audio onto digital media
> - rekeying of textual content
> - OCR of scanned textual content
> - tagging text and other digital content to create a marked-up digital resource
> - digital photography – especially for 3-D objects or large-format items such as artworks (Deegan and Tanner 2002, 34).

Digital imaging and the creation of related records, or metadata (see Chapter 7), has been the main focus of the application of technology in the library and archive sector ever since multimedia systems became readily available (see Chapter 2). Any item that can fit onto a scanning bed, or underneath the focus of a camera, can be scanned or photographed and a digital image representation can be produced. Items which are commonly digitized by memory institutions include (but are not limited to) printed books, printed journals, manuscripts, maps, photographs, photographic transparencies, music manuscripts, woodcuts, line drawings, paintings, archaeological site plans, archaeological finds, blueprints and architectural illustrations or plans, medical illustrations, documents, correspondence, newspapers, papyri and ostraca. The range of digitized material captured as digital images is as broad as the range of material held in libraries, archives, museums and private collections.

There are many reasons institutions bother to undertake the costly and time-consuming endeavour of digitizing a collection. From a user's point of view, current access to high quality digital resources, for free or little cost, is paradise. From an institution's point of view, the opportunities to provide and enhance digital resources 'for learning, teaching, research, scholarship, documentation, and public accountability' (Kenney and Rieger 2000, 1) are large, although 'they recognize that changing user behaviour may jeopardize these resources and their stewardship' (ibid.). Keeping up with user expectations can provide financial headaches, not only because of the cost of technology involved but the cost of training and employing people to undertake the digitization work and to safeguard the digital investment in the long term. It takes time, effort, expertise and funding to undertake a digitization program, which is not as simple as just taking a photograph of everything in the collection, and it takes time and effort for funding to be secured for digitization. For example, at the British Library digitization is:

> still seen as expensive. Specialist photographers were needed, plus considerable input from conservators in the planning and setup of projects. Also, for some classes of materials, conservators were needed on a continuing basis during the digital capture of, for example, the Gutenberg Bible, Shakespeare Quartos and the Chaucer Canterbury Tales. With funding having to be sought externally for each project, the overall amount of digitisation undertaken remains small in terms of the overall size of the BL's special collections (Smith 2006, 9).

As a result, the motivation for the creation of digital surrogates which can be used in some cases in place of the original, both within and beyond the physical institutional boundaries, requires considerable consideration. Electronic surrogates, such as digital images, are superior to other forms of surrogates in various ways (such as microfilm, prints, photocopies) as they can be copied, used to create other derived reproductions, manipulated and distributed more easily than their physical counterparts. 'Increased access' to material is often cited as the main reason digitization is undertaken, although this is a phrase seldom qualified and can mean anything from improving intellectual access, adding to the scope and content of representation, and ensuring the accurate representation objects, documents and artefacts; to improving physical access to physically remote objects, collections which have been dispersed, or precious or fragile items not available for public display; or improving access to information for potential users who have disabilities and are unable to consult materials in traditional settings, extending the user base to those who cannot, say, use a mouse or see a computer screen clearly through good use of design criteria which can facilitate equal access for all.

Digitization, done successfully, can add value to both the end user and institution. Deegan and Tanner (2002) summarize succinctly the wide range of reasons given for digitization, and the advantages digitization of materials can hold for memory institutions:

- immediate access to high-demand and frequently used items
- easier access to individual components within items (e.g. articles within journals)
- rapid access to materials held remotely
- the ability to reinstate out of print materials
- the potential to display materials that are in inaccessible formats, for instance, large volumes, or maps
- 'virtual reunifaction' – allowing dispersed collections to be brought together
- the ability to enhance digital images in terms of size, sharpness, colour contrast, noise reduction, etc.
- the potential to conserve fragile/precious objects while presenting surrogates in more accessible forms
- the potential for integration into teaching materials
- enhanced searchability, including full text
- integration of digital media (images, sounds, video, etc.)
- the ability to satisfy requests for surrogates (photocopies, photographic prints, slides, etc.)
- reducing the burden of cost of delivery
- the potential for presenting a critical mass of materials (32–33).

Additional benefits not present in this list include the expertise acquired by internal staff, the potential for commercial licensing and the raising of revenues through this new channel, raised profiles of institutions, and the potential for experts and users alike to comment on original source material. Deegan and Tanner (2002, 30–57); and Hughes (2004, 1–30) discuss all of these reasons in full.

The potential benefits digitization can bring vary from institution to institution, and are dependent on the needs, facilities and requirements of each individual digitization project. For example, at the Victoria and Albert Museum, converting the picture archive (from which users request surrogate copies of images for research) into digital form meant that:

> There is a great deal of time saved … After scanning, the image printing can take place unsupervised as a batch process during down time, such as overnight, and more importantly, the file can be re-used for further printing at a later date. With traditional analogue photography, once a print had been made and handed over to a client, it was gone. For a repeat order, the whole process had to be undertaken again from start to finish. For digital files, however, subsequent prints take only a short time to produce (Stevenson 2006, 88).

For the National and University Library of Iceland; Cornell University; and the Árni Magnússon Institute, digitization allowed the virtual reunification of dispersed manuscript and book collections of an entire range of Icelandic sagas, ballads, poetry and epigrams, aspiring 'to give access to the 'collection of record' for the chosen subject' (Sagnanet n.d., http://sagnanet.is/). For the First World War Poetry Digital Archive at the University of Oxford (www.ww1lit.com), digitization will allow the virtual collection of geographically dispersed primary source material, such as manuscripts and letters, from five major British poets from the First World War. As well as images and transcripts of the documentary material, contextual information such as images, video and audio will also be digitized (showing that digitization is not merely digital imaging), and the project aims to actively explore how to imbed digital resources in the learning and teaching experience in primary, secondary and higher education. Aims and benefits of digitization are thus specific to each organization.

Although some benefits of digitization are unpredictable (such as increased publicity and public interest in institutional holdings), those planning to undertake a digitization project are advised to consider why they are planning to invest the finances and effort in providing digital resources, so that the results can be designed for the institution and the institution's core users. Institutions generally cannot afford to digitize everything: although commercial companies, such as Google, may be able to adopt this approach (see below) in an institutional setting careful planning, and careful selection of material to be digitized, is necessary (see Hughes 2004, 31–53). Indeed, if digitization:

> is done without fairly broad-based institutional consideration and buy-in on the decision of what collections to digitize, the drain of money and professional time in such projects could easily derail other important programmes (Hughes 2004, 50).

The opportunity costs to an institution may be high: resources required for digitization are large, and may necessitate diverting scarce resources from other parts of the institution, running the risk of potential resource misdirection if the digitization effort has not been well thought out, or alienating the potential user base of the institution (Kenny and Rieger 2000, 2).

There may be also good reasons not to attempt digitization. Hughes (2004, 50–52) details issues which may bring a sharp halt to digitization projects, including unresolved copyright issues, lack of adequate funding, lack of institutional support, technical drawbacks and the potential for digitization to damage or compromise fragile or rare original materials. Additionally, Hughes debunks common myths about digitization, stressing that: digitization is not preservation and is not a substitute for proper preservation strategies, as digital masters contribute to preservation only in reducing wear and tear of the original and surrogates can never replace the original; digitization is not a cost effective way to save space, as although digital files will take less physical space to store than the physical collection, the costs involved in long-term storage of the digital files are still prohibitive; digitization does not save money, as the technical and intellectual investment required to undertake the digitization is large, costs are never recouped through subscription or accession fees, and there are unpredictable costs involved in maintaining digital files in the long term; not every object in every collection is worth digitizing, and digitization should focus on items that will give the most benefit to users; and that digitization is not a substitute for proper, structured collections management. The development of detailed, up to date catalogues and metadata of institutional holdings may be a by-product of digitization, but this should not be the primary motive for carrying out the digitization in the first place (Hughes 2004, 51–52).

A Brief History of Digitization

Early Years: Before the WWW

It may seem that digitization is a recent phenomenon in memory institutions, but the current state of affairs where libraries, archives, museums, galleries and even private collections are expected to make their holdings available in digital form follows a period of experimentation with and appropriation of available digital technologies that dates back almost 40 years. Institutions began to utilize computer systems in the 1970s:

> with the creation of electronic catalogues. The analogue card catalogues that provided access to the collection items were replaced by databases. The bibliographic information on the catalogue cards was converted into database fields. The electronic catalogue provided automatic access to analogue objects such as books, works of art and documents. In the 1980s the conversion of printed source material, such as books and articles, into digital files started to become widespread. Two types of digital files were created. The first file type represents the storage medium of the original analogue document; this is often called a digital image. The second file type represents the coded content (for instance, characters and figures) of the original document, and, depending on the type of original, can be an electronic text, table, or database (van Horik 2005, 12).

In the 1980s, interest in the application of digitization and image processing in the arts, humanities, libraries and archive sector began to grow. Small-scale, in-house projects of limited scope and interest were undertaken by individual institutions experimenting with the application of the newly available (but still expensive) technologies (González 1992), but towards the end of the decade large-scale projects were launched by various institutions, including pilot projects aiming to investigate the appropriation of digital technologies to the handling of large volumes of information.

One of the first digitization projects was launched in 1984 by The National Archives and Records Administration (NARA) in Washington. Their project

'Optical Digital Image Storage System (ODISS)' aimed to test the utility of digital image and optical disk technologies for the reproduction, storage and retrieval of archival documents. Digitizing 220,000 pages of documents, the ODISS project found digital representations of their holdings to be easy to use, with significant time saving for searching and retrieving information, improvement of legibility for documents digitized in high resolution, reduction of storage space, and reduced handling of original documents, although they were perhaps optimistic with their predictions of the longevity of the digitized material – suggesting 100 years! (see NARA 1991; González 1992, 1998 for an overview).

Another early adopter of digitization was the 'Archivo General de Indias' in Spain, a 200-year-old archive of extremely valuable documents illustrating the history of the Spanish empire in the Americas and the Philippines. Started in 1986, the pioneering and ambitious digitization project saw three public and private organizations join forces (The Spanish Ministry of Culture, IBM Spain and the Ramón Areces Foundation) to develop a computerized information system and undertake large-scale digitization of the archive holdings. By 1992 the archive had digitized seven million pages, with eleven million completed by 1998, halting the deterioration of original papers caused by handling in the research rooms (González 1992 gives a full overview of the system and its architecture, and the processes used for digitization; González 1998 reflects on 10 years of the project). Although not without its technical and legal problems, the digitized archive, which now has tens of millions of digital images of manuscript material and electronic texts, is available for consultation in the archive itself (its online presence is rather minimal, although the database can now be searched (www.mcu.es/archivos/MC/AGI/index.html).

In the library sector, various experiments were undertaken on printed library material (which has fundamentally different characteristics to archival material). One of the pioneers was the Library of Congress in Washington which, early in the 1980s, launched a pilot project to look at both optical disk (for use in the digitization of general periodicals) and videodisc (for non-printed material such as photographs) – both storage mechanisms which are long since defunct[1] (Price

1 The majority of digitization projects in the 1980s used videodisc (Philip's LaserDisk) as the delivery media: a technology which was soon superseded by CD-ROM, and eventually the Internet. Videodiscs needed their own players – now unavailable: as a result the majority of the output of these early projects is now unreadable. The most high profile example of this was the British Broadcasting Corporation's Domesday Project, where schools around the UK were asked to survey their areas to produce a database of how Britain looked to the British in 1986, 900 years after the original Domesday Book was compiled (Finney 2007). The resulting database of statistics, maps and photographs was saved onto videodiscs for posterity, but by 2000 the majority of videodisc players were defunct, and a lengthy and costly programme of conversion and emulation was begun in 2002 by LongLife Data, taking 16 months to recover the videodisc data and recreate the original application (Darlington et al. 2003). LongLife Data created a web version of Domesday 1986, which is now available at (www.domesday1986.com).

1984; Parker 1985; Fischer and Swora 1986). The advantages which were found in undertaking the research included the saving in storage space compared to that taken up by the original material, although the process of digitization itself was found to be time-consuming.

Another pilot project in the library area was the joint development by Cornell University and the Xerox corporation, supported by the Commission on Preservation and Access, which attempted to develop a prototype for digitizing damaged, or 'brittle', books and providing high quality laser copies on request from users, at great speed and fair prices. In December 1991, one thousand 'brittle' volumes were digitized and digital editions prepared, ready to print. The project also investigated whether digitizing was a convenient alternative to the production of microfilm: finding that the time taken was actually similar, although the possibilities of access were higher (Council on Library Resources 1986; González 1992, 100). Around the same time, Yale University Library, one of the earliest developers of preservation microfilming practices:

> engaged in the first stages of a long-term and comprehensive effort to develop practical systems for the conversion of microfilm to digital image, and thereby to develop an understanding of the appropriate relationship of the two technologies in future preservation practice (Waters 1991, 1).

During this period, interest in imaging technology was also growing in the visual arts sector, with many art galleries and museums beginning to undertake projects using imaging technologies, which were becoming increasingly affordable. An attempt at cataloguing the projects that took place in the 1980s and 1990s was undertaken at the European Visual Arts Centre at Ipswich. In 1990, a meeting was hosted to discuss possible European collaboration in the form of a European Visual Arts Information Network (EVAIN) whose aim was to 'maximise the potential development and effective use of image-based interactive multimedia applications within museums and galleries' (Pring 1991, iii). This led to the setting up of a database of projects in order to circulate developments and applications in the visual arts area and, in 1991, EVIAN began to publish the bi-annual database of *Image Technology in European Museums and Art Galleries: ITEM* (Pring 1991). Concentrating on European projects, ITEM organized a joint exchange of information with the Clearinghouse of Art Documentation and Computerization, based at the Thomas J. Watson Library of the Metropolitan Museum of Art, New York, which had documented imaging projects in art galleries and museums in the US since the late 1980s (Stam 1987; Barnett 1991, iv). The goal of the Clearinghouse was 'to provide a gateway of information concerning relevant automated projects and activities' based on the premise that 'a substantial amount of information on computerization can be shared by researchers and systems alike'. Before the days of the Internet, 'this scattered but crucial information was unavailable in any one place, and required time-consuming, often redundant investigation' (Barnett 1991, iv).

The first ITEM database detailed 112 projects, covering a broad range from inter-institutional projects funded at government level, to individual institutions undertaking digitization of their own holdings. For example, an entry on the Europe Museums Network, details its aims to:

> demonstrate how new media can be developed, gain experience of multimedia design, gain experience of working with multimedia databases and computer system, and gain ideas for new services using broadband telecommunications networks (Pring 1991, 6),

and 'meet the needs of museums and the telecoms industry' in 'working to create new paths to art and culture for their visitors, to show that new media cannot replace art, but can lead people to it' – although there is little mention of their actual findings or recommendations. Early individual institutional digitization programmes are also catalogued, such as the Musée d'Orsay's *Galérie des Dates* videodisc project, which produced an interactive videodisc programme covering nine events in each year of a 68-year period. Completed in 1986, this two videodisc collection contained 15,000 slides and 14 hours of sound, allowing visitors to the gallery to explore the historical events through video clips, stills and textual information (Pring 1991, 41).

Towards the close of the 1980s:

> Federal agencies ... [became] increasingly interested in using digital information technologies to store large amounts of information economically and efficiently. This [was] particularly true of programs designed to provide Federal information to citizens, since a corresponding reduction in the creation of paper records could potentially reduce costs and improve the delivery of services to the public (Peterson 1994).

The National Archives and Records Administration (NARA) of the United States, in conjunction with the National Association of Government Archives and Records Administrators, conducted studies into digital imaging and optical media storage technologies at both State and local government levels, recommending image capture, storage and sustainability models (NARA 1991). By the close of the decade, all forms of memory institutions were embracing digital technologies, and in particular, image solutions, to begin to make their holdings more accessible, searchable and available to both government bodies and the general public.

Even at this early stage, prior to the invention of the World Wide Web, what is surprising about early digitization projects was the volume of material which was digitized. Most entries in the ITEM catalogue contain thousands of digitized images: The Italian government funded *Galleria Spada* project produced more that 5,000 images of the Spada Gallery in Rome by 1986 (Pring 1991, 85). The Arts du Costume du XXé Siècle project, at the Union Française des Arts du Costume, produced a videodisc of 33,000 images of their fashion collections, one containing collections from the eighteenth and nineteenth centuries, the other haute couture collections of the twentieth century, in 1987. La Storie dell'Arte Italiana (Pring

1991, 87) had digitized over 45,000 images of art, plus 30 minutes of video, in a project completed in 1988. The Henry Moore Sculpture Trust (UK) produced a *Sculpture Interactive* MediaBase Resource on videodisc containing 5,000 images and 70 minutes of film and radio extracts in 1990 (Pring 1991, 75). A considerable investment in time and effort was necessary to digitize such large collections, even without a ready vehicle for distribution (most digital records were consulted in the institution on stand-alone machines, or towards the late 1980s, distributed on floppy disc). There clearly was a passion for, and a belief in, this new technology.

Another interesting point to note regarding many of these early projects, across all of the library, archive and heritage sectors, is the consideration, at an early stage, of the need to instil 'best practice' in the digitization process (or to determine what best practice could actually mean when applied to digitization), and the ramifications for making large amounts of material available to the general public. Many early projects were undertaken at world leading institutions: being able to attract, or provide, the funding required for such large-scale digitization. The focus on the majority of early projects tends to be large scale, with large volumes of material being captured, with the hope that Optical Character Recognition technologies would then turn the resulting images into electronic text. Much of this research was optimistic, but the trial and error approach adopted by pioneering projects, and published as bona fide research, helped to establish many useful guidelines for subsequent digitization attempts.

However, many institutions were optimistic about the type of activity digitization could allow, and how easy it would be for the user to access these images (without home computers or a networked environment). Much of the rhetoric surrounding early digitization programmes was filled with:

> hollow pronouncements and promises … when early experimentation with desktop technologies and remotely accessible materials for instruction and research gave senior administrators in libraries and universities, as well as funding agencies and government departments, ideas that new technology would save millions of hours of teaching time and increase academic productivity, based on the assumption that a CD-ROM of a term's coursework could replace instructors and face to face classes. Such claims raised expectations unreasonably, and many enthusiastic 'early adopters' of digital technologies discovered at great expense that there are hidden costs and pitfalls to developing and using digital content (Hughes 2004, 7).

It took a while for institutions to realize that digitization is a costly and time-consuming exercise, which will not reap financial rewards but provides benefits for users, expanding skills, expertise and services, while requiring ongoing maintenance, development and funding.

It is also interesting to note that many early digitization projects were funded by, or carried out in tandem with, industry: in the early 1980s Kodak carried out a study with the Geneaological Society of Utah regarding the possibility of digitizing its millions of rolls of microfilm (see González 1992, 101), and IBM was involved in a variety of digitization projects including those with the Archivo General de Indias (Spain); the lifetime collection of American painter Andrew Wyeth's works (USA); the National Museum of Ethnology in Osaka (Japan); The Hebrew Union College (USA and Israel); Yale Library (USA); The Vatican Library (Italy); and the National Gallery of Art (USA) (Mintzer et al. 1996; Gladney et al. 1997). Such projects were beneficial to both institution and industry: providing the culture and heritage industry with access to expensive, advanced technology and providing the industrial partners with real life test cases for research and development, publicity and often financial benefits, such as tax-breaks, when working alongside charities, education or governmental institutions.

However, international and national policymakers and funding bodies were taking notice: for example, 'DigiCULT' – the European Commission's programme for undertaking 'EU-funded research on digital culture and digital libraries deal[ing] with leading-edge information and communication technologies for expanding access to and use of Europe's rich cultural and scientific resources' (European Commission 2007) – emanated from interest in this early digitization work and was established in the late 1980s. Policy development and funding streams for digital libraries and heritage effectively began at European level at the same time: with the European parliament drawing attention to the importance of the emerging digital environment, and fostering technology-based, applied research programmes for libraries under the Third and Fourth Framework Programmes in the early 1990s (Manson 1998). By the close of the 1980s, funding bodies across the world, lead by the US and the UK, were beginning to develop programmes to provide funds for institutions to undertake digitization projects.

The excitement in the humanities and heritage sector regarding the possibilities of digitization in the late 1980s and early 1990s was palpable, with much published research emanating from early pilot projects regarding the technicalities and possibilities of digitization. Thaller declared that 'image processing in many ways has been the "hottest" topic in Humanities computing in recent years' (1992a, 1) after a series of workshops were held in Glasgow, Tromsø and Firenze on the topic. The exponential growth of digitization in the arts, cultural and heritage sectors was heralded as:

> a curious and unprecedented fusion of technology, imagination, necessity, philosophy and production which is continuously creating new images, many of which are changing the culture within which we live (Colson and Hall 1992, 3).

The introduction of the networked global information environment in the early 1990s, the resulting public policy encouraging the production of these resources and the emergence of funding streams to create online resources, was to further encourage unprecedented investment and development in digitization within the heritage and cultural sector.

The 1990s

The exponential growth of digitization projects being undertaken in the close of the twentieth century meant that 'to the librarian at the very least, [the 1990s] could be termed the "decade of digitization"' (Lee 2002, 160). The increase in digitization efforts was due to a complex interplay between different forces: the increase in performance and availability of new technologies (see Chapter 2), an increase in awareness of the possibilities of these technologies, the resulting changes in public policy which increased the availability of funding for memory institutions undertaking technological projects and provided infrastructure to facilitate digitization efforts, and the changing perceptions within memory institutions themselves regarding how technology could be appropriated to meet user needs and offer new possibilities. This culminated in 'Countless millions of pounds, dollars, francs and marks [being] ploughed into digital projects that have involved the conversion of library, museum and archive collections' (ibid.).

In many ways, the 1990s began as the 1980s had ended, with small-scale digitization projects being undertaken of treasured holdings. For example, The British Library's earliest and most prominent digitization project was that of the Beowulf manuscript and, shortly afterwards, the Bodleian Library began putting digital surrogates of its Medieval and Celtic manuscript material online. Early projects tended to build on and reinforce research efforts into best practice (the research involved with digitization rarely invented new technologies, but ascertained how technologies invented elsewhere for other purposes could be appropriated in memory institutions). Faced with limited computer storage and network speed, expensive capture technologies that had not yet reached maturity, and software which needed tweaking to fit the needs of memory institutions, these projects were pioneering experiments into what could be done and how best to attempt it.

However, the development of the World Wide Web in the early 1990s (see pp. 25–26), which provided a vehicle for dissemination of digital information, encouraged scoping studies and research to be undertaken to ascertain how the new imaging and networked technologies could be appropriated, such as Peter Robinson's seminal study *The Digitization of Primary Textual Sources* (1993). Growing interest from the research councils themselves led to funding streams which encouraged an exponential growth in the creation of digital surrogates, on a worldwide-scale, shifting the emphasis rapidly from small, in-house projects of limited scope, to large-scale ambitious projects aiming to bring access to a high volume of resources to the masses.

In the early 1990s, following interest and resource provision by centralized sources, digitization began to gather pace. In 1993 in the UK, the Joint Funding Council's Libraries Review Group published a report known as The Follet Report (after Sir Brian Follet who chaired the investigation) which was a major review of the needs of libraries in the changing digital environment (Joint Funding Council's Libraries Review Group 1993). Following publication of the report, the UK government's Joint Information System's Committee (JISC a centralized initiative funded by all four of the Higher Education funding bodies for Scotland, England, Northern Ireland and Wales) announced funding of a string of initiatives to encourage the development of Electronic Libraries (or ELib) related resources, infrastructure and services to support the use of digital content in Higher Education and the institutions which serve it. More than £100 million was spent in this area by JISC by the close of the 1990s. In addition to this, JISC provided over £15 million of funding for the ELib programme (which looked into how digital libraries may be developed, including individual small-scale studies into digitizing particular content, see Wissenburg 2000; Rusbridge 2001), £50 million on networks and £24 million on data services (Rusbridge 1998). Other funding bodies were quick to follow, including the Leverhulme Trust; the British Academy; the National Heritage Fund and its related lottery counterpart the New Opportunities Fund; and the Arts and Humanities Research Board (AHRB). It is difficult to ascertain how much money in total went into digitization initiatives in the UK in the 1990s, but fair to say that it rapidly became an industry in itself, with most major academic, library and museum institutions bidding for finances in an increasingly competitive funding environment.

To facilitate best practice in the creation of digital resources in the UK and provide long-term storage facilities for resulting digital artefacts, it became clear that centralized services needed to be provided by the funders of digitization projects to ensure that standards were met, that the resources created were not lost upon the close of individual projects (Burnard and Short 1994), and that resources could be used by as wide a constituency as possible. In the library sector, the Consortium of Research Libraries in the British Isles (CURL, www.curl.ac.uk) was founded in 1992, funded in part by JISC, to provide tools, infrastructure and leadership, creating a cross-searchable library system to encourage easy access to digital resources by 'helping to build the Distributed and Hybrid Research Library of the future' (CURL n.d). The Arts and Humanities Data Service, formed to 'collect, preserve and promote the electronic resources which result from research and teaching in the arts and humanities' (AHDS 2005) was founded in 1996, funded jointly by the JISC and the AHRB, incorporating the existing History Data Service and the Oxford Text Archive (AHDS 2006, http://ahds.ac.uk/index.htm). The Technical Advisory Service for Images (TASI), providing advice and guidance to the UK's Further and Higher Education community regarding the creation of digital images, managing digitization projects and delivering these to users for a variety of educational purposes (TASI 2002c), was funded in 1997 by the JISC as a 3-year project, and given full status as a service in 2000 (www.tasi.ac.uk). These initiatives, and many others like them, served to provide the infrastructure to ensure that the quality of digital resources produced was high, and that the resulting digital resources would be made available to users.

In addition to creating digital images, surrogates of objects, and digital records of existing physical holdings, it was also necessary to investigate the infrastructure in which these records and digital representations could be hosted, searched, stored and delivered to the users. The concept of the 'Digital Library' as an all encompassing provider, store and search mechanism emerged throughout the 1990s:

> Digital libraries are organizations that provide the resources, including the specialized staff, to select, structure, offer intellectual access to, interpret, distribute, preserve the integrity of, and ensure the persistence over time of collections of digital works so that they are readily and economically available for use by a defined community or set of communities (Digital Library Federation 1998).

Much work was devoted to establishing digital library initiatives and providing digital content for such endeavours from the early 1990s. However, it is still not clear what constitutes a digital library:

> The digital library, the electronic library (generally taken to be synonymous with the digital library), the virtual library, the hybrid library, the library without walls are all concepts that librarians seems to be dealing with all the time. What do they mean? Do they mean the same to everyone who uses the terms? Do they all mean the same thing? Do we all mean the same thing when we talk about a library? … Every library is different, every digital library is different, and different players are advancing many definitions for the digital library (Deegan and Tanner 2002, 20).

Implementations of digital libraries from the 1990s onward explored the concept and the various possible interpretations of the term. There is much writing on the topic, which is a separate area in itself, such as Deegan and Tanner (2002); Witten and Bainbridge (2003); Lesk (2005); Dahl et al. (2006); and Earnshaw and Vince (2007).

In the US, the National Digital Library Program was initiated by the Library of Congress in 1994, reaching its goal of making 5 million historical American items, from over 90 collections and various US institutions, available on its American Memory website (www.loc.gov) by 2001. A public–private partnership, over $130 million was donated to the Library, from government, businesses and individuals (Library of Congress 2001). Another programme, the Digital Library Initiative, was launched by the United States National Science Foundation with the National Aeronautic and Space Administration (NASA) and the Advanced Research Projects Agency (ARPA) in 1994, giving digital libraries a major boost and allowing exploration of some of the major issues confronting the establishment of digital libraries on a large scale. Phase 1, running from 1994 to 1998, funded six digital library projects with a total of $30 million. Phase 2 (DLI2, www.dli2.nsf.gov) running from 1999, provided $55 million to fund 36 projects that aimed to extend and develop innovative digital library technologies and applications. Clearly, a lot of activity was going into the creation of digital resources, but also investigating the infrastructure necessary to provide them. Other funding bodies in the US also began to support digital library and digitization initiatives during this phase, such as the Research Libraries Group (Erway 1996); JSTOR (Schonfield

2003); The Getty Institute; the Andrew W. Mellon Foundation; the Coalition for Networked Information; and the Art Museum Image Consortium (AMICO) programme. Some of the funding bodies did not and do not limit their support to the US, but are active in pursuing international collaboration that builds research collections without regard to their physical location.

The centrally funded infrastructure which underpinned these initiatives in the US mostly centred round the concept of the Digital Library. Digitization initiatives followed long term attempts to share library catalogue information: founded in 1967, the OCLC (Online Computer Library Center, www.oclc.org) is a 'computer library service and research organization dedicated to the public purposes of furthering access to the world's information and reducing information costs' (OCLC 2007) through the sharing of library records, providing services for locating, acquiring, cataloguing, lending and preserving library materials now used by over 60,000 institutions in 112 countries, and funded by a variety of international governments, institutions and charities. The Coalition for Networked Information (www.cni.org), founded in 1990 by the library and IT Communities to 'enhance scholarship and intellectual productivity' (CNI 2006), rapidly grew to a current membership of 200 institutions representing higher education, publishing, network and telecommunications, information technology and libraries, and library organizations. The Digital Libraries Federation (www.diglib.org), founded in 1995, comprises of a consortium of the main academic and public libraries, providing leadership and support for large-scale digitization programmes, together with guidelines and forums for sharing experiences between members. In addition to such consortia and forums, vehicles for disseminating research and reporting best practice in digitization were established. D-Lib Magazine, an electronic publication with a focus on digital library research published by the D-Lib Alliance, launched its first issue in July 1995, and is still publishing related research and developments today for a wide international readership (www.dlib.org). The Research Libraries Group (now part of the OCLC) started publishing their newsletter, Diginews, an online newsletter for digital imaging and preservation in April 1997, which ran for 10 years, and is now preserved at http://digitalarchive.oclc.org/. The founding (and funding) of such broad initiatives ensured that the communities undertaking digitization were sharing information and expertise, and working towards common goals.

A similar tale is to be told across most of the developed world. The European Union's Telematics for Libraries Programme, running from 1990 to 1998, (http://cordis.europa.eu/libraries/) provided over €30 million to develop innovative library services and tools, as well as bibliographic resources and library networking infrastructures which underpin such services, across Europe. A national programme was started in France in 1992 (Beagrie 2003), with the Bibliothèque Nationale de France undertaking an ambitious digitization programme of material in the national library and associated collections. By 2008 this ongoing digitization effort, one of the costliest and largest in Europe, had succeeded in making 10 billion documents available online (http://gallica.bnf.fr/). National reports for countries involved in the preservation of digital information, including historical information about digitization programmes, and covering Australia, France, the Netherlands, the United Kingdom and beyond, can be found in Beagrie (2003). A summary report of the digitization efforts of all the EU member states has been produced annually since 2002 by the Minerva project (Ministerial NEtwoRk for Valorising Activities in digitisation, www.minervaeurope.org) which also provides guidelines for best practice in digitization (Minerva 2007). DELOS, a Network of Excellence on Digital Libraries, provides guidance, advice and forums to encourage the integration of efforts in Digital Library research and development across Europe (www.delos.info), and its records also demonstrates the range and interest in digitization at this period.

The shift in digitization projects in the 1990s from the small-scale and focussed to large-scale and all encompassing can be seen in the approach taken by one of the world's largest and finest memory institutions: The British Library. Founded in 1972 by the amalgamation of various UK institutions, with a collection of over 150 million individual items gathered over 250 years that cover all ages of written civilization, the British Library began to seriously consider digitization in the early 1990s. The British Library's digitization projects began with the *Electronic Beowulf* in 1992 (Kiernan 1997; Prescott 1998), a collaboration which:

> linked access, scholarship and conservation of the fire damaged manuscript. Early concentration on material such as Beowulf which was unique, valuable, at risk (in conservation terms), and of high scholarly importance, was typical of the first steps by major libraries in the early 1990s (Smith 2006, 9).

Initial experience gained through the Beowulf project at the British Library 'was built upon and improved through rapid advances in and general availability of technology' (ibid.), which 'saw an important shift in the mid-to-late 1990s from digitisation as experiment to digitisation as an operational task' (ibid.). Since 2000, the BL's digitization strategy has focused on large-scale digitization of textual materials to build a 'critical mass' (ibid.) of material, such as the major newspaper digitization projects: the digitization of a million pages of the Burney collection of eighteenth-century British newspapers (www.bl.uk/collections/burney.html), and the digitization of two million pages of nineteenth century local, regional and national newspapers (www.bl.uk/collections/earlynewspapers.html). The library's materials are increasingly now produced:

> primarily – or solely – in digital form, and the Library's digital collections are large and rapidly expanding ... For the BL, digitisation offers an important way to open up its unique heritage collections, and make more widely accessible items of national and international appeal (Smith 2006, 5–7).

At the start of the 1990s, then, 'In the early days of the Web, museums provided some of the best content and some of the most compelling reasons to go online' (Peacock et al. 2004). Towards the close of the millennium, 'A decade of digitisation and documentation for the Web ... created a rich array of cultural and historical information across the museum, library and archive sectors' (ibid.). The development of the World Wide Web was the cause of the growth of digitization efforts in the library, cultural and heritage sector, and its increasing popularity with users fanned the expectation and desire to see digitized material online:

> The internet has stimulated a demand for online access to information. Institutions, like museums and libraries, correctly perceive that digital images – at the same time as they reduce the need for direct access to the originals – can be used to provide improved access to those works in their collections that are considered most important (or most 'in demand'). Importantly, such access is location- and time-independent. That is, scholars anywhere in the world can retrieve or view web pages (Grycz 2006, 33).

With the growth of material online in the latter part of the 1990s, it became almost impossible to track and trace all digitization projects. Efforts such as ITEM database switched from being a print publication in 1995 (Pring 1995) to being an online resource, but folded in 2000, given the impossibility of the attempts to keep cataloguing this type of online resource, and the success of the Internet search engines.in allowing individuals to search for the type of projects they wanted online. The act of finding relevant material, including digital image material, among the host of information available online became the subject of much scholarly effort itself (see Chapter 7). Around the same time, the process of digitization, explored and experimented with by early projects, and ratified into procedural and technical guidelines along the way (see pp. 120–122), became less of a scholarly endeavour within itself and more of a standard means to provide digital information to a wider audience. By the end of the decade:

> Digitisation is not a per-se research issue but is part of a wider context related to the information society and the effective use of the digital content by cultural institutions (Minerva 2003, xxiii).

Post 2000

Much digitization effort accompanied the hype surrounding the millennium celebrations, with many funding programmes put in place to provide the resources to create digital content. These efforts continued into the new century: for example, in July 2001, the UK Government's lottery-based New Opportunities Fund (NOF) announced the largest single coordinated funding initiative in the UK for digitization, with grants totalling £50 million for more than 150 UK local and national organizations to document a wealth of UK achievement and heritage in science, culture and social diversity under its NOF-digitize programme. Such a wide reaching programme was undertaken to create a 'communities bank' of Internet resources, primarily for use in learning and targeting, in particular, 'lifelong learners'. For a summary of the scope of these projects, explore (www.enrichuk.net). The JISC also announced a large-scale digitization programme in 2004 (www.jisc.ac.uk/digitisation_home.html), aiming to 'change the world of authoritative e-resources through its investment in digitising content from some of the UK's greatest collections' (JISC 2007). The first phase, with funding of £22 million:

> began in 2004 and included the 18th century parliamentary papers, Archival sound recordings, British Library 19th century newspapers, Medical journals backfiles, NewsFilm Online and Online historical population reports (ibid.).

The second phase, with a further £12 million:

> features projects that will enable all users, regardless of location and time, online access to a range of authoritative digitised e-resources previously difficult or impossible to access. Together, the projects represent a diversity of rich and vivid perspectives on the history, culture and landscape of the UK and beyond. They capture a wide variety of aspects of UK life, from Cabinet papers to First World War poetry, radio news to East End music hall, political cartoons to British borders, and in a wide range of media, including sound, film, images, journals, newspapers, maps, theses, pamphlets and cartoons (ibid.).

Funding councils, then, are now aiming to create a knowledge base of high quality resources, from established projects, institutions and repositories, under their watchful eye, demanding observance of strict technical guidelines with aims for reuse in national repositories. The majority of these resources are (but are not exclusively) digital image-based.

Around the same time as the launch of large-scale, centrally funded initiatives, such as the JISC digitization programme, came the emergence of proposals from large commercial firms to digitize holdings of institutions wholesale. By avoiding the 'cherry picking' tactics of the funding councils, they aim to digitize everything possible, with the view that searching mechanisms to allow intelligent and useful analysis of large-scale digital collections will soon become sophisticated enough to allow users to find their potential needles in the digital haystacks. Such digitization programmes are rife with copyright problems, and can often cause complaint and consternation from traditional memory institutions, although many are carried out in cooperation with world leading, large institutions to allow large-scale digitization of holdings that they could just not afford to do on their own.

Funded by the corporations, the financial model of these large-scale projects differs from that of the funding councils (who use public funds to create freely available digital resources). In some public-private digitization partnerships, free access to the digitized records is available from terminals within the institution building, but those general users consulting the digitized collection via the Internet are charged for access to records. For example, the UK's National Archives (TNA) have joined forces with the American company My Family Incorporated, more commonly referred to as Ancestry.com, to digitize and provide online access to the historic census records of England and Wales (1841–1901), and other related historical records (www.nationalarchives.gov.uk/census/). The combined scale of the digitization, with over 165 million individual records, required much investment from Ancestry, which was just not possible for TNA to provide, given their limited budget and facilities. Access to the census is free to those using the dedicated machines in TNA at Kew itself, and although it is free to do some level of searching of the databases on Ancestry's website (www.ancestry.co.uk), detailed access to images of the records (which contain all the information, as some fields are not digitized) requires some payment or subscription to the service. The public interest in the historical census is phenomenal, and more than enough users utilize this facility to make it profitable, as the overwhelming demand at the launch of the 1901 census shows: the TNA expected 1.2 million visitors per day, and instead, the site crawled to a halt after dealing with 50 million requests per hour, requiring the withdrawal and redesigning of the service, which has since kept up with this incredible demand (Inman 2002).

The largest of such digitization projects, though, is currently being carried out by the commercially owned search engine and information provider Google (www.google.com), which has brokered agreements with some of the world's largest and best equipped libraries to carry out a mass digitization scheme of some of their holdings. Known as 'Google Print' at its launch in October 2004, the service is now known as 'Google Books' (http://books.google.com/), providing the facility to read books online by giving access to images of the digitized texts compressed in PDF format. At present, this service is free to all users, but access to some materials can be restricted depending on agreements with specific institutions, and the geographical location of users.

The list of organizations joining the Google Books programme continues to grow. The University of Michigan will have its entire print collection of seven million books digitized over a six-year period (BBC 2004). The 40,000 books from the University of Harvard will be digitized. New York Library, Stanford University and the University of Oxford's Bodleian Library have all pledged to allow out of copyright material to be digitized. Mysore University library, the largest and oldest library in the southern Indian State of Karnataka, will have 800,000 Sanskrit or Kannada texts digitized (Techtree.com 2007). In total, over 20 of the worlds most esteemed libraries or archives are now allowing Google access to their collections, allowing Google to amass the largest ever corpus of human knowledge in digital form.

Google is able to achieve this by establishing high throughput digitization centres at each of its collaborating libraries: the digital scanning and processing unit at Oxford, for example, is 'capable of producing as many as 10,000 electronic books per week' (Carr 2004). The universities themselves benefit as digitization is carried out which they could not afford to do, and they are given a digital copy of the text for themselves, for example, at Oxford:

> The scanning operation will lead to the creation of two digital copies of each book: one for Google, and one for Oxford. The Google copy will be fully indexed and searchable through the Google search service, while the Oxford copy will be linked directly to the relevant catalogue record in the Oxford Libraries Information Service (OLIS) (ibid.).

The Google Books digitization programme is then presented as a 'win-win' (ibid.) opportunity for contributing libraries. However, recently there has been concern about the restrictive legal conditions Google (and others) place on texts they have digitized, as restrictions prohibit electronic texts from being included in commercial search engines other than themselves:

> some libraries and researchers worry that if any one company comes to dominate the digital conversion of these works, it could exploit that dominance for commercial gain (Hafner 2007).

Google's efforts are not without their detractors. Google asks publishers to 'opt out' of the digitization programme, insisting that any authors or publishers who do not opt out can have their works digitized under 'fair use' laws. As a result, the publishing industry and writers' groups have criticized Google Books for infringing copyright, with various legal challenges being made to Google's 'brazen violation of copyright law' (Authors Guild 2005). Additionally, the bias towards English language material is questionable (Jeanneney 2007). The quality of the scanning and the lack of benchmarking procedures can be worrying, with some pages being cut off when placed wrongly on the scan bed, the robotic scan arm being visible, or even the fingers of scanner operators being captured forever in the image of the digitized text (Theage.com.au 2007) although Google does provide the facility to report these errors. Additionally, trusting a commercial company with providing access to this information for perpetuity is risky: it may be free now, but will it always be? Also, if the texts are restricted to search results from only one search engine does this carve the Internet into distinct sections, rather than providing an online environment for free dissemination of information?

Naturally, after Google's announcement of Google Print, its major competitor – Microsoft – announced its own large-scale digitization programme, MSN Book Search (http://books.live.com), in October 2005 (Microsoft Corporation 2005). Working with libraries which did not sign up to the Google Books programme, such as the British Library and Cornell University Library, and a range of publishers under the 'Live Search Books Publisher Program' which encourages in-copyright material to be submitted to the service, Microsoft has been building up its own vast collection of digitized material, accessible though its own search engine. Although its terms and conditions prevent text it has digitized from being searchable in other commercial search engines (such as Google), its restrictions are not as harsh as the Google license, allowing other search engines to point to the material, if not to undertake full text searching on records available in text form. The MSN Book Search suffers from many of the same issues as Google Books, though, with worries that restricting full access to one search engine threatens to limit, rather than improve, access to information.

This commercial mass digitization is not limited to the production of images of, and machine readable versions of, text, however: Corbis Images, another commercial company owned by Bill Gates, has been acquiring the digital rights to images and digitizing vast image archives, since 1989 (www.corbis.com, Süsstrunk 1998). With an archive of 100 million historic, art, entertainment, news and creative images, the company is the leading broker of quality digital image material across the world. It too has links to major institutions: in this case, archives, art galleries and museums, such as the National Gallery (UK); The Bettman Archive of Photographic Images; and the Hermitage Museum in St Petersburg. In 2007, Corbis announced a partnership with the Smithsonian Museum, aiding in the creation of digitized versions of the holdings of the 17 individual museums, and controlling licensing of these images for editorial and commercial use worldwide (Corbis 2007). Corbis' licensing terms are strict: however, it does provide a relaxed licence for use in art and design education (http://education.corbis.com/). Although such arrangements safeguard the revenue streams of institutions and individuals against the easy, unlicensed and unwarranted reproduction of their images and abuse of their intellectual property, and provide a legal framework to pursue those making unlicensed profits from use of famous images, there is concern within the photographic industry regarding how much power a large company like Corbis can wield over individual photographers and institutions (Covington 2001).

In response to these restrictive commercial ventures, the Open Content Alliance (OCA) (www.opencontentalliance.org) was formed in 2005 as a consortium of:

> cultural, technology, nonprofit, and governmental organizations from around the world that will help build a permanent archive of multilingual digitised text and multimedia content (Open Content Alliance n.d.)

that will be available without restrictions online, in conjunction with Yahoo! and the Internet Archive. The OCA operates a significantly different license to Google Books: asking owners of books in copyright to opt-in to digitization. Books which have been digitized are freely available from the Open Library website, although it is still in demo form (http://openlibrary.org/). The Open Content Alliance has a relationship with Microsoft, and many other commercial companies, working towards making as many digitized texts as possible freely available online. It will be interesting to see how this resource progresses without the commercial heft of a company like Google to fund its mass digitization attempts.

As a result of both the commercial and publicly funded efforts to provide high quality material online, it is now difficult to remember a time when institutions did not provide digitized representations of their holdings. The results of years of investment of effort and resources by the cultural, heritage, commercial and voluntary sector provide a rich, online environment for users to browse, analyse and study:

> Do you want to read Shakespeare's Hamlet in the first quarto edition of 1603? You have only to go to the British Library site and click on the heading 'Treasures in Full'. Do you need to consult a Finnish journal for a certain date in 1805? Go to the University of Helsinki Library site and the appropriate issue will appear on your screen. To consult descriptions of monuments in Egypt and Nubia, click on the site of the Maison de L'Orient et de la Méditerranée. And so forth (Jeanneney 2007, 19).

Indeed:

> The possibility of examining rare and unique objects outside the secure, climate-controlled environments of museums and archives liberates collections for study and enjoyment (Besser and Trant 1995, 7).

Digitization Standards and Guidelines

The need for technical digitization guidelines was highlighted by early digitization projects (Besser and Trant 1994; Cartolano et al. 1995; Canadian Heritage Information Network 1996), and by the late 1990s, best practice in undertaking digitization was firmly established in the library, archive and heritage sector. (An overview of the main imaging guidelines produced from the 1990s onwards, and a history of the development of these guidelines, can be found in Puglia and Rhodes 2007.) It is important to understand that, in general, digitization programmes aim to create consistent images of documents and artefacts which are fundamentally individual and inconsistent, presenting a variety of physical attributes and capture requirements to the digitizer. As a result, guidelines produced for the scanning and photographic process, the cataloguing of material, and the delivery and long-term storage of digitized objects, documents and artefacts, aim to ensure that the digitization process is as consistent, and the quality of images produced as predictable, as possible.

Digitization guidelines, whether practical, managerial or technical in nature, are the first point of reference for those about to undertake a digitization project and there is no need, nowadays, for an institution to figure out every detail themselves (as was the case with early digitization projects, when much trial and error was necessary to ascertain how best to capture images of every type of object). Institutional decisions will have to be made, though, regarding every aspect of the digitization process, and projects should attempt to undertake digitization to sector standards:

> The idea of following 'best practices' – accepted, documented, methodologies for doing things efficiently and well – is long established in the library, archival and museum world, as well as other sectors, including industry. In relation to the digitisation of cultural and heritage materials, best practices, like their analogue antecedents, are simply working practices and procedures that can provide a safety net for practitioners

> as they navigate all aspects of the digitisation workflow. Following these markers will give a reasonable expectation of success and add value to projects in terms of their long-term consistency (Hughes 2004, 199).

However, technology is far from static, and changes too rapidly for any one set of standards to be applicable. While it is true that certain technical requirements such as resolution (see pp. 40–43) and choice of file format (see Chapter 4) have settled into patterns of adoption, other issues such as colour management and quality control (Chapter 8) have yet to be resolved, and the technical infrastructure which underpins digitization is constantly changing. Therefore:

> The best solution … is not to work towards rigid standards but to develop sets of best practices, or current practices, around key topics. These can be then applied or modified according to the needs of specific institutions, collections and projects (ibid.).

Projects are advised to consult specific guidelines for the sector, such as The National Initiative for a Networked Cultural Heritage (NINCH)'s *Guide to Good Practice in the Digital Representation and Management of Cultural Heritage Materials* (NINCH 2002). The Arts and Humanities Data Service's Guides to Good Practice series for humanities digitization projects covers best practice in areas as broad as the creation of digital resources for the visual arts, archaeology, history, the performing arts, literature, language and linguistics (http://ahds.ac.uk/guides/): although funding for this service has been withdrawn, and at time of writing its future is unknown, these guides should still exist in some form and be applicable to many undertaking digitization. The Technical Advisory Service for Images (www.tasi.ac.uk) provides excellent, freely available, up to date online guides regarding all aspects of digital imaging, with a slant towards the provision of digital images for use in education. (Those within the UK's Higher Education sector can use the TASI helpdesk to ask specific questions regarding digitization projects which are not addressed in the wide coverage of information provided online.) The Digital Library Federation maintains an up to date and comprehensive online list of standards which it identifies, documents, organizationally endorses and promotes (www.diglib.org/standards.htm); the Canadian Heritage Information Network also provides an up to date overview of standards, including useful introductory material (www.chin.gc.ca/English/Standards/); and Minerva maintains a select list of guidelines regarding the digitization of paper-based documentary heritage (www.minervaeurope.org/guidelines.htm).

Useful, trusted sources of up to date technical standards include those produced by established and well known institutions, such as the *Library of Congress Technical Standards for Digital Conversion of Text and Graphic Materials* (Library of Congress 2007), or guidelines produced by established governmental bodies, such as the USA's National Archives and Records Administration, which produced technical recommendations for digitization (NARA 2004). Guidelines pertaining specifically to issues of Digital Curation and the longevity of digitized collections can be found at the UK's Digital Curation Centre (www.dcc.ac.uk/tools/).

It will be seen from these guidelines that there is a broad spectrum of acceptable digitization practice, and institutions will have to carefully choose which approach they will adopt to face the many issues involved in digitization, such as how to select materials to be digitized, which technical standards and documentation they should utilize, how they should be cataloguing and archiving digitized materials, and how best to display and deliver digital surrogates to users. Becoming aware of the wealth of material and guidance out there should be the first stage of those attempting to undertake a digitization project: 'Examining existing guidelines will allow the extrapolation of the best and most recent standards currently available that can be modified to fit the intended purpose, institution, and budget' (Hughes 2004, 200). There are also some primary texts on the subject that no project should begin digitization without consulting: these are listed at the end of the chapter.

Current Issues in Digitization

The shift in digitization projects to the large scale, and the growth in use and user expectations regarding the provision and quality of digitized material, results in a change in research questions that need to be asked by professionals working in the area:

> We're getting pretty good at digitizing material at scale … If you look at many of the projects … you will see there are lots and lots of materials being digitized. Our museums, our libraries, our archives, our historical societies, are all running digitisation programs … We have a wealth of experience and a large number of successful projects (not to mention some highly educational failures) to build upon. With the exception of relatively esoteric materials in specialized formats or that have some really unusual characteristics, this is not really research any more. Or to put it another way, the research questions are less about how to do it at all and more about how to optimize – how to do it more efficiently or effectively, how to be sure that you've chosen the most appropriate strategies and technologies (Lynch 2002).

At time of writing, research questions remain about use and usefulness of digitized collections, how new and developing technologies, such as those touted as 'Web 2.0' can be integrated into digital online collections to be of benefit to users, and how to integrate the vast swathes of online ephemera digitized by amateurs into our thinking about digitization, collections and corpora.

Use and Usability of Digitized Collections

The vast amounts of digitized material being made available online by both professional corporations, public institutions and private collections, and the growing use of imaging technologies in personal life (see Chapter 6), adds to user expectations of what should be available, nowadays, and results in an increase in demand by users for high quality material. For example, the increase in demand for digital images from the Victoria and Albert Museum (www.vam.ac.uk) has been put down to a number of coinciding factors:

> It is interesting to observe how this client demand is stimulated. The more that internal staff see digital images on museum databases, the more they realise their versatility. External client demand also plays a part; indeed this has been one of the drivers for digitisation needs … However, for many non-creative staff, it is their personal use of digital cameras and computers that show them how these technologies can be applied in the workplace. It could be that their children's schoolwork illustrates the advantages of working in this way. Whatever the reason, the demand for digital images of the collection and museum events and activities is steadily growing month by month (Stevenson 2006, 72).

However, this has been juxtaposed by increased user expectations:

> As we have created more digital output, the users of these images have become more critical of quality and their expectations have been raised (ibid. 85).

But:

> the more that digital images are seen, the more demand there is to re-use them for other projects … This database … is now routinely used on most museum projects such as exhibitions and publication preparation, and by curators for preparing talks and lectures. This familiarity with using images for research purposes has stimulated projects where digital images are used in their own right. The museum website is an obvious showcase for the collection (ibid. 89).

Digitization at such a large scale would seem to be a self-promoting vehicle: the more that is provided, the more the resource is used, and the higher the demand for other resources of high quality.

What is it that users require from images provided by memory institutions? Users, who will tend to spend most of their online time on professionally produced commercial websites, are displaying increasingly sophisticated knowledge of information environments, and expect the surrogates and representations provided by information institutions, and the infrastructure which hosts, provides and displays them, to keep up with modern developments. Beth Sandore, in her contribution to Kenny and Reiger (2000), suggests that *What Users Want from Digital Image Collections* is fast retrieval, image and text versions (to conduct full text searches of documents), completeness and legibility of images without scrolling down the page, multiple sizes of images to support differing research needs, consistency across image databases, tools (such as zoom and pan) to deal with large images, simple user interfaces, hypertextual links between structural and intellectual content and the ability to manipulate digital images (such as zoom, being able to examine images side by side, save searches, results and annotations). Users also need a variety of search functions, which provide a variety of user options to enable cross-database searching and, more importantly, a standardized interface and query language across different systems, as different and bespoke implementations of systems can yield very different search results with the same terms, depending on the cataloguing and metadata captured (see Chapter 7) (Sandore 2000; also see Sandore and Shaik 1988).

The question of what users want also has to be juxtaposed with issues of how institutions choose to present images to users, and what attempts they will make to contextualize the materials:

> while much of that information is now available via the Web, it is not always true to say that it is readily accessible. By accessible here we mean not just findable, regardless of literacy, disability or bandwidth, but usable and valuable as knowledge, not just information. A range of barriers, only some of them technical, impedes the effective flow of knowledge from source to searcher via museum Web sites. Among the most significant is the fact that much of the museum content that can be found remains as raw information, not readily assimilated into knowledge by the user. The value of that information remains a rich but largely untapped seam, notwithstanding advances in database-generated content, search engines and interface design (Peacock et al. 2004).

Providing large digitized collections of raw material, and some fairly simple access tools, is not enough to allow users to get the most out of digitized collections and institutions will have to investigate the provision of:

> sophisticated systems for ongoing use or apparatus providing interpretation …We need to study the lines of demarcation between raw cultural heritage materials, if you will, and interpretation or teaching, or presentations of these materials. This is a boundary line that I don't think we really have a very clear understanding of. It gets to the historic mission differences among museums, libraries and archives, and the growing confusion about those distinctions in the digital world; it involves the historical and perhaps changing roles of scholars, teachers, curators, and librarians. It invites questions about which audiences or user communities we are teaching to use uninterpreted databases of raw cultural heritage materials, and the methods we are teaching them to use in exploiting these resources. We have to ask questions about just how 'interpretation-neutral' a collection of raw materials can really be (Lynch 2002).

Institutions must develop an understanding of the online environment which informs users' behaviours and desires, while being creative with their own delivery of information and digital surrogates, to challenge and inform the user:

> the best results are achieved when digital interpretations extend the context of objects and collections beyond the physical boundaries of museums and archaeological sites,

> for them to become everyday realities. In this sense, digital cultural heritage may be seen as a branch of architecture, with the agenda of creating new *virtual* spaces for museums and sites limited by their physical boundaries … These are spaces where objects may be displayed in continuously changing contexts, according to the personal tastes and needs of visitors and curators, who will be able to create their own stories (Bianchi 2006, 464).

There is much to be done to explore how best libraries, archives and museums can provide an online presence of their digitized collections that enhances the user experience and makes the most of the opportunities the digital medium presents. In the first instance, those developing front-ends and user interfaces to digital collections should be aware that integrating users into the design and development process is a fundamental part of delivering a resource which will prove useful, and perhaps even become well used, and should consult readily available guides to producing usable online resources, such as Jadav (2002) and Krug (2005).

Given that there is now a plethora of digital information that has been made available by institutions in the library, archive and cultural and heritage sector, what can we say about how users are using this material, and what they are using it for? Anecdotal reports, such as those from the Victoria and Albert Museum, above, are common but surprisingly, there is a dearth of evidence which gives hard, clear statistics about how such digitized collections are used. This is worrying, considering the financial and temporal investment necessary to undertake a digitization project. The anecdotal evidence suggests that while some projects become popular and well used, others become relatively quickly forgotten. Research looking at available (but limited) log files of portals to information resources, which capture the requests given to the server and so can give a quantified illustration of what is used, suggest that almost a third of humanities based digital resources available online are rarely, or seldom, accessed (Warwick et al. 2006). However, this is equitable to the number of academic papers published which are never cited (ScienceWatch 1999), or books never taken out of store in library collections. The difference is that the costs of publication for books and journals are borne by (usually commercial) publishers, while the costs for digitization of objects usually, in some part, comes from the institution itself. Evidently, there is a lot of material being produced which is never used. Additionally, once individuals have left the website, or purchased the CD-ROM, there is no way to know how they are using the digital surrogates afterwards or what they are using them for.

There is also the issue of trust – or mistrust – in the use of digital images in research. In a study undertaken on user perceptions of digital images of manuscript material it is reported that there is:

> a chasm in perception and usage within … digitisation. In a user group consisting predominantly of users from the academic community … use was shown to be heavily influenced by undergraduate students utilising the digital surrogates as teaching aids. The levels of satisfaction with the digital surrogate from the postgraduate and academic staff user groups were quite low. Therefore, there seems to be a dividing

> line in the academic value of the digital surrogate between the levels of undergraduate, postgraduate and academic staff (Tawse 2003, Chapter 5).

As a result:

> digitisation would seem to be supplying access to a large percentage of those people to whom it is not strictly necessary to see manuscripts, rather than to those who must see it for their work related research (Tawse 2003, Chapter 4).

In Tawse's study, academics did not trust digital images of manuscripts for research – unless they had created the digital images themselves. This should be borne in mind by those creating digital image archives – images may be useful and interesting to the general public, or those engaged in learning activities, but digital images archives rarely propagate new, robust, academic research from those images, unless they were created for that purpose in collaboration with the researchers in question.

Evidence of use is a thorny issue, and one which the research councils and funders are becoming increasingly twitchy about. In the UK, the Arts and Humanities Research Council has recently cited 'Evidence of Value of ICT' (Information and Communication Technologies) as one of two main review areas of its research programme (the other being the problematic issue of the sustainability of digital resources after project funding ends), declaring that:

> Collecting and highlighting all the evidence relating to this is important not just to persuade funders to support ICT use in the future, but also to increase uptake in the academic community. It should be the main basis for the discussion of future needs and opportunities (AHRC 2007a).

The lack of evidence of use, or uptake of services, means that funding can and will be withdrawn from funding programmes and support services. In May 2007, the AHRC announced it was withdrawing funding from the Arts and Humanities Data Service from March 2008 (AHRC 2007b), although it was a world leading service and provided much needed advice to those undertaking digitization, and other ICT related projects, within the UK. It may be that, as further evidence of use fails to materialize, we see a further scaling back of research programmes and services tied to digitization, after this period of strong growth and proliferation of digitized content. The question of who will pay to maintain digital collections once they are created, and who will ensure that they are available for use in the future (particularly given the present funding crisis) is one which is also unresolved:

> we must consider the life of digital archives and their place in the technology, for although completely modern, they are as fragile as ancient books. All research must anticipate future evolutions, so as to ensure that the digitized texts or images can be reformatted without the original texts having to be re-input, thereby risking further

> deterioration. Digitization in itself offers no guarantee of longevity; it must constantly adapt to the pitiless changes of ongoing technology. And this fact must be an obsession for those in charge (Jeanneney 2007, 64).

If collections are not used, should they been maintained? If they are not maintained, how can they be used?

Web 2.0 and Memory Institutions

The majority of institutions undertaking digitization provide the resulting images, texts and other digital media via an online presence. Most of these websites are fairly static, and allow little interaction or input from the user, rather than them being able to choose which resources they wish to see or access. In what has become known as the standard 'Web 1.0' model, pages are delivered to a user, who then requests another, but cannot add to or input any details to the page itself that can be seen or used by other users.

'Web 2.0' was the term coined, in 2003, by Tim O'Reilly (of the technology book publishers) to describe the next generation of service-based websites that provided tools and facilities for online communities to interact with material and utilize the collected intelligence of many visitors to shape and change the resulting user experience. (See O'Reilly (2005) for an introduction to the many facets of the term Web 2.0 and also for an introduction to those who rubbish it as mere marketing hype; and Anderson 2007 for an unbiased overview of how these tools can be used by educational institutions.) These tools and technologies are becoming increasingly popular on commercial and social networking sites, such as Flickr; MySpace; Bebo; Facebook and other sites where the majority of Internet users spend a good deal of their online time. The popularity of these sites, and the different model of interaction with digital media they afford, such as user tagging (see pp. 180–181) and RSS feeds, has affected user expectation and demand for material provided by institutional websites:

> Put simply, libraries must now begin to use these Web 2.0 applications if they are to prove themselves to be just as relevant as other information providers, and start to deliver experiences that meet the modern user's expectations (Chad and Miller 2005, 8).

As a result, libraries, archives and museums are currently locked in a debate regarding what the term Web 2.0 means, what it means for them, how they can best utilize the available tools, how they can afford to implement and support the tools available, the effect this will have on both their institutional control and online branding, and their control over the user experience (Crawford 2006). If there is a Web 2.0, should we be thinking about Library 2.0, Museum 2.0 or Archive 2.0? And if we are, what is it that we are thinking about? If there is a bandwagon, how can we get on – or off – it?

Meredith Farkas, on her 'Information Wants To Be Free' blog (http://meredith.wolf water.com/wordpress/index.php) attempted to define what 'Library 2.0' may mean, in a definition that could be embraced by all memory institutions:

> The idea of Library 2.0 represents a significant paradigm shift in the way we view library services. It's about a seamless user experience, where usability, interoperability, and flexibility of library systems is key. It's about the library being more present in the community through programming, community building (both online and physical), and outreach via technology (IM, screencasting, blogs, wikis, etc.). It's about allowing user participation through writing reviews and tagging in the catalog and making their voice heard through blogs and wikis. It's about making the library more transparent through its Web presence and its physical design. We need to make the library human, ubiquitous, and user-centered. This involves a change in our systems, our Web presence, and our very attitudes. It will take a lot of work for a library to be completely 2.0, but the idea should inform every decision made at the library (Farkas 2005).

However, there is considerable backlash in the community about the problems adopting Web 2.0 technologies in the LIS sector may pose:

> There is a lot of talk about what Library 2.0 is, what Web 2.0 means to us, and what technologies can benefit us (RSS, tagging, etc). Fine. ILS vendors are going to see this as a potential gold rush and try to capitalize on it at, what I fear, is our expense. And we may quite possibly be enabling them. Why do I say this? Well, first, let's look at what's at stake here. Essentially it's our data: our catalogs, our patrons, our website content, our library programming, etc. This is our precious gold. This is the raw material that we will use to shape the future of library services. The traditional business model that ILS vendors have pursued (and forced on us) does not give us the freedom to use our own data in the way that we're ultimately going to want to use it (Blyberg 2005).

There is additional concern that the adoption of these technologies has actually been talked about by librarians and information specialists for a considerable amount of time, and no amount of branding the discussion as Web 2.0 will present a novel case, when providing user services which best suit user needs should be paramount (Crawford 2006; Anderson 2007). Discussions among the library, archive and museum communities on this topic, particularly in the blogosphere, are lively, and likely to rage with strong opinions for some time to come (Miller 2005, 2006; Ellis and Kelly 2007).

The few institutions who have, so far, forayed into the Web 2.0 phenomenon and actually implemented Web 2.0 type services have met with general success, and a great deal of interest from members of the public, particularly when using the technologies to increase usability of their digital image collections. Traditional means of searching catalogues meant that users would have to know the artist, title or proper way to refer to an object captured in an image. Image tagging, which allows users to assign their own tags or labels to images, popularized by sites such as flickr.com, creates a user-based taxonomy or 'folksonomy' of image tags which others can search on (see pp. 180–181). The Power House Museum in Sydney, Australia (www.powerhousemuseum.com); the Cleveland Museum of Art (www.clevelandart.org); and the Smithsonian Institution (www.si.edu) have all implemented prototype image tagging on their websites. The Metropolitan Museum of Art ran an interesting experiment, documenting the tags members of the public are likely to use and comparing that with the traditional curatorial description provided, showing the differences between the terminologies used by experts and non-experts, and showing that social tagging is a useful and fun way to engage visitors to the website (Chun et al. 2006). It is likely that we will see more use of these technologies in the cultural and heritage sectors in the future, but again, they have to be weighed up with issues of purpose, usability and use, in order to provide services that improve the existing user experience.

Online Museums

A seldom considered, but growing, online phenomenon is the rise of online museums created by amateur enthusiasts, generally containing digital images of holdings and artefacts. These museums can vary from the ramshackle and quirky to the glossy and guidelines-compliant documentation of ephemera which traditional, established institutions are either not interested, able or willing to catalogue, digitize and provide online. The Museum of Online Museums (http://coudal.com/moom/) maintains a registry of such creations, including the World Carrot Museum (www.carrotmuseum.co.uk); the Gallery of Audio Cassette J-Cards (www.polaralert.com/exhibition/top100/index.html); and Devil's Rope: The Barbed Wire Museum (www.barbwiremuseum.com/index.htm), all featuring exhaustive documentation and digitized source material of their chosen topic.

In many cases, these function as twentieth-century cabinets of curiosities, and can be viewed as amusing, eccentric or even worrying obsessions with a particular type of ephemera which the rest of the world has chosen to leave undocumented. *The Guardian* newspaper described the Museum of Online Museums thus:

> The internet has brought advancements, but nowhere has it been more successful than in the field of meaningless rubbish. Here, vast swathes of tat are housed in one handy place for easy navigation (2007, 31).

However, just as the quality of how they are constructed varies, the importance of the content ranges from the amusing, to serious attempts at providing information resources to both scholarly and amateur researchers that are just not available anywhere else, and can be useful even if they lack the institutional backing and institutional guidance of their official online counterparts. Often these repositories, archives and museums would not exist without the Internet as a means to share and disseminate their holdings.

A prime example of this is the well used, and award winning, Museum of Menstruation and Women's Health (www.mum.org). Contained in the house of its director, Harry Finley, and in development since 1994, the museum has had an online presence since 1998, providing historical overviews of sanitary products, the varied and changing approaches to advertising, and the social and cultural aspects of women's health, encouraging academic and social debate. The site itself can be rather maze-like, and shows no sign of using imaging or web publishing standards, but the importance of MUM was stressed when the former Tampax company, Tambrands and then Proctor and Gamble, donated thousands of items from their own archives to the Museum. MUM is the place to consult for primary source material regarding menstruation, as Harry Finley explains:

> As far as I know most of the material on MUM is found no where else … I try to provide all the information I have about the objects … Many people have asked permission to use information and pictures from the site for projects and I always say yes. I suspect many people use the pictures and information without asking. Teachers from high school and college have told me they use information from MUM for classes; someone even said it was MUM that started the academic interest in the history of menstruation, nice to hear but I kinda doubt that. Researchers have asked to use pictures for articles, a Professor at Duke University asked for a copy of one, etc., etc. and many publications also have used material from the archives … I don't check the number of users but am aware of page views, which have increased in the past few years. I can tell when something like a magazine article mentions MUM because the numbers temporarily increase (Finley 2007).

Other commercial and academic institutes have approached the museum for use of its archive in patent or scholarly research: a few have even tried to buy the entire archive, which is not for sale, as a new, permanent physical museum is planned for the future. At the moment, MUM is a one-man operation, and couldn't function in any way except online, as Harry Finley describes:

> It's impossible for one person (or at least me) to run a physical museum and especially without funding; I tried it once for four years and it almost killed me! The online museum reaches around the world and updating can be done when I want to. It's open 24/7. It's cheaper online, especially if ad revenue covers costs; the physical museum was free. I express myself about the same way – I didn't hold back in the museum in my house – but once I say it online I don't have to repeat myself; it's there until I take it off … But I must admit it was more fun talking to people in the flesh; the mutual enthusiasm and exchange of ideas was great. That's the advantage of the future museum (ibid.).

Online museums, such as MUM, are often the result of the passion of individuals such as Harry Finley, and due to funding constraints or the attitudes of funding sources to topics such as this one which are viewed as taboo ('I have taken a bit of a beating from some quarters, which has hurt me' (ibid.)), online museums resulting from amateur digitization projects can provide a rich source of primary material for both scholars and the general public, and their democratizing nature is worthy of further consideration.

Advanced Imaging Applications

The majority of digital imaging undertaken within memory institutions is generally carried out to produce a two-dimensional digital surrogate of an object, artefact or document, which can be used to generate relatively low resolution representations for inclusion on a web page. It is recommended (in the guidelines, above) that one high resolution image is captured, and subsequent surrogates produced from that high quality image, to scan 'once for all purposes' and avoid wear and tear on the object. Such imaging is relatively straightforward: although choices must be made about what is to be photographed (some objects can be approached from different angles, using different lighting, etc.), the resulting two-dimensional image is created by general digital photography or scanning, and post-processing or manipulation of the image is kept to a minimum to allow the integrity of the image to be maintained.

However, there is a niche, but growing, interest in using computational technologies to facilitate the analysis and understanding of cultural and heritage objects. This can be accomplished through digital imaging in two ways: the nature of the capture of the digital image can be adjusted, allowing the creation of digital images which expand our understanding by capturing information the human eye or brain is not capable of processing independently, or digital images can be analysed and interrogated computationally through algorithms known as 'image processing' to reveal patterns or features in the image which would not otherwise be noticeable. Finally, the capturing of high resolution images can facilitate ways of delivery, access and integration of digital images into cultural heritage which extends above and beyond the provision of digital image surrogates on institutional web pages.

Advanced Capture Techniques

In some cases, straightforward capture techniques do not suit the individual characteristics of objects being digitized, and projects may choose to investigate and refine particular photographic techniques. For example, these have been developed to facilitate the imaging of architectural sites for conservation (Beckett et al. 2006); the recording of archaeological and heritage sites (Bryan 2006); the study of easel paintings (Saunders et al. 2006); and to deal with the inherent problems when photographing stained glass windows (Macdonald et al. 2006). However, there is also opportunity to capture visual representation of information in a different way to how it is normally perceived by the human eye–brain system.

The most common advanced imaging technique is to capture images utilizing different regions of the light spectrum, for example, infrared reflectography, which has proved a powerful, non-destructive investigative imaging technique for the examination of paintings and ancient documents, such as papyri. The technique, based on acquiring and storing images in the infrared spectrum region between 1 and 2 microns wavelength, makes use of the fact that infrared radiation can pass through layers of paintings or documents, except when partly or totally absorbed by a medium such as charcoal or carbon-based ink. The contrast between a charcoal sketch and its background, or handwriting and its document, can then be seen in the resulting black and white images, and used to aid in making visible the hidden traces contained within the artefact.

Infrared imaging has been in use for this purpose from the start of the twentieth century, and was first undertaken with special, analogue photographic film (Gibson 1978). Recent development in technology has made it possible to use digital imaging capture devices to produce high quality digital images in situ, with on the spot visualization of results possible. The resulting digital images can also be reproduced easily for dissemination, and as a result, infrared imaging is increasingly carried out with digital cameras. However, there is not a market large enough to justify the costs of research and development of special sensors for the cultural and heritage sector, and most projects repurpose sensors originally designed for military applications (Bertani and Consalandi 2006), or use simple filters placed across the camera lens to block out regions of the light spectrum other than infrared. In many cases, digital infrared imaging is more successful than analogue infrared capture, improving the range and quality of images available.

A successful example of digital infrared imaging of documents can be found in the digitization of the ink tablets from Vindolanda, a Roman fort on Hadrian's Wall, which consists of carbon ink writing on slivers of fir wood. Once excavated, the ink oxidizes in the air, turning black and making the writing hard to read. Even after conservation, all the details of the ink writing can only be revealed through infrared photography, which has been undertaken since their discovery. The first photographs were taken using analogue technology (Birley et al. 1993, 103–106), but since the late 1990s, digital imaging has been used to capture the infrared representations. The additional functionality of the digital imaging equipment, and the increased control over the capture environment, meant that researchers 'were able to achieve further improvement in legibility … Digital scans of the tablets offered a range of quality in the images which was in most but not all cases an improvement on the conventional black and white infra-red photographs' (Bowman and Thomas 2003, 14). The resulting images can be seen on the Vindolanda Tablets Online website (http://vindolanda.csad.ox. ac.uk/index.shtml).

Other imaging techniques which are now moving into the digital include ultraviolet imaging (using light from the opposite end of the spectrum to infrared, which can also aid in the detection of handwriting), and X-Ray analysis of paintings to allow analysis of underlying sketches and plans. Again, both were fairly common analogue imaging techniques which have now been implemented digitally, allowing more control over the imaging environment and quality of the resulting image.

An example of a project in the cultural and heritage sphere which is using these approaches, and developing novel experimental techniques, is the work being done on the Archimedes Palimpsest, held at the Walters Art Museum, Baltimore, and currently being studied by a host of scholars from the University of Oxford;

Stanford University; John Hopkins University; Rochester Institute of Technology; and others, to reveal the treatises of Archimedes originally written on the vellum, before it was reused as a prayer book (www.archimedespalimpsest.org/index.html). The project has had numerous successes in using infrared, ultraviolet and X-Ray imaging of the text to read the remains of the excised text in the manuscript. The team are currently experimenting with outlier methods such as the use of LED imaging (illuminating manuscripts with specific bands of light, rather than using filters to remove certain parts of the light spectrum) and X-Ray Fluorescence Imaging (generating secondary X-Rays from an X-Rayed document to produce alternative representations of the manuscripts) to read any areas of text which still remain indecipherable.

Image Processing Techniques

Image processing, the manipulation of digital images by a computer to change the images for effect, display or analysis, is a large and complex field within Engineering and Computing science (Gonzalez and Woods 1993). The earliest computer processing of images began in the 1950s at the National Bureau of Standards on the SEAC, the first electronic computer in the US government with an internally stored program (see p. 21) and the need to automate the processing of surveillance photographs for defence encouraged the development of automated techniques for image-enhancement, restoration, editing and basic manipulation of size, colour, brightness and contrast. Automated processes can also be used to analyse images and pick out patterns that the human eye cannot see, and image processing is now routinely used in defence, security and medical imaging analysis, to automatically highlight areas of concern in particular images.

Basic image manipulation tools have been available on desktop PCs since the early 1990s, with Adobe Photoshop being the industry standard for image manipulation (more complex analysis will have to be programmed using an advanced imaging programs, such as Matlab, www.mathworks.com/products/matlab/). Individual projects in the cultural and heritage fields have used the facilities provided in image manipulation and analysis tools since the earliest production of digital images in the sector (Thaller 1992b). The Archivo General de Indias project (Gonzáles 1992) developed different algorithms to be able to improve the quality of digitized images, allowing users to select the range of tonalities viewable, blackening letters and separating them from the image background. Image processing is used to improve the readability of portions of manuscripts which have become unreadable due to a reduction of contrast (caused by oxidation, humidity, etc.) or to aid in reading the eroded surface of objects such as incised documents, coins or inscriptions where letters cut into the surface are no longer clearly visible (Terras 2006). Manuscript material which has been erased can be virtually restored using image processing techniques to reconstruct overwritten portions of text (Twycross 2006). Image processing can also be used to segment images into constituent parts, which can be useful, say, in the study of stained glass windows, allowing possibilities for the production of surrogates, inspecting and interpreting of the windows (Macdonald et al. 2006). Filters can be used to remove background noise and produce 'clean' images that researchers can use as a further alternative information source. Image processing can also be used to create watermarks, or identifying elements, within an image to hinder the unauthorized use of the digital image in publication or distribution (Gladney et al. 1997; see also pp. 200–201).

Much of this use of image processing in the arts, humanities, library, archive and museum sector borrows tools and understanding from computing science, although some advanced projects investigate the development of new and novel imaging techniques specific to their own application, which, if successful can, in turn, be applied in other areas. However, the tools currently available to facilitate research in this area are limited, tending to be tied to specific research projects, in particular research groups, and are not readily available to those creating digital image corpora:

> the promised research opportunities that are inherent in the new technologies has not been matched by tools that enable historical scholarship. Even the image databases themselves that are available … are limited in scale, detail, fidelity, resolution, and flexibility – indeed, in the processes of creating … corpora we are probably in the same stage that text was in the 1980s (Hockey and Ross 2008, 65).

Although an effective method, depending on the research question, there are yet to be image processing tools developed specifically for the arts, humanities or cultural and heritage sectors.

Additionally, there can be issues in using manipulated images for research and illustration of academic findings. Van den Berg et al. (1992), in an early paper on the use of image processing in the art historical discipline, argue that the main issues in the use of image processing in the study of the arts and humanities are not technical, but intellectual 'What do we study and how do we study it?' and conceptual 'How do we present the results of our studies?' (ibid. 5). However, due to the different ways in which objects are viewed and treated within the various sectors of the humanities 'it is difficult to conceive of "image processing in the humanities". It is even difficult to conceive of image processing within the limited area of history studies as a single field of interest' (Ore 1992, 135). Thaller asks, 'Is image processing a genuine and independent field of computer based research in the Humanities, or is it an auxiliary tool?' (Thaller 1992a, 1). Although it can be used successfully to manipulate and analyse certain types of images, there are ethical concerns to be aware of when using image processing to produce manipulated images which will be used as primary evidence in research (see pp. 194–198), and all changes made to images, however slight, should be noted in technical metadata to explain the image's provenance (see p. 169).

High Resolution Images

The creation of high resolution images of cultural and heritage material for public consumption is a relatively new by-product of the digitization efforts in memory institutions. Previously, high resolution images were created as a 'scan once for all purposes' digital master and although creating very high resolution images can be a potentially invasive process, often requiring more light to be cast on the original work to be able to capture the image successfully (Kilbride 2004), scanning or capturing in this way can reduce overall wear and tear in the original. The resulting, high resolution master images are very large, and it is only in recent years that the average personal computer could store, manipulate or display them. Recently, many memory institutions have been investigating other spin-offs which can be generated from these high resolution images, often for commercial gain or blurring the boundaries between the digital surrogate and original artefact by the production of high quality facsimiles of art works and manuscript material. Very high resolution capture may also yield insights into documents and artefacts which were hitherto unavailable, for example, high resolution digital images of Chaucer manuscripts have allowed the identification of Chaucer's scribe, Adam Pinkhurst (Mooney 2006) which has been described as 'one of the most significant medieval discoveries of recent years … This would have been impossible without access to high quality digital images' (Hughes 2008, 38).

There are problems in allowing users access to high resolution images of materials for their own study: making high quality digital images freely available opens up institutions to the possibility of unauthorized use of images for the user's profit, in the creation and selling of counterfeit objects featuring the image. Some institutions provide zoomable images on the websites, allowing users to focus in on particular aspects of an image (using Java technology) and never delivering the complete high resolution image to the user's machine. This can be a popular feature of websites, and can be useful for researchers. However, another solution to this problem is to not provide the general public with high resolution images themselves, but high quality facsimiles of image-based material, which have been generated from the institutionally held digital images.

Since 2003, the UK's National Gallery has been operating a 'Print on Demand' service, offering users the opportunity to print any work in their collection at any size between A4 (210 x 297mm) and A0 (841 x 1189mm). Reasonably priced, these reproductions are colour matched to the originals, printed with UV-stable pigments, and made on semi gloss paper, giving as close a replica as possible of a varnished oil painting surface through digital imaging production techniques (www.nationalgallery.co.uk/shop/). The service has proved popular and raises much needed revenue for the institution and many other institutions have since followed suit, such as the Tate art galleries (http://tate.artgroup.com/); the Fine Arts Museum of San Francisco (www.famsf.org/store/); and certain museums of the Smithsonian Institution (www.smithsonian store.com/home.jsp). Often third party commercial organizations are employed to manage the production process, and commercial bodies who also own the digital rights to various cultural and heritage images, such as the Bridgeman Art Gallery (www.bridgemanartondemand.com) and publishing archives, such as the archive of the fashion magazine Vogue (http://vogue.artgroup.com) now also provide a professional printing service of images for users. Although reproductions and facsimiles of artworks have been available for years in gift shops, or by requesting a copy of available photographs from institutional archives, the difference with this service is that users have the choice of exactly what they want reproduced and, often, how they want it to be presented: a facility that has only become possible through the availability of high resolution images of the art in question. The digital image, then, is changed from an endlessly transmittable and reproducible digital representation, to the means of producing an accessible, physical facsimile of unique and unobtainable imagery.

Individual digital images can be stitched together (using image processing) to form panoramas, which are often used to display sights of historic architectural interest (Aru et al. 2006). High resolution panoramas, or stitched together representations, can now be reproduced in high enough quality to replace missing or displaced originals. For example, Paola Veronesse's 'Wedding at Cana', a sixteenth-century seven by ten metre masterpiece featuring 130 guests, cooks and musicians, has hung in the Louvre since it was taken from its Benedictine monastery on the Venetian Island of San Giorgio, by French troops in 1797. Rather than attempting the legal effort to repatriate the looted painting, a surrogate of the original has recently been placed back in the monastery, based on 1,591 individual digital photographs of the painting, stitched together to total 500 gigabytes of image material, printed on a canvas with similar weight and weave to the original. Artist Alan Lowe, who headed the digitization project, commented that it was not a facsimile:

> This is not a Poster ... Facsimile has a derogatory context – I see this not as a falsification but a verification ... In any case, we could not have brought the painting back here because there is too much daylight and no climate control (Kington 2007).

Although projects such as this raise questions of verisimilitude and authenticity, with proper documentation, it can be argued that it is better to experience a detailed, well made facsimile in place of an empty, barren wall where an original once was found, but has no chance of ever returning.

The crossover and relationship between the real and the virtual has become ever more complex with the high quality images of historical artefacts, and in particular, art works now available. One of the most popular art exhibitions in Italy in recent years was 'Caravaggio: Una Mostra Impossibile!' at the Loyola University Museum of Art, presenting the complete works of Caravaggio to an expectant audience. However, the exhibition did not contain the original paintings, which are scattered throughout public and private collections worldwide and have never been shown together, but high resolution, true to scale, colour referenced digital images of 57 works, backlit to mimic the artist's famous chiaroscuro (interplay between dark and light). More than 300,000 visitors attended the exhibition: the company in question (Rai-Radiotelevisione Italiana, the Italian government's broadcasting agency) has more plans to produce various other 'impossible' exhibitions according to artist or theme (Burghart 2006). The digital image, in this case, has gone from being a product of the memory institution to the sole contents of the memory institution, with all the philosophical debates which this appropriation of digital technology demands of those within the information profession.

Conclusion

Digital imaging technologies have been readily adopted by memory institutions and, following a period of experimentation, it is now commonplace for libraries, archives, museums, art galleries and private collections to undertake the costly and time-consuming effort of producing digital image surrogates of their collections, usually for delivery online, to provide the accessibility to and digital coverage of collections that users have now come to expect. There are interesting times ahead for the information professional in dealing with the wealth of digital information now available, keeping up with the changing nature of Internet technologies, and coping with resulting changes in user expectations and needs. Being informed of the issues surrounding digital media, and digital images, is the best way for those working within the industry to understand the developing and changing information environment and provide useful services to users of digitized collections.

Further Reading

A variety of texts have been produced to aid the information professional in creating, managing and delivering digitized material, most of which are geared towards the capture and provision of digital images, given that this is the most prevalent digital capture medium. Most are readily – some freely – available and consulting these can contextualize and explain the issues surrounding digitization within the library, archive and information studies sector, in more detail than has been covered here.

Besser and Trant produced one of the first introductory booklets for the use of images in heritage institutions in 1995, with *Introduction to Imaging, Issues in Constructing an Image Database*. The specific technologies mentioned in the original publication are now dated, but Besser updated the pamphlet in 2003, which is available in print (Besser 2003) and freely, online (www.getty.edu/research/conducting_research/standards/introimages/index.html). The booklet covers the main digital imaging primitives that are still applicable today, including resolution, compression, etc., and still remains a useful, if short, introduction to the issues surrounding the creation of an image database.

Kenney and Rieger's book *Moving Theory into Practice: Digital Imaging for Libraries and Archives* (2000) provides an excellent overview of imaging projects and the issues which confront them, featuring many case studies of projects and the opinions of many experts in the field, giving short, in-depth and balanced coverage of many relevant issues. Focusing on the management issues (such as selection, digital benchmarking, quality control, metadata, access, image management systems, digital preservation and developing digital imaging programmes from individual projects) it provides a very useful and usable guide to how libraries and archives can use digital imaging effectively in their work.

Lee's book (2002) *Digital Imaging, A Practical Handbook*, has a rather misleading title, as it mostly deals with managerial issues in undertaking digitization, such as selection criteria, implementing the digitization workflow, funding opportunities, etc., rather than the implementation of specific imaging technologies, but is an excellent reference to aid those in charge of making institutional decisions about why, what and how to digitize collections. The book contains many flow charts, decision matrices and aids to costing, which will help those planning a digitization project for the first time.

Hughes' text *Digitizing Collections, Strategic Issues for the Information Manager* (2004) details both practical and strategic issues that staff in memory institutions need to understand before making cultural material available online. The book presents the strategic decisions which will precede a digitization initiative, such as the advantages and economics of digitization, developing institutional procedures and strategies, and confronting topics such as risk management and copyright before they become insurmountable issues. The book then deals with the many complex issues involved in running a digitization project, providing case studies from a variety of institutions and covering topics such as project management, procuring funding and dealing with rare and fragile collections.

MacDonald's edited book *Digital Heritage, Applying Digital Imaging to Cultural Heritage* (2006) contains various chapters written by those working on important, well established, projects in digital imaging of all aspects of culture and heritage, including 'research and general libraries, museums, commercial photographic collections, fine art auction houses, and the built heritage' (xv). Many chapters are presented as case studies of individual projects and approaches, describing both previous and current leading-edge research in digital imaging, but all stress issues of usability, giving a historical and holistic view of the evolving nature of user requirements over the past decade or so. A section on 'Technologies' provides seven chapters which span 'well-selected axes of digital heritage: digital cameras, infrared reflectography, image processing, colour management, image compression, and – a neglected Cinderella in the field – image quality' (xvi), providing an accessible and useful introduction to the technologies which underpin digitization projects.

In addition to these specific, focused texts, there are a host of more general publications which cover broader areas which the library sector is currently negotiating. The Digital Futures Series, by Facet (formerly Library Association

Publishing), provides overview texts on the changing information environment, and the impact on information institutions and information professionals. Deegan and Tanner's *Digital Futures, Strategies for the Information Age* (2002) considers the rapid expansion of the Internet and electronic communication, mapping the transition of the library sector 'into the wired world' (xi), covering creating and collating digital content through to its delivery and management, providing an overview which assumes little prior knowledge from an interested reader. Hughes' book (2004), the second in the series, was recently followed by *Digital Preservation*, edited by Deegan and Tanner (2006), which presents chapters written by a select number of widely acknowledged experts giving perspectives and overviews of different aspects of digital preservation, such as strategies, metadata, costing and the challenges of preserving online material. The text introduces both the main issues in digital preservation and various national or international initiatives that are addressing the problem, arming the information professional with an overview of this pressing issue.

Other, slightly broader texts worth becoming familiar with include those dealing with preservation of digital data, such as Borghoff and colleagues' *Long Term Preservation of Digital Documents: Principles and Practices* (2006) and Gladney's *Preserving Digital Information* (2007); and texts exploring issues surrounding Digital Libraries, such as Lesk's *Understanding Digital Libraries* (2005); Dahl and colleagues' *Digital Libraries: Integrating Content and Systems* (2006); and Earnshaw and Vince's *Digital Convergence: Libraries of the Future* (2007).

Finally, online resources can provide overviews and tutorials on digital imaging for the library and heritage sectors. Cornell University Library's online tutorial *Moving Theory Into Practice, Digital Imaging Tutorial* (2002) provides a well illustrated overview of many of the issues covered in this chapter (www.library.cornell.edu/preservation/tutorial/contents.html). The Technical Advisory Services for Images website (www.tasi.ac.uk) remains the first port of call for up to date, well explained, authoritative information about digital imaging technologies for those wishing to undertake a digitization program.

Chapter 6
Personal Digital Image Collections

What is your most treasured possession?
Old pictures of my family.

Alek Wek, Supermodel, Q&A, *The Guardian* (Greenstreet 2007).

Just as water, gas and electricity are brought into our houses from far off to satisfy our needs in response to a minimal effort, so we shall be supplied with visual or auditory images, which will appear and disappear at a simple movement of the hand, hardly more than a sign.

Paul Valéry, Pieces Sur l'Art (1931), translated in Benjamin (1936), reproduced in Benjamin (1992, 221).

The way we take photographic images has changed phenomenally over the past decade. Although film cameras have been an affordable and popular household item for the past century, the growing use of digital imaging technologies is permanently transforming the way in which we take, share and comment on photographic images, encouraging us to take many more pictures than ever before, which are accrued on cameras, computers and mobile phones. However, problems with the long-term viability of digital image data mean that many personal digital photography collections will not survive for future generations. Unless the problem is confronted, our visual understanding of the early twenty-first century will be compromised.

This chapter discusses the growth in use of digital imaging technologies by the general public, before giving an overview of what is known about our changing photographic habits and how and why digital cameras, and the resulting digital photographs captured, are utilized and stored. The phenomenon is so new, there has been very little academic consideration of the impact this has on use and users of photographic technologies. Many of the sources used in this chapter are commercial reports, which should be treated with the knowledge that they have their own agenda: the personal content industry focuses on selling technology to encourage consumers to capture and create their own personal digital collections. Nevertheless, contextualizing the growth of personal digital collections and, in particular the use of the digital imaging technologies, will provide those in the information profession with an understanding of user behaviours formulated in everyday situations that informs and affects behaviour towards institutional resources. Additionally, there is scope for those in the information profession to become more involved with the wider community to highlight the risks present to the longevity of personal digital image collections. Without further education and information, the future of personal digital photography collections looks bleak.

The Growing Use of Digital Imaging Technologies

In 2004, the UK's cost of living index, which calculates economic inflation through tracking the costs of a 'basket' of 50 popular goods routinely bought by the average household, lost a toaster and gained a digital camera (Thornton 2004). In 2006, 98 million digital cameras were sold worldwide, reaching 50 per cent of households in the United States, Japan and leading nations in Western Europe (Lyra Research Inc 2007). In 2007, 6 in 10 people in the UK claimed to have a digital camera and, in addition, 83 per cent of mobile phones sold came with a digital camera integrated into their system (Ofcom 2007, 38–39). Currently, there is a rapidly expanding emerging market for digital cameras in China, India, and Latin America (Hsu and Hwang 2008). The total number of digital cameras in use worldwide is expected to reach 400 million in 2008 (Wray 2007). In contrast to this, although many households still own traditional film cameras, sales of film cameras and film itself have fallen away precipitously, after 150 years of popularity. Sales of still film cameras in the UK halved from 600,000 in 2005 to 300,000 in 2006, resulting in a market value of just £14 million for film, against an estimated £1 billion for digital. The overall sales ratio suggests that, in the UK in 2006, digital cameras outsold film cameras 20 times over (Lyra Research Inc 2007). It seems obvious that:

> Film cameras are being replaced by digital cameras in consumers' minds … Film is likely only to survive only in a few niche areas – such as in disposables and amongst professionals … [The photographic industry] is having to readjust to deal with the consumer trend (Sabbagh 2004).

This astonishing switch from analogue film-based media to near saturation of the consumer market with digital imaging technologies took place in under a decade, although uptake of digital cameras was initially slow. Digital camera systems became commercially available in 1986, with the Canon RC-701, but its price tag of $27,000 was prohibitive to it being used by anything other than industry. The first digital camera aimed at consumers, the Apple Quicktake, with a fixed lens capable of capturing 640 x 480 pixels (only 0.3 megapixels in today's parlance) became available in 1994 with a price tag of $1000, which was costly for a piece of equipment which produced such low quality images (Ang 2005). Yet it was not only the cost of the digital cameras which held back uptake: in the mid-1990s, most home computers were not capable of dealing with large image files. By the late twentieth century, most systems could comfortably handle the processing and memory requirement necessary to create, manipulate, store and display digital image files (see pp. 22–24) and higher quality home printers became available which allowed those photographs to be printed for use. Once the environment for handling digital image files was available, demand increased for peripheral technologies such as cameras, scanners and printers, and resulting manufacturing costs plummeted. Aggressive competition between camera makers and the adoption of cost saving components (such as cheaper LCD screens and less expensive image processors) helped to drive down prices further. The market for digital cameras exceeded the market for still film cameras in 2002 (Schofield 2002). The popularity of camera phones, commercially available since the late twentieth century (see p. 30) but now more popular than mobile phones without imaging facilities, extended the ubiquity of digital cameras. By placing a digital camera in nearly every pocket, the camera phone has encouraged the documenting of both everyday and newsworthy events by digital photography and video:

> A camera inside a telephone seems like something that might have appeared in a Victorian catalogue of detective cameras – minute, invisible, and much more convenient to operate discretely than a camera concealed in a bowler hat. Eliminating the camera from the practice of photography removed a barrier to spontaneous image capture, allowing anyone with a telephone to participate in the documentation of their immediate environment (Rubenstein and Sluis 2008, 13).

The use of digital photographs in the mid-1990s (by those who could afford a digital camera and multimedia computer) centred around the home PC, with few facilities to share or disseminate the resulting images, save burning them to disk, CD-ROM or other peripheral storage device. Programs became available to aid those in ordering their digital images, such as PicaView by ACD-Systems or Cartogra's PhotoManager, but these programs, which often came bundled with digital cameras, focused very much on individual users who were limited to use and display of images on their own machines. Additionally, few printers were commercially available which allowed high quality photographs to be printed out in any quality. Merely capturing images is not enough, however: people like to show the resulting images to friends, family and strangers with related interests. Sharing digital images online takes the possibilities of self-expression presented by the Internet to its logical conclusion, and is only one of a range of tools and facilities available which allow countless individuals to create, document, share and comment on text, images, sound and video. Without the Internet (and specifically, the World Wide Web) as a network for communication, it can be argued that the uptake of digital imagery would not have been as strong.

When the Web became popular, towards the late 1990s, users sent each other pictures via email, which, given the speed of available Internet connections, often meant waiting for a long period for files to upload or download, causing frustration and, often, animosity. To avoid this problem, people began hosting their personal photographs on their personal, or professional, web pages and circulating the URLs rather than the digital photographs via email, although it required the user to have an understanding of authoring for the Web as they had to create the pages themselves. At the time it was estimated that 'still images … represent 85–90per cent of the media files currently on the Web' (Future Image Inc 2000, 11). The 'multimedia' revolution mostly consisted of digital text and image.

Early photograph hosting websites began to facilitate the process of putting images online by providing an environment for people to upload and share their images. Some analogue film processing companies, such as Kodak and Walmart, added the functionality of scanning in the resulting images and hosting them online, creating a hybrid process which both bolstered the threatened film-based photography industry while facilitating the uptake of digital imaging technologies (Vroegindeweij 2002). By the close of 1999, there were over 130 'dot.com'[1] companies devoted to hosting photographs online, mostly based in the US, and usually presenting the users with some facility to print out images via mail order. The most popular of these were Photopoint.com, Zing.com (both no longer operational) and Shutterfly.com (www.shutterfly.com) (Rand 2000, cited in Vroegindeweij 2002, 26), although the revenue generated from online photographic printing services in 2000 was only 13 million dollars, 'a mere speck in the overall 40 billion dollars photofinishing industry' (Vroegindeweij 2002, 26). However, as more households acquired digital cameras (and phones with integrated cameras) demand for online services continued to grow, eventually outstripping that of traditional, analogue film processing. In 2007, printing from digital images represented 68 per cent of the photo finishing market in the US and 72 per cent of all photos printed commercially in Europe. Home printing of digital photographs (and the printing of traditional film photographs anywhere) continues to decline (Wells 2008).

Facilities to backup, host and share photographs online have become increasingly sophisticated. The latest generation of photo album websites have experimented with the means by which users can label and search online image collections. In late 2004, social websites such as URL tagging website (http://del.icio.us/) and the photo sharing facility Flickr.com (www.flickr.com) started experimenting with online forms that would allow users to 'tag' their own entries, creating a 'folksonomy' of terms unbounded by traditional metadata terminology or structured vocabulary, and allowing comments and labels of media to be searched and accessed by other users (Schofield 2005; see pp. 180–181). This commenting and searching facility, coupled with access to ever faster networking technologies, and ever cheaper digital cameras capable of taking higher quality images, has encouraged users to create, upload, share, display, search, tag and print large volumes of digital images. The most popular online facilities, such as PhotoBucket (http://photobucket.com/); Slide.com (www.slide.com); and Flickr, often increase their market share further as a result of deals with social networking sites: for example, PhotoBucket allows members to post multiple photos to social networking profiles on websites such as Bebo.com and MySpace.com.

---

1 Dot.com is the name given to organizations which do most of their business online, from a .com website.

The number of users utilizing these online tools, whether for free or willing to pay a fee to have access to increased facilities and tools, is astounding. At the time of writing (early 2008), PhotoBucket declares on its home page that it has 58 million users, and Slide.com claims to have '134 million unique global viewers each month' (Slide.com 2007). More than 14 million digital photographs are uploaded to the social networking site Facebook.com everyday (Facebook.com 2008). The exponential growth in users can be seen in the statistics of usage regarding Flickr.com. Launched in 2004 as a photo sharing website, with much input from users in designing the interface, display and searching mechanisms, Flickr allows users to upload photos (via email, through a web interface, from a mobile phone) and push them out (via Flickr itself or via user's blogs). Due to the success of its design, and the ease in which people could now share photographs, Flickr accrued 0.27 million users and 5 million photographs by April 2005 (when it was bought by Yahoo.com for US$30m). 'By Spring 2006 its membership had grown to 3 million, with 130 million photos … By April 2007 it claimed to have 7.2m members and 400 million photos' (Cox 2007, 3). In November 2007, 2 billion photos in total had been uploaded to Flickr (the two billionth photo was a picture of a gum tree, taken in China Town, Sydney, see Flickr 2007) and the site continues to expand.

The convergence of image capture, network, telecommunications and computing technologies has turned the Internet:

> into the most mass medium of them all. Nothing more than a mass medium, permeating our daily lives to the point of becoming invisible. Its numerous users are busy working, having a good time or expressing themselves, and they have almost perfect tools and services at their disposal. Connection never breaks, distinction between a server and a hard disk, between your desktop and that of another person has almost vanished, and there's nothing that could contribute to the development of user-media relationship, nothing to provoke us. Web 2.0 propagandists can't stop talking about the multitude and power of today's web amateurs, the new users who love to dance, compose songs, write encyclopedic articles, take photos and film videos, write texts and publish it all on the Web. And yet, they are rather indifferent to the Web itself (Lialina 2007).

Many users now view the Internet as an essential service, like the provision of drinking water from the tap or electricity from the socket: it is only noticed when it is broken. Digital imaging technologies slot into this service and become part of the fabric of our day to day lives: for many people, taking a film to be processed is now a forgotten task from a different age. Once consumers are converts to digital cameras, they tend to keep up with the latest available technologies: half of all digital camera sales (not including camera phones) in the US and European territories are to those who already own a digital camera (Ang 2005). Traditional, film-based photography is becoming a niche hobby or specifically chosen artistic approach.

The uptake of digital imaging is affecting other industries, including medicine, journalism, law enforcement, tourism, space exploration and fine art (Rubenstein and Sluis 2008, 1), and affecting media, reportage and the relationship between news reporters and viewers. The majority of the photographic coverage of the 7 July 2005 London bombings was provided by amateurs, indicating that digital photography had come of age, and was 'all but universal among the urban population' (Ang 2005). The BBC encourages the general public to send in pictures of newsworthy events to its yourpics@bbc.co.uk email address, and this facility has proved popular. On routine days, between 100 and 150 users will email or message in 150 to 250 images from around the globe. On days when something UK-wide happens, such as the blizzards which covered the country on 8 February 2007, thousands of users contributed: in this case, the BBC received over 7,000 images in 24 hours (BBC 2007a).

On 22 November 1963, the fatal shooting of John F. Kennedy, the President of the United States of America, was captured on grainy, shaky, silent film footage recorded on home 8mm film cameras. On 27 December 2007, pixelated and noisy digital footage captured on mobile phones and digital cameras recorded the assassination of the Pakistani Presidential candidate, Benazir Bhutto. Aside from the differences in the media used to record these seismic, horrific murders, there are differences in the circumstances of recording. It was by chance that JFK's assassination was captured, at a time when few consumers had access to such technology, and before professional news agencies covered every moment of a presidential procession. Photographs showing the sea of supporters surrounding Bhutto's cavalcade, all wielding digital cameras in the seconds before her death, suggest that nowadays, it is only by chance that such an event would *not* be recorded. The all-pervasiveness of digital imaging technology and society's obsession with documenting every aspect of reality, ensures by the time the traditional news agencies have arrived, the footage has been captured and possibly even distributed. All main news agencies now encourage the general public to submit relevant photographs and video footage, including CNN (ireport@cnn.com); Reuters (pics@reuters.com); and Fox (ureport@foxnews.com), although this often gives the news agency exclusive rights to the footage, with no payment passing to the photographer. No news coverage of extreme weather, atrocity, tragedy or 'act of god' is now complete without the shaky, pixel, still images or hand-held video footage captured on a mobile phone or digital camera by a passing member of the public. Such primary, image-based evidence is also appealed for by police, for use in criminal investigations (BBC 2005b).

Are you a member of the public who has caught a newsworthy image, paparazzi shot or video footage on your camera or phone? Users can sell photographs on through one of the online websites which will broker a deal with international news agencies. Sites such as (www.shutterpoint.com) (www.mrpaparazzi.com) and (www.thesnitcherdesk.com) allow users to upload their photos directly to a website or send them by email from their home computer or mobile phone, piping profitable snapshots into a syndication network which can be accessed by traditional news outlets. A percentage of any resulting profits are shared between agency and photographer. In a 2007 newspaper article, Mark Frith, editor of the UK celebrity gossip *Heat* magazine (www.heatworld.com):

> recalls how, back in the 90s, the daily delivery of paparazzi picture to Smash Hits, where he then worked, would arrive in a single A4 envelope. Today he receives between 10,000 and 20,000 electronic images every day (Aitkenhead 2007, 22).

The market moves so fast, and volumes of images submitted are so large, that automatic image recognition software is now used to scan every photo, 'to ensure no sale escapes'. It is no wonder that celebrities complain of 'suffocating persecution' (ibid.).

As the popularity of digital imaging increases, the traditional photographic industry is in disarray, with well known, household names (Leica, Agfa, Polaroid and Kodak) stopping the manufacture of film cameras and film, and the provision of film-based services (ZDNet 2004). High street stores are removing film cameras from their shelves. At a time when photography has never been so popular, those who have been in the business for a hundred years are suffering and disappearing. Additionally:

> the restructuring of the profession is more subtle, profound and distressing: experienced photographers are finding themselves marginalised, [and] their darkroom skills discounted … Working practices have changed (Ang 2005).

In the period of 10 years, the way we create, process and distribute images has changed irrevocably, providing the seamless means to capture and share images with friends and family, but economically affecting individuals and industry along the way.

Nowadays, digital imaging technologies are all pervasive. Disposable, single use digital cameras are even available for use in situations where you would not want to risk losing or breaking expensive technology. As a result, it is difficult to know how many images are now taken. In 2002, 75 billion prints were made of photographs taken on analogue film cameras, according to the Photo Marketing Association International: they know this as 2.5 billion rolls of film were sold worldwide (Lyman and Varian 2003). With today's technology:

> it is impossible to be accurate, but with a world population of digital cameras exceeding a third of a billion on top of millions of film using cameras still in use, it is likely that more pictures are taken every year than in the previous 160 years of photography put together. In addition to the other pollutions we have unleashed on ourselves, we may well have to thank digital photography for giving us image pollution (Ang 2005).

Use and Usefulness of Digital Image Technologies

The statistics, above, give us some indication of the recent popularity of digital imaging, but tell us little about how digital cameras are actually used or reasons for their comprehensive uptake.

Due to the wiring of the human eye-brain visual system (see pp. 3–4), we attempt to capture most of our memorable moments visually, which nowadays means through photography (rather than, say, painting). It is important to remember that, since it was commercially available, photography has always been an important part of our society and our home life:

> Cameras go with family life. Not to take pictures of one's children, particularly when they are small, is a sign of parental indifference … Those ghostly traces, photography, supply the presence of dispersed relatives. A family's photograph album is generally about the extended family (Sontag 1979, 8–9).

Collections of photos declare the connections between individuals, friends and family. Viewing family photos enforces links betweens different generations. Given the ubiquity and ease of use of imaging technology, we now have the opportunity to photograph the most poignant, important and happy times of our lives: births, weddings, birthdays, Christmases, anniversaries and family gatherings (This is juxtaposed with times of loss and unhappiness, which can be just as important, but where we take far fewer pictures.) Collections of photographs build up, documenting our lives, in a way that other media cannot:

> To collect photographs is to collect the world. Movies and television programs light up walls, flicker, and go out, but with still photographs the image is also an object, lightweight, cheap to produce, easy to carry about, accumulate, store (ibid. 3).

The widespread availability of film photography in the twentieth century allowed users to capture large collections of photographs over a lifetime, but we now take many more images than the 24 or 32 that were offered on a film reel. One reason for this is the different economic model of digital imaging versus still film photography. With analogue film, the market mechanism saw industry profit from users every time they wanted to process film, and for most users the cost of processing was prohibitive to taking too many photographs. With digital cameras, the cost is borne at the time of purchase of the equipment, rather than processing, and as a result, it doesn't matter how many images you take or if any are disposed of (and psychologically it is better value to take as many pictures as possible). Digital imaging is relatively limitless (depending on the memory capabilities of camera, computer and backup facility) and as a result, encourages users to document not only the special moments in life, but the everyday.

The convenience of digital imaging technologies is also another reason for their incredible popularity, for both professionals and amateurs. Devices are becoming increasingly small, allowing users to have access to a digital camera at all times (particularly when they come bundled with a mobile phone). Hundreds of images can often be captured on one device without the need for organizing or pausing. Pictures can be viewed instantly, rather than waiting for film processing and the images taken can be checked immediately, on site, for quality and relevance. Images can then be transferred to a computer and manipulated, cropped, resized, and so on: the computer operator has access to darkroom techniques which would previously have to be carried out by an expert, at cost, and can also insert additional information into a file, such as metadata (see Chapter 7) which was not possible with previous analogue technologies. Images can be emailed, posted to websites or transferred between hand-held devices, such as mobile phones, with very little effort. Copying the image does not pose any threat to the original or cause degradation. Images can be selected for print, rather than hoping that photographs will have turned out, while having to pay for the processing of a whole reel of film anyway. It can be argued that digital images have reduced environmental impact when compared to traditional film photography, due to the smaller amounts of chemicals necessary in production, although this should be tempered with calculations regarding the energy needed to capture and use the computational technologies.

Wide access to digital imaging technologies has facilitated the development of online systems which could not have operated successfully without them, such as online dating websites, which would not be successful without allowing users to post photographs of themselves; online auction houses (in particular, eBay) which allow users to post pictures of items for sale; and the development of academic and community-based websites around specialist topics, which may rely on photographic imagery, from archaeologists to genealogists, to horticulturalists. From providing a facility to capture pictures of our immediate community, photographic technologies have now expanded their remit, and now can often aid in increasing the scope and coverage of the communities and individuals we regularly interact with.

Although these wide cultural trends can be easily surmised, what can we tell about the habits of those who have access to digital imaging technologies in the home? What research has been done to ascertain how and why individuals are actually using these technologies? Previous research into the motivation of why people take pictures at all, undertaken prior to the switch to digital imaging, provides considerable evidence that people capture life moments to share them, allowing communication and story telling (Chalfen 1987). Research into the motivation for use of digital technologies found that user's aims, purposes and application were similar, using photos as a memory aid and a tool to reminisce about past events. (Balabanović et al. 2000; Vroegindeweij 2002; Bentley et al. 2006). However, the ubiquity of digital imaging technologies, the number of images we accumulate and the speed at which we can disseminate and share images, seems to be changing the aims and function of photography:

> taking photographs seems no longer primarily an act of memory intended to safeguard a family's pictorial heritage, but is increasingly becoming a tool for an individual's identity formation and communication … In recent years, we have seen profound shifts in the balance between … various social uses: from family to individual use, from memory tools to communication devices, and from sharing (memory) objects to sharing experiences … Individuals articulate their identity as social beings not only by taking and storing photographs to document their lives, but by participating in communal photographic exchanges that mark their identity as interactive produces and consumers of culture (van Dijck 2008, 1–63).

It would seem we are taking many more photos than ever before, not only to document our lives for future remembrance, but to affirm personal bonds (with both family and peers) and to interact with each other immediately, rather than retrospectively. The immediacy of digital imaging encourages us to treat it as a disposable and transient medium, for instantaneous entertainment. This can be seen, in particular, in the uses of camera phones by teenagers, who often capture and circulate images among peer groups, in effect to facilitate relationships and build related experiences. Photography moves away from a means of recording the present for those in the future, to be ever fulfilling the needs of those in the present, capturing both the significant and the mundane (ibid.). The main photographic uses of camera phones are creating and maintaining social bonds, constructing personal and group memory, providing a vehicle for self-presentation and providing a means for self-expression (van House et al. 2005, 1845).

There is also an increased use of digital imaging as a cultural art form, and websites designed to encourage users to share and disseminate creative images, such as certain Flickr-based groups and FFFFound! (http://ffffound.com/) allow users greater opportunities to share their digital born art. However, the greater volume of photographic images taken does not mean that we are all artists, and does not mean each image has intrinsic value:

> We live in a world of instantly recordable images. Our mobile phones are equipped with cameras. Even the cheapest digital device will reliably focus and correct our errors. But while we may all have cameras in our pockets, that does not make us photographers (*The Observer* 2007, 30).

Concerns about the nature of photographs and their relationship to art is not new, as this was felt even with the popularity of traditional film photography:

> Photography has become almost as widely practised an amusement as sex and dancing – which means that like every mass art form, photography is not practised by most people as an art. It is a social rite, a defence against anxiety, and a tool of power (Sontag 1979, 8).

The online tools which are used to share and disseminate digital images also provide a vehicle to criticize the mass of images produced, and the artistic pretensions of those with no discernable talent:

> I went on to Flickr and it was just thousands of pieces of shit, and I just couldn't believe it. And it's just all conventional, it's all clichés, it's just one visual convention after another (Stephen Shore, quoted in Soth 2007).

The volumes of pictures we now take and accrue are accumulated for various reasons including self-expression, reminiscence, social bonding, family history, boredom, amusement, artistic endeavour or plain experimentation with the technologies available. Whether or not others think they are of any worth, many people are devoting their time to documenting and creating through digital imaging technologies.

What do we do with these photos once we have taken them? Recent research suggests that keen users of digital cameras undertake various tasks, termed 'photowork', to enable their recent pictures to be utilized, including downloading, selecting, organizing, editing and filing (Kirk et al. 2006). This tends to be done, if at all, shortly after the photos were taken: older photos tend to be left and ignored and are rarely revisited for any maintenance tasks (ibid.). After these initial stages, the majority of digital images are shared or made available to others: it is 'consistently reported that 80 per cent of photos are shared publicly' via email or websites (see Cox 2007, 4) although the percentages given by various studies regarding sharing and use often do not square with estimates of the percentages of images neglected given in other studies, below). This use of email, the Internet and online photo-sharing systems has changed the photographer and viewer dynamic, and the aims of the digital photographer seem to be evolving:

> [Traditional film photographers] all described sharing primarily within an existing social group and taking photos to archive, while the [users of digital technology] took to share, and share primarily with strangers. Privacy was an important dimension for [traditional] participants, while [digital users] assumed that anyone could see their photos and were comfortable sharing them … a different set of behaviours may be emerging around the online mechanisms … and offline practices intended to support those (Miller and Edwards 2007, 5).

As digital photography continues to become more popular, individuals now have the opportunity to push their images out into the world, predominantly via online sites, for everyone to see.

And what of the photos after they have been taken and shared? How do users store them? When organizing digital images (*if* they are organized), people tend to use photo management software, such as iPhoto (www.apple.com/iphoto/) and Picasa (http://picasa.google.com/) or the facilities presented by online systems such as PhotoBucket, Slide and Flickr, to group their photos around time-based 'events', storing photos in a virtual album linked to titles and a date stamp, giving a chronology to the collection (Gargi et al. 2002; Graham et al. 2002). People find managing their digital photos far easier than their traditional print photos, given the labelling, sorting and browsing features of most basic photographic management software, and the ability to flick through and view volumes of images at speed, but tend to not make use of advanced features such as content-based image retrieval (Bentley et al. 2006; and see pp. 181–183). Even the tagging facilities provided by online systems, such as Flickr and photo management software like iPhoto are only used occasionally: 'manual tagging rarely occurs due to the added effort that it requires and the simple ease of use of browsing large numbers of thumbnails by events or time' (Bentley et al. 2006, 668).

Most digital images stay as digital images and are rarely printed out, whether at home or by a professional print service. It was estimated in 2005 (Ang 2005) that one in ten digital images are physically printed: most reside on users' computers, with a selected few published or stored online and some are never copied from the cameras or phones which took them. Of course, not all of these pictures are worthy of being kept or preserved, but people rarely discard digital photographs, even if they are bad or poor, as they can still prompt memories of events (Bentley et al. 2006, 673). Additionally, many devices (such as mobile phones) have large enough photo memories to not require any sorting or deleting to take place, and users may not discard images until their device is changed. Many digital photographs are never looked at again, causing 'feelings ranging from discomfort to guilt' (Vroegindeweij 2002, 77), and in many cases people do not ever get around to organizing their digital images in any way. This was always the same with traditional film photography:

> People tend to spend very little time annotating their personal photos. How many family photographers are diligent enough or have enough time and energy to get a roll of film back from being developed, go over the pictures, and put them into albums, instead of just sticking the pictures in a shoebox? How many people go through their digital photos and give each one a unique file name in an appropriate directory instead of leaving them in the default directory created by the camera software? Not many … As a result more and more people find themselves with thousands of digital photos with little organization and little utility, and they are resigned to gaining no more benefit or enjoyment from them than the thousands of printed photographs stored in shoeboxes around the house (Kustanowitz and Shneiderman 2005, 1).

However, the lack of collections management of digital images has much more serious ramifications than the lack of management of print images and leads to concerns over the longevity of personal digital image collections, and what will be available for both ourselves, our families and historians of the future in merely a few years time.

The Longevity of Personal Digital Image Collections

In summer 2007, the worst floods in living memory devastated many areas of the UK, waterlogging entire towns and neighbourhoods, and causing the biggest natural disaster on record for many towns in the north of England. For those who lost their homes and belongings in the flood waters, the most precious, irreplaceable, items often mentioned in reports were photographs:

> My parents and my granddad all say that the most distressing thing about the clear-up operation the day after the flood was finding my granddad's photos … soaking wet under the bed … I remember my mum calling me, close to tears. 'There were so many memories there' … She knelt in the car park outside the flat that day, painstakingly separating each one, laying them across the boot and back seat of her car. My parents spent the next week drying them all in the batches in their house (Bachelor 2007, 32).

Many accounts of natural disaster, and the loss of personal affects, focus on the loss of photographic images: 'My parents had a house fire years ago and they lost all their photos and it was the hardest loss of all for them. They told me that not saving them was their biggest regret' (Jackson 2005). For many in the insurance industry, this is a common tale ('Furniture can be replaced but family photos cannot. I still feel numb.' BBC 2007b), although, with today's technology it is avoidable:

> If you were … in a fire in a house and you could only take one thing with you, what would it be? … And most people say photographs, pictures, photo albums. And yet, it's possible to make copies of photographs … It's certainly very easy to scan entire photo albums. But people don't do it (Joseph 2004).

Computational technologies can be used to store and preserve personal photograph collections in two different ways: digital images of existing analogue, still film photos can be acquired through digitization, which can be stored in case of loss of originals; and backup procedures can allow both digital born photographs and digitized images of traditional photographs, to be securely archived for long-term storage.

Home digitization of existing personal film photography collections is a growing hobby, and with the correct investment in capture equipment and the necessary time to devote to acquiring, labelling and storing each image, it can be relatively straightforward to digitize old photo albums and create a digital archive of copies of the originals for personal use and sharing among friends and family (McMahon 2008), much in the same way as memory institutions create digital representations of their holdings. At present, though, this is not something considered by the majority of households who would stand to lose their photograph collections in the unlikely event that their home environment be destroyed.

Of greater concern, however, is the lack of interest in methodically storing digital photographs, whether they are digital born or a digitized representation of an original, in a way which would ensure they could be accessed easily in the future. A recent survey suggested that one third of digital camera users in the UK make no attempt to backup their photographs (BBC 2006). Up to 70 per cent of digital camera users in the US consider their personal computer to be the main source of storage for their images (PMA Foresight 2007): a major issue when the computer outlives its natural product cycle and ceases to function. Much of the problem stems from public misunderstanding about the nature of computer systems, which are often sold as entertainment, when they are complex technologies, prone to obsolescence, breakdown, infection and corruption. Often, users do not know where or how they have stored collections on a computer, or do not consider why it is necessary to store images carefully. Users upgrade home computer systems and do not port over data collections to new machines; discard old mobile phones and cameras and do not bother to check that images are transferred to other media; and do not understand the nature of different file formats and the necessity of metadata (see Chapter 7) so store unlabelled, poorly compressed images in increasingly jumbled volumes on untended hard drives. Such users only become aware of what they have lost after their hard drive permanently crashes and the data stored within becomes unobtainable.

Other options are available, and (thankfully) are increasingly used to store images. Almost half of households in the US claim to backup images regularly to external media such as DVDs or CD-ROMS (ibid.), which is an easy and useful basic attempt at backup, especially if stored securely, off-site from the main home computer, ensuring the data's safety in case of household disaster. Photo management software can aid in organizing routine backups of image data to removable media. However, DVDs and CD-ROMS still suffer from problems of obsolescence and are not nearly as durable as professionally produced photographic prints physically stored in archival quality albums. Recently, there has been a move towards printing out photos for long term storage, with an increasing number of households choosing professional printing as a means to store, display, share and disseminate favourite digital images (ibid.). How many of these choose to store printed pictures off-site are debatable, but printing out images would prevent loss when a computer ceases to function and the digital files are lost. (It should be noted that the quality of printed images is dependent on the type, quality and combination of paper and ink used, determining the 'brightness, colour saturation, density, ink drying properties, tone and image permanence' of an image (Hirsch and Valentino 2001, 244), and it is recommended that those printing out digital images for posterity should use professional print services to ensure that their images will not rapidly fade or discolour.)

Eleven per cent of households are now using online facilities to store their images (ibid.). Online facilities come in two flavours: freely available user accounts which place a limit on the number and total file size of images that can be stored online and, occasionally, a limit on the bandwidth used to upload (and download) images by the owner each month; and professional, paid for accounts which give unlimited access to backup services. Free services may seem good value and are usually tied to the uploading of photographs to professional print sites for mail ordering print copies of images, with a vague promise to keep a version of the uploaded digital photos available in the long term. However, there is little information given to the consumer regarding how long the images will be preserved and enquiries to commercial companies regarding this matter are usually politely rebuffed or ignored (Campbell 2007, 24). Even more worryingly, Truprint.co.uk (www.truprint.co.uk), a popular photo printing site which claims on its homepage to have millions of users, states that although they offer free, unlimited storage for online photos that are uploaded to the users account and will keep accounts open as long as users purchase photos at least once a year, high resolution, original images are only stored for 90 days, during which prints should be ordered as they are afterwards deleted from the system and replaced with a highly compressed low resolution version created by Truprint themselves (ibid.). This compressed version is of much lower quality than original images and is, therefore, not a suitable backup version. Although this resampling and deletion is mentioned clearly in the terms and conditions set out when setting up a user account, it is debateable how many users would actually read and digest the legalese. As a result, many users may be trusting off-site storage of their photographs to a system which does not actually provide a backup service.

Uploading personal photos to a paid for account with an online backup facility is a much more reliable preservation strategy. For a small monthly sum, private backup facilities can be used to upload all manner of digital information, keeping a secure, off-site copy of all digital data selected for backup in a virtual safe deposit box, only available to the account creator. Popular commercial providers of such services include Data Deposit Box (www.datadepositbox.com); British Telecom's Digital Vault service (www.bt.com/personal/digitalvault/); Thinking Safe (www.thinkingsafe.com); and Remote Backup Systems (http://remote-backup.com/). However, such systems only host copies of digital data and do not allow others to view or download content. Where photos are concerned, many people want to share their data with others.

Online photo sharing sites often offer professional accounts which, for a small fee, give unlimited space on their server for hosting copies of digital images. Usually, the photographer has the choice whether the images will be kept private, made available to only friends and family or made available to everyone who would care to view them. Images posted on sites such as Flickr are often viewed as transitory and ephemeral, and part of a 'photostream', 'feed', 'pool' or 'slideshow' representing an individual, of which the most up to date is the most important: however, professional accounts also act as a backup service, archiving a copy of the digital file securely, off-site, for as long as the account is kept active (and the commercial company is operational). For those concerned about the longevity of their personal digital image collections, this option is recommended, perhaps in conjunction with printing and storing of local copies of digital files. However, given that only 11 per cent of households opt to archive images in this manner, there is still the potential for the loss of massive amounts of digital image data in society as a whole (PMA Foresight 2007).

The variety of backup options, and the time taken to organize and backup collections, juxtaposed with the ease in which digital photos can be individually copied, also causes its own problems:

> It is still a tedious task for typical users to manage personal digital photo collections, much like the old 'photo shoeboxes' ... One new problem is that files often need to be organized across different storage and viewing devices. Putting photos on a web server enables easy sharing among friends and families. But issues like slow Internet connections, storage cost, and privacy restrain people from uploading all their photos to the web. Local PC disks will still be a primary device for storing personal photos. In addition, many users would like to archive their photos on removable media such as CD. The problem is that applications on these different devices are not directly linked to each other. Photos, once uploaded, are no longer associated with their corresponding local copies. Instead, multiple copies of the same photo are stored in different places, and each can only be accessed using a separate application. When a collection grows to thousands of photos, it becomes very easy for a user to lose track of their files (Gargi et al. 2002, 1).

A digital image which is lost track of is one which is not likely to survive in the long term.

Why does this matter? This is an issue which, until recently, has received little mention in consumer literature, user guides or in the press. Even a commonly available book designed to promote and encourage saving and sharing personal life events in digital form, suggestively titled *Digital Photos, The Future of Memories*, contains no consideration of the long-term storage or backup requirements necessary to ensure these memories will indeed have a future (Howard 2004). Given the ubiquity of digital imaging technology and the frequency with which it is used, each owner of a digital camera may be at risk of losing thousands of photographs, among which may be irreplaceable records of events. Descendents, family and academic historians of the future, and library and information professionals will be confronted with a period of time, from the late twentieth century onwards, which will be remembered as 'the digital Dark Ages' (Kuny 1998). Family, amateur and even professional photographs will not have survived: digital images will not be found in a suitcase in a loft by chance. The same, of course, is true of all our digital data: music, documents, emails, spreadsheets, and so on: without careful archiving and care, and migration to current formats and systems, data will be lost to future generations (see Deegan and Tanner 2006 for a full exploration of digital preservation approaches, techniques and issues). However, our strong link to the photographic image and our fascination with reminiscence, memory and the passing of time, makes the loss of personal collections of image data particularly poignant.

The irony of this is that the longevity of some digital images may itself be the root of problems. The relationship between individuals and cameras is complex, with many people willing (or unknowingly) playing up to the camera in a way which would not be expected:

> If I were just curious, it would be very hard to say to someone 'I want to come to your home and have you talk to me and tell me the story of your life'. I mean, people are going to say 'You're crazy'. Plus they're going to keep mighty guarded. But the camera is a kind of license. A lot of people, they want to be paid that much attention and that's a reasonable kind of attention to be paid (Diane Arbus, in Sontag 1979, 191).

Add to that the ubiquity and frequency of use of digital cameras, and there is a good chance that candid, embarrassing or incriminating shots of individuals in less than upright circumstances will be taken, shared and circulated between peer groups and beyond. The issue is that once such images are presented into the public sphere, they will be out of the control of the individuals within them, or those who took the pictures, and have a tendency to re-emerge at a later date as a source of concern:

> Few people realise that sharing experience by means of exchanging digital images almost by definition implies distributed storage: personal 'live' pictures distributed via the internet may remain there for life, turning up in unforeseen contexts, reframed and repurposed (van Dijck 2008, 68).

Nude portraits, taken between consenting adults, have a tendency to circulate after the demise of a relationship (Scarcella 2007). Digital images of various relatively harmless incidents of common student behaviour – such as drinking alcohol in dorm rooms and celebrating after exams – are circulated widely after the event. As a result, they have been used as evidence for prosecution by Universities (Chalfont 2005; Smith 2005; Foster 2007). Illegally kept pets are confiscated (Sheridan 2006), and landlords revoke leases (WFTV.com 2006) after incriminating photos are naively posted online. In 2007, John Darwin, who claimed to have come 'back from the dead' after five years with little memory of how his life was spent since a canoeing accident, was shown to be a fraudster after a simple search on Google brought up a picture of him and his wife featured on a Panama estate agent's website (Moore 2007). We are not careful with our digital images and have little control over how and why they are used, once circulated. As well as the potential for losing our digital image collections, we are loosing control over the use of individual digital images.

Recommendations and Advice

Until recently, there has been very little consideration of the issue of the longevity of personal digital image collections. In 2005, the International Imaging Industry

Association (www.i3a.org) Management Committee approved a Consumer Photo Archiving Project, acknowledging the problem:

> Is the imaging industry responsible for helping people preserve their memories? Absolutely. The veterans of the imaging industry know that relationships with customers have been built on trust … The advent of digital imaging hasn't altered the trust factor, but the technological obstacles to memory-keeping – currently lurking under the surface of consumer understanding – could drastically alter the equation. Observations of consumer behaviours and attitudes regarding digital photography create a mandate for industry action (International Imaging Industry Association 2005).

The work of the resulting pan-industry task force, including contributions from Kodak, Hewlett Packard and other leading providers of digital imaging 'solutions', resulted in a website, launched in February 2007: www.savemymemories.org. The website provides an overview of: the importance of preserving image collections over the long term; guides to the problems encountered with hardware, software and other factors such as technological obsolescence, theft or loss, and the usefulness of online storage services; brief guides to file management, including naming, organizing and search strategies; how to attempt to recover files after a system crash; and a collection of links to other useful articles. A site such as this has the potential for informing the general public on basic data management procedures and is written in accessible, easy to follow, bite size chunks:

> If you have all of your digital photos stored on your computer but have yet to do anything else with them, take steps to protect them right away. Make prints, copy to CDs or DVDs, a second hard drive, or upload them to an online service for storage (International Imaging Industry Association 2007).

However, the success of the website seems to be limited: a year after launch, very few other websites are linking through to the initiative, which indicates that it is not a popular resource. Although promised, the website does not seem to have been updated since launch. Adoption of the recommendations would seem to be low, and the industry has to find a way to connect with the general public regarding such issues. To many people backup is 'a boring task that consumes valuable picture-taking time' (Rouse 2005, 8) and although:

> back up solutions abound … if we can only get consumers to understand the importance of backing up their images, we might begin to take some giant steps forward (DarConte 2007).

Where are the voices of librarians, archivists, curators and historians regarding this issue? The sector has been undeniably quiet. However, it is important to gain an understanding of how the general public are utilizing imaging technologies at a time when the library, museum and archive sector are spending so much time, effort and money producing their own collections of digital images (see Chapter 5), as the behaviour formed by users outside institutional environments will inform their behaviour and use of digital images provided by memory institutions. Users will expect online environments to work in the same way as their commonly visited web destinations: 'Users spend most of their time on *other* sites. This means that users prefer your site to work the same way as all the other sites they already know' (Nielsen 2000). Those producing digital versions of holdings for use by the general public had better keep abreast of how the general public are using imaging technologies outside memory institution's environments, if they want their own offerings to be well used.

As for the issue of the longevity of digital image data, there is no doubt that the available guides and recommended approaches produced for the information sector do have insights which could benefit the general public in understanding the issues of long-term preservation of digital image data (such as those produced by the Technical Advisory Service for Images 2006e, 2007a, 2008). However, how many members of the general public are likely to read such documentation? Likewise, comprehensive overviews produced for the information sector, such as the *Digital Images Archiving Study* produced for the UK Government's Joint Information Systems Committee by the Arts and Humanities Data Service (Anderson et al. 2006), are unlikely to reach a wide audience beyond the reaches of institutional libraries, archives and museums.

However, librarians and information professionals have a role in educating the public about such pressing issues. In 1998, it was said that:

> We are … living in the midst of digital Dark Ages; consequently, much as monks of times past, it falls to librarians and archivists to hold to the tradition which reveres history and the published heritage of our times … Despite the present lack of public interest in digital preservation, it is necessary to believe, perhaps as an article of faith, that the efforts of librarians and archivists will be appreciated in the future. The traces of information that we are able to save from our digital vellum will be valuable sources of information to the future. Even if the task of digital preservation remains thankless, it is a vital one and must still be undertaken. The objective is a noble and necessary one even as the many problems appear insurmountable (Kuny 1998).

Kuny was referring to the digital holdings of libraries, archives and other institutional bodies but the same problems now apply to personal data collections, particularly collections of digital images. Without intervention, publicity and advice from information professionals educated in the problem, it is unlikely that the digital images we have all accrued on our hard drives will survive intact for future generations.

Conclusion

Over the past ten years, the exponential growth in the use of digital image technologies has radically changed the way we take, use, share and conceive of personal photography. Ease of use of capture devices and telecommunication systems designed to support them, has encouraged frequent use of digital cameras and as a result, we take many more photographs than we ever did with still film devices. The relationship of individuals to their personal collections is changing, with the focus of photography shifting from capturing images for perpetuity, to becoming a tool for social interaction, bonding and entertainment. However, due to the vagaries of digital technology including issues such as technological fatigue and obsolescence, and the general public's misplaced faith in the longevity of computers and peripheral devices, our growing collections of digital photographs are at risk if we do not take steps to preserve and archive them for future generations. This is an issue which affects many, but an understanding of how to avoid widespread loss of photographic data has not permeated into general society. Information professionals have a role to play in educating the public in general issues regarding digital preservation, particularly that concerning digital image data, although little has been accomplished in making this issue known.

Further Reading

Due to the recent emergence of digital imaging as the dominant form of image exchange, not much research has been done regarding the use and users of these technologies. Very little has been published regarding how these technologies are being appropriated by the general public (this can be contrasted with the raft of publications available which encourage people to purchase and use digital cameras). Interesting work is emanating from researchers in Human Computer interaction and Sociology, and papers analysing the way users' modes of behaviours are developing and changing in response to using these technologies can be found in conference proceedings and journal articles such as those featured in this chapter. van Dijck's work on digital photographs, society and memory, featured above, is more fully covered in her book *Mediated Memories in the Digital Age (Cultural Memory in the Present)* (2007). It can be expected that further studies regarding this topic will be published in the near future; meanwhile, the personal content industry will continue to generate reports and statistics encouraging users to purchase and utilize digital imaging and communications technologies.

For those wishing to educate themselves on matters regarding the long-term preservation of digital data, Lazinger (2001); Borghoff et al. (2006); Deegan and Tanner (2006); and Gladney (2007) are good places to start. Juxtaposing these with particular issues regarding the longevity of image collections (see www.tasi.ac.uk), particular aspects of preserving personal digital image collections (www.savemymemories.org) and guides which are beginning to appear on this issue geared to professional photographers (Krogh 2006) will provide the tools necessary to evangelize about the necessity of caring for the output of our digital cameras and camera phones.

Chapter 7
Image Metadata

> an image … is beautiful, but not very useful, before it is connected to a description (Thaller 1992a, 2).

> Now we have another impossible thing to do and we have to do it knowing that it is impossible – a thought that would never have occurred to, say, Melvil Dewey! This new impossible thing is to bring order out of chaos, to trap lightning in a bottle, to take an electronic document with the life-span of a May bug (and most likely, the cosmic significance of a May bug) and make it part of an arranged and harmonious world – in short, to apply some kind of bibliographic control to the disorder of the Internet and the Web. If there are, as politicians and futurists claim, untold intellectual riches out there in cyberspace, what use are they if they cannot be found, and found, and found again? (Gorman 2003, 6).

Capturing image data through the use of digital equipment is one thing, aiding users in their attempt to locate and find digital images is quite another. The creation and maintenance of image metadata, or information about images, is crucial to current approaches to image searching, which generally involve entering a string of text that describes the subject or concept required, and querying a database which is expected to hold detailed and accurate textual records regarding the images. In order to provide access to relevant images, good, detailed, systematic and consistent descriptions of their contents and provenance is required. Concept-based image retrieval is therefore currently dependent on the creation and maintenance of good quality metadata. Additional information can be recorded about other image attributes such as format, creators, provenance or time and place of creation, which is essential information for the technical and managerial upkeep of digital image collections.

This chapter provides an overview of the concept of metadata and surveys current approaches to the creation of image metadata in memory institutions. Formal standards-based metadata approaches have recently been eschewed by the average Internet user and content creator, however, and different approaches to labelling and finding images, such as the use of folksonomies, are an alternative, useful way to search and retrieve digital image data. A brief background to automated image processing-based searching through Content Based Image Retrieval is also presented, mainly to indicate how far off we are from moving to widespread use of non-textual tools to aid in the searching of digital images. At present, the provision of good, systematic, textual metadata is the best approach for organizing, managing and allowing users to discover digital image collections. An understanding of metadata issues is therefore fundamental for those undertaking digitization projects or dealing with collections of digital images.

What is Metadata?

Metadata is literally 'data about data':

> structured, encoded data that describe characteristics of information-bearing entities to aid in the identification, discovery, assessment, and management of the described entities (Association for Library Collections and Technical Services Task Force on Metadata, 2000).

By providing structured terms about an information object in defined fields, the condensed representation of the object can be used to find, search and manage digital objects:

> At the most basic, metadata can be considered as *data about data*. In essence metadata is the extra baggage associated with any resource that enables a real or potential user to find that resource, to decide whether or not it is of value to them; to discover where, when and by whom it was created, as well as for what purpose; to know what tools will be needed to manipulate the resource; to determine whether or not they will actually be allowed access to the resource itself, and how much things will cost them. Metadata is, in short, a means by which largely meaningless data may be transformed into information, interpretable and reusable by those other than the creator of the data resource (Miller 2004, 4).

However, 'metadata' is a relatively ubiquitous term perceived and understood in various ways by different communities:

> Traditionally, cultural heritage and information professionals such as museum registrars, library cataloguers, and archivists have used the term metadata to refer to cataloguing or indexing information that they create to arrange, describe, and otherwise enhance access to an information object. Since the 1960s, libraries, aided by internationally recognized cataloguing rules and content standards … have shared descriptive metadata using automated systems such as online public access catalogs. Descriptive theory and practices vary considerably owing to the differing professional and cultural missions of museums, archives, and libraries, however (Gilliland-Swetland 1998, 1).

The concept of metadata has its genesis in the idea of Universal Bibliographic Control: the possibilities of the interconnections that could be afforded by standardization, cataloguing and automation of library records discussed in the international library community from the 1970s (Kaltwasser 1971) and the management of scientific data in the 1980s, where standard vocabularies were adopted to describe the differing qualities of data sets to allow searching and retrieval of experimental data. Over the past thirty years, it has become a busy, broad field of interest to information professionals and data managers. With the arrival of the Internet in the 1990s, a great deal of work has gone into resolving issues of metadata and cross-record searching, and comprehensive access to information for users. Agreements on national and international approaches and standards for library and archive material have been reached to facilitate data exchange (Gorman 2003; Intner et al. 2003). Technical issues regarding interoperability and methodological issues about the type and use of metadata continue to be explored, to facilitate the management, creation, use and preservation of both digital and non-digital objects. The creation of efficient but effective metadata schemes is important to avoid time-consuming, laborious manual data entry, while ensuring that enough data is captured to facilitate the discovery process.

Metadata differs from exhaustive cataloguing (which although effective in describing content and content relationships, is expensive) and keyword searching (which is cheap but ineffective) by producing a standardized set of structured fields of information which creates 'a cloud of collateral information around a data object' (Clifford Lynch, quoted in Association for Library Collections and Technical Services Task Force on Metadata (2000)). Resources can often be described with very few terms:

> In many cases, a great deal of detail may be recorded about a resource, much of which will be essential for particular uses of the resource, or for maintaining it in some fashion. It is normally the case, however, that only a small number of elements are actually required to capture the essence of a resource, thereby facilitating the discovery process (Miller 2004, 7).

Metadata is generally textual, describing a resource with a few specific fields of information, but of course can be used to describe non-textual objects, such as images. Metadata can be applied at an individual item level, for physical, born digital and digitized materials, but also at the collection level, to aid in the management and the finding of bodies of material. Because of its efficient nature, metadata is now routinely created alongside digital objects in libraries, archives and information environments:

> Who will create Metadata? The most likely persons to do this work are librarians, metadata specialists, subject-matter specialists, and resource creators. When will metadata be created? It can be created when the resource is created, or any time after the resource is created. How will users create metadata? With file editors or with metadata editing tools; and, in the latter instances, either manually or automatically. How will metadata be stored? It can be embedded in the resource, or in a searchable database or index, or both (Jul 2003, 152).

Creating and maintaining metadata about objects and in particular digital information objects, is obviously time-consuming and costly, and a tension exists between the two metadata functions of discovery aid and resource description: metadata creators have to provide enough information to be useful, but cannot afford to be exhaustive. However, the provision of metadata is important to: increase accessibility and the effectiveness of searching; retain the context of items within a wider cultural and heritage landscape; expand the use of items by facilitating access to new communities who would previously have not been able to locate the item; ensure different multiple versions of items are identified; track legal rights and information; aid in the long-term preservation of digital objects; and to aid in benchmarking technical data to make systems more efficient and effective (Gilliland-Swetland 1998, 6–8).

In the early days of digitization projects, metadata was seen as 'not the first priority' of those looking after an archive or collection, and it was stated that 'it is not likely that the curators of collections of visual material will on a broad scale succeed in getting these activities funded' (van den Berg 1992, 8.) However, it is now acknowledged that part of the process of digitization is the provision of reliable and consistent documentation, including metadata about each and every image, document or object in the collection. 'Organizations are realising the asset value of metadata and the amount of resources they have put into its creation, and are managing it as an investment' (Gilliland-Swetland 2004, 23). Those carrying out a digitization program will now be required to spend time providing adequate metadata about the resources they produce and metadata is now viewed, not as a poor cousin to traditional library cataloguing but as a critical component

> of digital resource development and use, and is needed at all stages in the creation and management of the resource. Any creator of digital objects should take as much care in the creation of the metadata as they do in the creation of the data itself – time and effort expended at the creation stage recording quality metadata is likely to save users much grief, and to result in a well-formed digital object that will survive for the long term. Well formed metadata is the most efficient and effective tool for managing and finding objects in the complex information spaces with which libraries are now dealing (Deegan and Tanner 2002, 114).

Metadata is therefore crucial for the preservation, management, description and use of a digital resource, including access restriction, resource discovery (finding), the documentation of resource behaviour and functionality, authentication, identification, record keeping, digital rights management (Gilliland-Swetland 1998, 3), and 'to place and sustain information objects within their cultural, historical, procedural, technological and other contexts' (Gilliland-Swetland 2004, 17). There are many different types of general metadata schemas: including those for technical, descriptive, administrative, rights, security, personal information, commercial management, content rating and preservation data (Schottlaender 2003, 22). All have an important role in uniquely identifying an object, placing it into its information structure in relation to other objects, and aiding users in finding, using and trusting a resource. An overview of the different types of metadata is provided in Deegan and Tanner (2002, 115–121); and Anderson et al. (2006, 72–84).

Digital Image Metadata

Digital images, like any other information object, need metadata to describe their provenance, content and technical characteristics. Standard library and archive-based metadata, cataloguing and bibliography schemes for 'traditional' library materials such as monographs and serials (for example, the Machine-Readable Cataloging (MARC); International Standard Bibliographic Description (ISBD); and Anglo-American Cataloguing Rules (AACR2) standards, see Gorman 2003; Intner et al. 2003) were developed for books and later generalized into standards for all types of library material. There is much discussion as to how electronic resources and documents can be brought into this 'architecture of bibliographic control' (Gorman 2003, 10), and the formidable technical issues that have to be resolved to allow this to happen. There are many problems encountered in trying to organize electronic documents and sites: electronic documents are mutable and less durable than their analogue predecessors, meaning that there is little assurance that a given document will exist in the same form when accessed in the future; there are vast numbers of electronic documents to deal with; there is little guarantee that an electronic document is what it claims to be; many electronic documents are for personal, local or temporary use (if they are of any use at all); and many electronic documents will not be of interest to libraries, archives and their users (ibid., 13). Add to this the fact that there is little standardization of presentation and format in digital documents, when compared to traditional, tangible library materials and it becomes clear that the existing standards are not suited to describing electronic data adequately (Polfreman et al. 2006).

Additionally, creating metadata for images (whether electronic or analogue) comes with its own problems. Although the basic metadata required for describing an image or work of art (or any non-text object, for that matter) may bear a strong resemblance to the metadata that describes traditional print documents, there will always be particular extra elements required to deal with the characteristics of non-textual resources. Textual data objects tend to be self-referencing: providing titles, author information and overviews from which keywords can be gleaned, but textual data regarding images (or image collections) has to be ascertained, created, inferred or decided by those interpreting the images:

> The description of non-textual data in text is problematic as there is more room for subjectivity of perception on the part of the cataloguer than with textual materials. Textual materials are often 'self describing': they contain textual information about subjects or keywords that can be extracted from the resources itself. With non-textual

> data, the metadata is created by individuals who, with the help of a range of reference works, make the most objective assessment possible about the object, but subjective bias is unconscious and cannot entirely be ruled out (Deegan and Tanner 2002, 117).

The relationship of pictorial information to textual metadata is the crux of the problem facing those trying to provide relevant, useful descriptions of image data. Indexers create textual metadata to create access points to images. The amount and type of terms used to describe an image resource varies, but they generally fall into two categories: structured information regarding numbers, dates and selections from sets of keywords or other controlled vocabularies to explain relationships between object and terms; and free text descriptions generated by the metadata creator, anticipating the terms users may employ to search for a particular image. There is no one size fits all approach to each image, however, and many images require in-depth consideration to describe them adequately:

> What metadata is needed to populate the database? The structure must be flexible. At an early stage, there must be the naming of objects, place, date and author of capture, as well as author of the work of art (if known). Some information is easily and immediately associated with pictures belonging to the archive, but most information needs research. A picture of an old man sitting on a chair, for example, has a different cultural value if one knows that the person portrayed is Théophile Gautier (a famous French author) (de Polo and Minelli 2006, 102).

Searching these fields is no different from searching in any other database application. However, it is well known that the words the metadata creator may provide and the words users may employ as search terms are based on personal interpretation, different levels of knowledge and education, and different vocabularies: they are often completely different (Jespersen and Jespersen 2004). As a result, 'language-based image indexing systems often fail the user in retrieval' (Jörgensen 1996). It is assumed that image content can be treated in the same way as other information objects, such as text or spreadsheets, when issues of interpretation, opinion, focus and scope can vastly change the type and quality of textual description of images. The granularity of terms is often problematic and the gulf between the knowledge of the metadata creator, and the user, can result in relevant images being lost in a search:

> Most of us are familiar with the abysmal searching functionalities currently available on the Web ... Searching for images is perhaps even more problematic than searching for text-based resources, as users must rely on how well the images are indexed with words if they can hope to retrieve them ... Anyone familiar with art information knows that often the subject matter or theme of a work of art is not reflected at all in its title. Hence if I want to quickly find images of 'Family life in the nineteenth century' which could have an infinite variety of titles, I can only find them if the descriptive terms family life and nineteenth century have been applied to them by a

> human being who has looked at an image; interpreted the title, the visual information, and other available data, and made the decision to apply these data values to it (Baca 2002a, 134).

Aspects of vocabulary control can be controlled by using a structured vocabulary or thesaurus, and specific metadata applications which deal solely with the technical, managerial and descriptive qualities of images have been developed. These are listed below.

Types of Image Metadata

Of primary importance to digital image data is technical metadata regarding the creation of the object, management metadata which documents the lifecycle of an image from creation onwards, and descriptive metadata which describes the content of the images being stored and provided for use.

Technical metadata describes the image as a digital asset, documenting its digital provenance, means of creation and the technical characteristics necessary to ensure that the image will be outputted accurately on other display devices, such as file format, resolution, colour space, etc. Technical metadata provides documentation which can be used to ensure that the digital file can be resurrected in the future, by providing an overview of the physical (rather than intellectual) characteristics of the image file and so aids in digital preservation. Technical metadata can also aid in workflow, by managing how and where images are stored or how images are labelled. It is becoming increasingly common for digital cameras to incorporate limited technical metadata within image files as they are created, using Exif data (see pp. 89–90), and some fields of (mostly) technical metadata can also be embedded within TIFF files (see pp. 82–87). Generally, though, further technical data will have to be captured by those creating a digital corpus to ensure its longevity.

Management metadata:

> is information documenting the life cycle of an electronic resource, including data about ordering, acquisition, maintenance, licensing, rights, ownership and provenance. It is essential that the provenance (custodial history) of a digital image object is recorded from, where possible, the time of its creation through all successive changes in custody of ownership. Users and curators must be provided with a sound basis for confidence that a digital image is exactly what is it purported to be … There should be a clear audit trail of all changes. (Anderson et al. 2006, 74).

It is very difficult to ascertain the relationship of a digital object to its original incarnation (for example, image files can be easily manipulated, cropped, resized, resampled and compressed) and maintaining good management metadata for digital images encourages trust in the veracity of the image object.

Descriptive metadata (also sometimes referred to as 'discovery metadata') attempts to capture the intellectual attributes of the image object, enabling users to identify, locate and retrieve suitable images. Systematically and consistently described visual material aids researchers in using image sources effectively in their work. Many of these attributes would have been catalogued in a traditional library system: for example, title, creator, date, subject, keywords, etc. Description of the content is rather more problematic and requires some interpretation on the side of the metadata creator in providing a 'content description' which can be applied at various levels of granularity, and can run to hundreds of related words, themes and concepts. Decisions need to be made about how to undertake this, whether through using arbitrarily chosen strings of words (often described as a 'word soup') or using structured and standardized terms from a carefully controlled vocabulary:

- Having considered the various kinds of subjects – of, about (or levels of description, identification, and interpretation), and literary works that an … image can be about – through which of them will you provide access?
- If you are providing access to more than one kind of subject, do you want to codify the distinctions between or among them?
- What level of analysis, or what depth of indexing, do you want to provide?
- What vocabularies will you use to record your subject analysis?
- What metadata schema or format will you use to describe … images?
- What type of information system will you use to retrieve and display the … images? (Shatford Layne 2004).

Without addressing these issues, it is unlikely that a cataloguer or team of cataloguers, will provide consistent, useful subject descriptions which can aid researchers when searching for images.

Other important metadata which may be captured about digital images includes information about the quality, veracity and authenticity of image data, information about the original object and information about rights management (Besser 1997).

It should be clear by now that the provision of such information regarding digital image files, within a cultural or heritage institution, is both necessary and essential to the use and usefulness of the images themselves. The need for management of the metadata is as critical as management of the digital image file itself:

> Digital images are beginning to stack up like cordwood as museums and archives plunge into more and more electronic application. Yet from a management standpoint, it is not at all clear that collections of digital files are any easier to manage than collections of film and prints. At least with photographic materials, institutions have had decades to

> develop filing and recording methods. This is not the question of how to describe the contents of an image, which is an entirely separate discussion. Rather, production and management data answer the questions of: what is the source of this image; how was it created, what are its characteristics, where can it be found, and what is it called. Pointers within each record maintain the interconnections among versions of images and where they reside. There is no one time or place where all of this information is acquired: reproduction data are entered when the file is received; image capture variables are recorded during scanning; image characteristics and linking references are added in a subsequent production step (Ester 1996, 18).

The creators of digital asset management systems tend to provide software facilities for capturing, storing and accessing metadata. Similar to library catalogue systems, but more flexible, expandable and configured to dealing with digital image resources, Image Management Systems (or IMS) are often the key to delivering large collections of digital image data: providing facilities to ingest, store, manage, search, retrieve and deliver images from the holdings, allowing users to interrogate, search and browse image data intuitively. To facilitate this process, the systems manage all types of metadata about the images to ensure that they can be found as easily as possible by creators, users and managers alike. IMS have only recently been adopted within the cultural and heritage sector (DigiCULT 2002), with some institutions adopting off the shelf systems and some investing in bespoke IMS for their individual needs (Weglowska 2006). Current vendors of full IMS systems, for dealing with large-scale digital image collections with complex metadata requirements, include Ibase Manager (www.ibase.com/manager/, used by The Tate; The British Library; and Glasgow City Libraries; among others) and System Simulation Ltd's 'Index+' software toolkit (www.ssl.co.uk used by the Victoria and Albert Museum and the Victorian Times digitization project, ibid.). Choosing and purchasing such a system requires careful consideration and much financial investment (TASI 2007b).

Image Metadata Schemes

Many implementations of metadata are localized and individual, existing on users' computers for their own use and discovery. Schemas offer a more formalized outline or description, and are used as the basis for cataloguing standards and categorization. However, much in the same way that file formats exist in proprietary and standard formats (see pp. 63–64), various schemas of metadata have evolved and although most metadata schemes (MARC, CIDOC-CRM) do not specifically cater for recording the particular qualities of images, various image metadata schemes are now in existence. There is no single correct way in which to implement metadata for all given image applications. Many image metadata schemes are only concerned with recording technical metadata, some exist solely to advise on the creation of descriptive or resource discovery metadata. Often, these schemas need to be used in tandem with a structured vocabulary or thesaurus (see below) to aid in standardizing the terms used to complete the desired fields. It is also possible to combine different schemas for a project to capture the information required for its own individual needs: 'It is not enough to use some metadata standard. A metadata standard appropriate to the materials in hand and the intended end-users must be selected' (Baca 2003, 54). Understanding the range of choices on offer is the first step in determining which are right for an individual project and various schemes are described below.

Dublin Core Metadata Element Set (DCMES)

The Dublin Core is a general metadata scheme: that is, it is not designed in particular to capture comprehensive descriptions of graphical metadata, but can be easily extended in that direction. The most widely used and supported metadata set in the library community, the Dublin Core provides a lowest common denominator in mapping and describing diverse information resources, and has become the most readily appropriated metadata standard for describing online digital resources.

Dublin Core takes it name from Dublin, Ohio, home of the Online Computer Library Centre (OCLC), where the first workshop in trying to ascertain a common, core list of metadata fields was held in 1995. DCMES was approved as an ANSI/NISO standard in early 2001, and as an ISO standard in 2003. Up to date information about the standard, including a dynamic list of appropriate terms, is maintained by the Dublin Core Metadata Initiative (http://dublincore.org/).

The core set of 15 simple data elements are meant to be used to describe and therefore facilitate discovery of, 'document-like' objects in a digital environment, capturing information regarding the title, identifier, creator, contributor, publisher, language, description, subject, coverage, date, type, relation, format, source and rights of an information object. None of these elements are mandatory, all can be repeated if necessary and expanded if required. The subject field can use Library of Congress subject headings, or some other defined classification scheme (such as those listed below).

The Dublin Core's basic nature means it is not suited to capturing descriptions with a high-level of granularity, but it is an easy to apply standard which focuses on simplicity, interoperability and international consensus, and as a result has been well used and heavily promoted in the library, archive and cultural and heritage communities. The New Opportunities Fund digitization program (NOF digitize, www.enrichuk.net) used DCMES as the minimum level of description projects had to provide about each digitized resource. The MINERVA project used DCMES as a basis for exploring the description of museum objects in their DC.Culture initiative (www.minervaeurope.org/DC.Culture.htm). The Open Archives Initiative Protocol for Metadata Harvesting (OAI-PMH) uses, as its basis, a simple DCMES record (www.openarchives.org).

Whether or not image data, and digital image data in particular, can be described as 'document-like' is up for interpretation. Indeed, the third Dublin Core workshop, held in 1997, specifically considered the application of the Dublin

Core element set to the description of images, concluding that individual images could be considered to be document-like objects when 'fixed': appearing the same to all users (Weibel and Miller 1997). Despite its limitations, Dublin Core is in widespread use as a relatively simple way to record descriptive and management metadata of digitized image resources and born digital images.

Exif

The Exif industry standard is a popular metadata schema used by digital camera manufacturers to capture and store basic technical data regarding the creation of an image. In particular, Exif data may typically store time and data of exposure, brand and model of camera used and further technical data about camera settings at the time of image capture. Its application for use in storing descriptive data (and as used as a finding aid) is therefore limited. See pp. 89–90 for further information about Exif flavour JPEG and TIFF.

DIG35 Specification, Metadata for images

DIG35 is a metadata standard which was developed by a wide consortium of manufacturers working in the digital image capture industry, first under the Digital Imaging Group, but since absorbed by the International Imaging Industry Association (www.i3a.org/i_dig35.html). Formed in 1999, the consortium worked towards:

> a standardized mechanism which allows end-users to see digital image use as being equally as easy, as convenient and as flexible as the traditional photographic methods while enabling additional benefits that are possible only with a digital format (International Imaging Industry Association 2008).

The main concerns of the initiative were to define a set of image metadata requirements which could be implemented across a variety of file formats and a variety of devices capable of creating, manipulating, storing and displaying digital image metadata.

DIG35 version 1.1 was released as a public draft in 2001 (Digital Imaging Group 2001) and details a scheme to encode digital image information in XML (eXtensible Markup Language). The metadata captured in the DIG35 schema is mostly technical, with six optional element types describing image parameters (such as height and width); image creation (technical and management data); content description (the geographical location, date and time of the image's creation, rather than descriptive keywords); history (of image manipulation); IPR (information about rights); and a further metadata field which can hold any of the optional elements recursively in an XML document tree.

DIG35 is similar to the information stored within Exif, and is used in a variety of capture devices and database management systems to capture and store generic technical image metadata. However, although it suits being used in a general purpose image library, because of its limited content description field, its application for those creating cultural and heritage information objects is limited.

IPTC-NAA Information Interchange Model

In 1990, the International Press Telecommunications Council (IPTC) and the Newspaper Association of America (NAA) began working together on a globally applicable model for describing digital objects within the newspaper and press industry. Launched in 1991, the Information Interchange Model provides 'headers' which can be inserted around digital image files as a wrapper, describing the type of data and the file format. Additional information, such as caption, news category or dateline can also be included (www.iptc.org/IIM/). Adobe Photoshop subsequently incorporated the data structure of IIM into its proprietary format (.psd, see pp. 91–92) which became commonly known as the 'IPTC headers'. Development of the model was frozen in 1997 in favour of XML-based metadata schemas, but the aims and concepts of the IMM influenced subsequent work in the field and the model is still used in picture libraries. However, it is now of little use to projects involved in creating new digital objects.

NISO Z39.87–2002 Data Dictionary-Technical Metadata for Still Images

In April 1999, the National Information Standard Organization (NISO); the Council on Library and Information Resources (CLIR); and the Research Library Group sponsored a workshop that specifically addressed how to standardize the recording of technical metadata for images. Acknowledging the contribution the DIG35 initiative had made, the standard does not attempt to duplicate or even address work on descriptive metadata schemes, but encourages a clear division between technical and physical properties of an image and attempts to describe image content, based on experiences in digitization centres. The result was a data dictionary, approved by the American National Standards Institute in 2006, which includes elements for recording detailed technical information (formats, compression), image creation processes, change and manipulation history, and any quality metrics applied (National Information Standards Organization 2006). NISO Z39.87 attempts to capture all aspects of technical metadata necessary for the management and preservation of bitmap images, but has no support for content description or rights management. No particular method of encoding the metadata information is recommended in NISO Z39.87, but the Network Development and MARC standards office of the Library of Congress maintains a NISO Z39.87 compliant XML schema called MIX which can be employed to store the resulting data set (www.loc.gov/standards/mix/).

PREMIS (PREservation Metadata: Implementation Strategies)

A working group jointly sponsored by OCLC and the RLG, PREMIS aimed to create a core management and technical metadata set, and a related data dictionary, needed to support preservation of all kinds of digital resources (i.e. not only digital images). In particular, the PREMIS guidelines are concerned with preservation metadata and have no focus in resource discovery or descriptive metadata (PREMIS Working Group 2005). As a result, PREMIS is not a comprehensive standard, but does provide the essential technical and management metadata for archiving digital documents, although these need augmenting with information of more granularity for capturing technical information specific to digital images (such as colour space and bit depth). PREMIS concluded its activities in 2005 (www.oclc.org/research/projects/pmwg/) but the data dictionary and XML schema continue to be maintained by the Library of Congress (www.loc.gov/standards/premis/), with the guidelines having reasonable uptake in the library and archive community. PREMIS still remains a useful basis for the capture of technical image metadata, but it is recommended that NISO Z39.87 is more immediately suited to the task of storing digital image metadata.

Categories for the Description of Words of Art (CDWA)

CDWA is a metadata schema which describes a set of categories and detailed guidelines which may be used to catalogue art, architecture and related cultural and heritage information. CDWA provides an inclusive framework for the description of art objects and their visual surrogates, which can be successfully used to classify digitized and born digital images if the subject focus is a work of art. There is no focus on format or technical environment: CDWA is concerned with the intellectual subject focus of the image, dividing subject into Description, Identification and Interpretation, and providing fields to cover the object's history and relation to other works. In total, CDWA provides 512 categories and further subcategories to exhaustively describe the object or artefact (Baca and Harpring 2006).

Work on CDWA began in 1995 by the Art Information Task Force (sponsored by the College Art Association of America and the Getty Trust, see Baca 2002a) which comprised of representatives from the potential user community, including art historians, art librarians and information specialists. It has since been well used by both academics and information professionals as a means to classify art works. CDWA maps to, or forms the basis of, a variety of other, more specialized metadata standards, such as the Foundation for Documents of Architecture/Architectural Drawings Advisory Group's *Guide to the Description of Architectural Drawings* data categories (Porter and Thornes n.d.); The Art Museum Image Consortium (AMICO) data dictionary (AMICO 2004); the Museum Documentation Association (MDA) Spectrum (www.mda.org.uk/spectrum.htm); and the VRA Core Categories (see below).

CDWA Lite is an XML schema created to describe core records for works of art and their image surrogates, based on a subset of CDWA. The CDWA website, at the Getty Research Institute, contains a full set of the guidelines and a thorough discussion of the issues involved in building art information systems (www.getty.edu/research/conducting_research/standards/cdwa/index.html). Harpring (2002) demonstrates how CDWA can be applied to describe, catalogue and index works of art and their related images.

VRA Core

The Visual Resources Association have been working, since 2000, on a metadata standard for the cultural and heritage community that can describe the correct approach to documenting visual documents, distinguishing between original works and surrogate images of the work and providing a generic metadata scheme for both. Based on CDWA, the VRA Core is a complete and informative system that is particularly useful for managing slides and digital images of art and architecture. The standard consists of a metadata element set (which provides basic information units such as title, date, location, etc.) and guidelines as to how these elements can be structured and stored, while allowing flexibility and extensions to the core set.

Various incarnations of the guidelines have been released: the current guidelines, VRA Core 4, were released in 2007 (Visual Resources Association 2007). An XML schema is now recommended for encoding and storing the metadata. Current developments are kept up to date on their website (http://vraweb.org/projects/vracore4/).

VRA Core was recently used as the base for the metadata guidelines produced by the JISC Image Digitisation Initiative to give this UK wide, wide-scale project a set of core descriptive metadata fields and terms that would be standardized across the projects funded by the initiative (JISC Image Digitisation Initiative 2002). The updated guidelines remain widely used in the cultural and heritage sectors. However, as VRA Core is not interoperable with Dublin Core, and does not contain a comprehensive set of technical metadata elements, those using VRA Core to describe digital images tend to use it alongside DCMES to ensure that technical and managerial metadata is also adequately captured.

Cataloguing Cultural Objects (CCO)

Cataloging Cultural Objects: A Guide to Describing Cultural Works and Their Images (CCO) (Baca et al. 2006) is a set of guidelines produced by the Visual Resources Association for describing, documenting and cataloguing cultural works and their visual surrogates. Mapping to both CDWA and VRA Core metadata sets, CCO is a broader manual that examines issues in assigning metadata to works of art and their related images, the description of relationships between objects and the analytical process necessary to describe complex works. Launched in 2006, CCO provides rules for descriptive cataloguing and guides to naming resources, in an attempt to help standardize the terms used to describe objects and facilitate user retrieval through descriptive consistency. In particular, CCO's contribution is to the standardization of data content, establishing the data values that should be used when completing records of unique cultural objects. CCO is designed to be used by professionals working with cultural and heritage objects and can be used alongside other more descriptive metadata sets (such as VRA Core or CDWA) or technical and management metadata schemes. Current documentation is available from the CCO website (http://vraweb.org/ccoweb/cco/index.html).

Sepia Data Element Set

In 1999, the European Commission on Preservation and Access (ECPA) set up the SEPIA (Safeguarding European Photographic Images for Access) project which investigated the long-term preservation of photographic collections, and aimed to define the role of technology in managing collections of photographic images. Among discussions of various preservation issues regarding photographic images, SEPIA provided recommendations and guidelines on best practice in metadata and the use of standards. The SEPIA Data Element Set (SEPIADES) resulted from these discussions (Aasbø et al. 2003) providing lists of core elements, over 400 optional commented elements, and detailed guidelines for technical identification of photographs. SEPIADES recommended the use of DCMES to capture technical and managerial data about photographic images. The SEPIA project (www.knaw.nl/ECPA/sepia/home.html) ended in November 2003, and the guidelines have not been updated since. Although the report and guidelines still have relevance for those cataloguing and preserving photographic image collections, it is advised that those beginning to produce metadata about image collections should look towards up to date standards, such as VRA Core, CDWA and CCO.

Structured Vocabularies and Thesauri

Users often have an idea of the objects, documents or images they are searching for but don't know how to describe or define the content, or have any real idea of titles, authors, provenance or dates, which could be used as a basis for retrieving records from a system. Those cataloguing the objects, through providing good metadata records using schemas, such as those described above, have to carefully choose the terminology they use to fill out subject fields to ensure that they provide terms and descriptions which are rigorous, dependable and predicable to users. Although cataloguers can provide their own keywords of terms they believe may be associated with an item, structured subject vocabularies are often used to provide a list of terms which are suitable in describing objects. These predefined lists of words can explicitly show the relationships between and among concepts and aid the user in resource discovery by providing a wealth of words to choose from, such as both broad and narrow terms to describe an object ('boat' and 'kayak'); the names of related or connected individuals (expressing the connection between William Wordsworth and Dorothy Wordsworth); alternative spellings of places, people and subjects ('Antwerpen', 'Antwerp' and 'Anvers', 'Fionn mac Cumhaill' and 'Finn McCool', or 'color-field' and 'colour-field') and alternative nomenclature ('dull gilt' and 'antique gilt').

The need for providing standardized lists of terms which can be used as a tool by those generating discovery records has been acknowledged since before the advent of digital technology. Tools, such as the Library of Congress Subject Headings (www.loc.gov/aba/); Library of Congress Authority files for Names, Subjects and Form-Genre (http://authorities.loc.gov/); the Union List of Artist Names (www.getty.edu/research/conducting_research/vocabularies/ulan/); and the Thesaurus of Geographic Names (www.getty.edu/research/conducting_research/vocabularies/tgn/) have provided standardized lists for cataloguers of all types of materials for decades, although obviously the fact that these tools are now mostly available online shows how important and useful the digital environment has become to cataloguers and metadata creators.

Structured vocabularies which can be particularly used to provide discovery metadata for image data have been under development since the 1980s:

> A single list of standard terms from which catalogers and researchers can choose indexing and retrieval vocabulary is needed … because of the great variety of media and pictorial types and because of the broad range of users of graphic materials, whose knowledge and experience vary. While an extensive and often informational vocabulary is employed in the descriptive portion of the catalog record, indexing terms should be controlled. Reconciling variant terms by designating a preferred indexing term not only simplifies the cataloger's task but also makes retrieval more efficient. For example, the standard term 'dry plate photonegatives' lessens confusion about 'silver gelatine glass negatives', 'glass plates' and 'dry plates' (Zinkham 1986, v).

The lack of vocabulary available to describe book illustrations led the Library of Congress Prints and Photographs Division to expand several of their physical description lists into the *Descriptive Terms for Graphic Materials*: Genre and *Physical Characteristic Headings* (Zinkham 1986), now expanded into the Library of Congress Thesaurus of Graphic Materials (www.loc.gov/rr/print/tgm2/toc.html). This remains one of the most important structured vocabularies for use in describing image data, whether it is analogue or digital. The Art and Architecture Thesaurus (www.getty.edu/research/conducting_research/vocabularies/aat/) is popular for describing art works, and ICONCLASS (www.iconclass.nl) is useful for describing the subject matter of image materials, providing a hierarchy of objects, events, people and abstract ideas that can be used to examine, describe and classify the content and subject of an image.

Choosing a Metadata Scheme and Structured Vocabulary

It is clear that those wishing to describe image data have a wealth of choices to make regarding which metadata schemas to use when describing image resources, but the choice of metadata schema itself should also be made in tandem with choosing the most appropriate structured vocabulary for the objects in question:

> Choosing the most appropriate metadata standard of standards for describing particular collections or materials is only the first step in building an effective, usable information resource. Unless the metadata elements or data structure are populated with the appropriate data values (terminology), the resource will be ineffectual and users will not be able to find what they are looking for, even if it is actually there. Again, there is no one-stop-shopping for the appropriate vocabulary tool for any given project. Rather, builders of information resources should select from the menu of vocabularies most appropriate for describing and providing access points to their particular collections (Baca 2003, 52).

The Library of Congress Subject Headings; the Library of Congress Thesaurus of Graphic Materials; the Art and Architecture Thesaurus; and ICONCLASS are all extensively used to provide consistent terminology to fill the 'subject' field in Dublin Core records of digital image material, thus allowing metadata creators to capture technical, managerial and descriptive metadata in a consistent and relatively straightforward manner.

However, it may be the case that these tools do not correspond to an individual collection, and metadata creators will decide that the most appropriate approach is to create their own structured vocabulary which suits and reflects the contents of their individual collection:

> Increasingly, institutions and projects, especially collaborative initiatives in a particular subject area, are finding that the most effective thing they can do to serve their internal and external users is to build their own thesauri and classification systems, using terms from established, broadly accepted subject vocabularies like Library of Congress Subject Headings, or the Art & Architecture Thesaurus, but also adding both preferred and variant terms from the specific field of study and from sources both printed and human, both expert and non-expert. Some leading museum collection management systems include built-in subject vocabularies and thesaurus building tools to facilitate this process (Baca 2003, 52).

As with most choices in the digitization process, projects who educate themselves about the metadata schemas and tools available prior to making a decision about the specific approach they will adopt stand to have the best chance of creating usable and useful digital image resources.

Folksonomies

The problem with metadata is that it is time-consuming and costly to create and depends on securing the services and attention of trained information professionals. Over the past few years, there has been a trend in online systems to rely on 'the wisdom of crowds' (Surowiecki 2005) to provide labels for objects, which can then be used as search terms by other users. Unstructured, un-policed, non-hierarchical and unchecked, these lists of informal keyword 'tags' have provided an alternative, useful means of browsing and searching collections of online resources. In particular, folksonomies are well used and useful, when created alongside collections of digital images.

In 2003, an online service for storing and sharing personal bookmarks (links to other websites of interest) called Delicious (http://del.icio.us) was launched. Although not particularly innovative as a bookmark manager, its major pioneering contribution to the online environment was allowing users to add their own keywords as a fundamental means of searching, labelling and managing their contributions, allowing users to 'tag' resources with the vocabulary of their own choosing. The photo sharing and management website Flickr (www.flickr.com) was quick to adapt this tool, allowing users to label their own images to facilitate image management and sharing of images with others in the online environment (Cox 2007).

The beauty of such a system is that as more users contribute, the more sophisticated the tag coverage becomes. The most popular tags become fairly obvious and are often graphically represented in a 'tag cloud' with the most commonly used terms featuring in larger text, aiding users in gaining an overview of the resource. The term 'folksonomy' – juxtaposing ideas of 'folk' and 'taxonomy'[1] – was coined by Thomas Vander Wal, a technology consultant, to describe these informal categories (Smith 2004).

The problem with folksonomies, however, is that they are generated by untrained individuals: one of the most popular tags on Flickr is 'me' (Mathes 2004). Ambiguity of terms is common, there is no control over the use of synonyms, and misspelling is rife. However, the opportunities provided by such systems should be weighed up against the problems:

> A folksonomy represents simultaneously some of the best and worst in the organization of information. Its uncontrolled nature is fundamentally chaotic, suffers from problems of imprecision and ambiguity that well developed controlled vocabularies and name authorities effectively ameliorate. Conversely, systems employing free-form tagging

1 'Note that despite its name a folksonomy is not a taxonomy. A taxonomy is the process, within subject-based classification, of arranging the terms given in a controlled vocabulary into a hierarchy. Folksonomies move away from the hierarchical approach to an approach more akin to that taken by faceted classification or other flat systems' (UKOLN 2005).

> that are encouraging users to organize information in their own ways are supremely responsive to user needs and vocabularies, and involve the users of information actively in the organizational system. Overall, transforming the creation of explicit metadata for resources from an isolated, professional activity into a shared, communicative activity by users is an important development that should be explored and considered for future systems development (Mathes 2004).

Many memory institutions, such as art galleries and museums, have incorporated user tagging systems into their websites (see p. 127; and pp. 180–181) with a variety of success, demonstrating that users choose and create different terms for objects and holdings than the words chosen by trained metadata providers (Chun et al. 2006), while the tools themselves provide a means for general members of the public to interact with websites, particularly in the case of image collections. An ongoing collaborative research project consisting of a consortium of major institutions and organizations (including The Guggenheim Museum and The Metropolitan Museum of Art) has been exploring the potential of user-based subject-oriented tags for museum collections since 2005. *Steve: The Art Museum Social Tagging Project* (www.steve.museum) continues to encourage debate on this issue, and ascertain how these technologies may best be appropriated by traditional institutions.

Understanding how users tag images and what terms they search for may also improve automated image retrieval tools. Online image search tools, such as Picsearch (www.picsearch.com); Google image search (http://images.google.com/); or their multilingual equivalent, PanImages (www.panimages.org) retrieve images from web pages based on keywords which are automatically extracted from the text on the relevant page using natural language processing techniques. This approach is rather hit and miss, with many images returned being not relevant to the search terms entered. Since 2007, Google has been running its 'Google Image Labeller' (http://images.google.com/imagelabeler/), an online game which encourages users to provide labels of images, assisting in image retrieval by helping to standardize tags and terms, and helping to improve the relevance of image searches on Google's databases. Such experimentation with user engagement and harnessing the collective efforts of the Web 2.0 (see p. 31; and p. 127) audience may help in improving the success rate of text-based image retrieval.

Content Based Image Retrieval (CBIR)

While traditional image retrieval systems (for both analogue and digital images) have relied on the textual descriptions provided by human cataloguers, problems with inconsistent labelling remain. An alternative means of searching and retrieving images is provided by automated Content Based Image Retrieval (CBIR) systems, which use image processing technology to compare, recognize and retrieve images based on the pictorial content of the images themselves, using features such as colour, texture or shape. The selection process is done automatically, by the computer, without relying on manually assigned keywords or any available textual description.

CBIR is a large research area in engineering and computing science. There have been various and varied attempts at automatically retrieving digital images based on image content. The successful development of systems may have ramifications for medical imaging analysis, web searching, trademark protection and security services. The literature on this area is wide (Gudivada and Raghavan (1995); Gudivada and Raghavan (1997); Eakins and Graham (1999); Marques and Furht (2002); and Vasconcelos (2007)) although the success of systems, even after years of development and research, is limited, and it is acknowledged that content-based systems cannot solve all image retrieval tasks by themselves, as they currently stand. The main issue is that although automated programs may be able to spot areas of colour or shape in images, there is little understanding at present of how to represent the higher-level semantic content of images. For example, a retrieval program may be able to identify images which have a large circle of red in the top right-hand corner or a stripe of blue across the bottom of the picture, but they will not be able to retrieve all images which portray sunsets or the sea. As a result, retrieval of image data by automated analysis of image content is fraught with difficulties.

Making effective use of the tools which currently exist for content-based image retrieval is an interesting challenge. Many museums and art galleries have experimented with CBIR to give an alternative means to search their image catalogue. IBM's Query By Image Content system (QBIC, http://qbic.almaden.ibm.com/) has been used by the State Hermitage Museum in St Petersburg, Russia since 2003, allowing users to 'search for artwork visually using tools that an artist would use' (State Hermitage Museum 2003). The tool allows you to choose colours, which you place in a grid, and QBIC searches the database for images which have similar colours in similar places (www.hermitagemuseum.org/fcgibin/db2www/qbicSearch. mac/qbic?selLang=English). QBIC returns a variety of image results which would be very different from those found through textual searching of keywords in the database: it may be the case that such tools could help those doing visual research to identify relevant images which they had not previously encountered, and so had no knowledge of the textual terms and references which may be used to describe them. However, another early adopter of the QBIC system, the Fine Arts Museum of San Francisco (www.famsf.org/), removed the facility from their website, perhaps because of its lack of use, lack of relevant image returns and problems in implementation and upkeep. Other available systems, such as the Rich Media products from Virage (www.virage.com) and VisualSEEK (www.ee.columbia.edu/ln/dvmm/researchProjects/MultimediaIndexing/VisualSEEk/VisualSEEk.htm) also suffer from the same problems, and uptake in the cultural and heritage communities has been limited. In 1992, Jaritz and Schuh (1992, 148) commenting on the current state of CBIR, stated 'We are more or less forced to be patient until further developments on the technical side become applicable for the historian'. Fifteen years later, we are still being patient.

The limited research which exists about how useful users find CBIR tools when searching cultural and heritage image collections (Holt et al. 1995, Holt et al. 1997) suggests that although interesting results can be obtained by the tools, basic textual descriptions and search facilities increase the relevance of the results returned, and text searches are much preferred when any details about an image or artist are already known. Descriptive information – or metadata – is still needed to facilitate image retrieval at the semantic level and, at present, only human cataloguers can provide and create this:

> As long as a human element is involved in the cataloguing process – something that will remain with us for the foreseeable future – the role of the cataloguer is destined to be the most significant in the entire classification process. It is only by understanding this crucial aspect of the process that end-user access to images can be enhanced (Hourihane 2002).

Conclusion

Due to the large size of most digital image collections created by memory institutions, facilities for user searching must be provided. At present, text-based queries are the standard method for searching and retrieving relevant images from databases. However, the quality of the results returned is dependent on the quality of the information provided about the images in the database: the metadata, which is generally created by trained information professionals. Although there are a variety of guidelines and tools to aid in the description of images and the provision of technical, managerial and descriptive metadata, there remain issues of standardization in the terms generated by a cataloguer. Folksonomies and CBIR may provide alternate ways to search image collections, but at present, relying on manually created metadata remains the best way to facilitate user access to image collections.

Further Reading

There are only a few publications devoted entirely to digital image metadata. Of course, attempts at the systematic classification of images have a long history, and many issues were well known before considering the classification of digital images in particular: Jespersen and Jespersen (2004) give an insightful overview of the application of textual description to image data. An early book entitled *Digital Image Access and Retrieval* (Heidorn and Sandore 1997) contains some useful papers on the subject, scoping the central challenges for libraries aiming to create, access and store volumes of digital images of their holdings, although the information landscape has changed exponentially from its publication. The most comprehensive introductory text available, an *Introduction to Art Image*

Access Tools, Standards, and Strategies, edited by Murtha Baca (2002b) provides selected essays on the topic of image retrieval, from the point of view of collection managers, cataloguers and users, and although designed specifically with art images in mind, is a useful introduction to many issues raised no matter what the genre of the images in question. The text also contains a wide bibliography on other related, interesting and accessible readings.

Stapleton (2006) provides an overview article on *Image Databases and Access*, addressing questions of database infrastructure, as well as metadata. Anderson and colleagues (2006) provide a useful chapter on image metadata, along with a 'recommended minimum element set for use with archival digital still images' (84–90), using as its source Dublin Core, PREMIS, and a few elements drawn from NISO Z39.87. This overview is a useful starting point for those wishing to begin providing metadata for digital imaging collections. Polfreman and colleagues (2006) provide a comprehensive overview of issues in generating metadata to aid in the resource discovery of digital objects.

The UK's Digital Curation Centre (www.dcc.ac.uk) provides accessible overviews on general metadata issues, such as Higgins (2006), with plenty of external links to related resources. General text books, such as Lazinger (2001); Intner and colleages (2003); and Gorman and Dorner (2004), are useful in understanding wider issues regarding the usefulness of metadata and how it is used throughout the library and archive community.

Chapter 8
Current Issues in Digital Imaging

> As I hold the future well-being of photography very dear I must see to it that these forces which militate against it be opposed and destroyed (Alfred Stieglitz, 1910, 8 cited in Arts Council of Great Britain 1978, 12).

Although digital imaging technologies have evolved and been appropriated over a number of years, and may seem to be present themselves as a mature, stable technology, there are many issues which remain regarding digital image creation, digital image quality, digital image management and digital image longevity. In particular, the issue of accurate colour management, particularly when creating digital surrogates of original objects and documents, remains an area of concern and research. This, in turn, raises questions of quality: how can those creating digital images ensure that they are accurate and truthful representations? The issue of 'truth' in visual evidence is one that has a long history, although the tools available to manipulate digital images make it a pressing issue in the current information environment. Aside from these issues of representation and accuracy, institutions creating and dealing with image material should be very careful of legal issues surrounding digital image material, particularly copyright and rights management. Finally, issues of sustainability and longevity are becoming ever more important as institutions realize that digitization is not only about the creation of digital images: digital image corpora require maintenance and management if they are to survive after the duration of the digitization project itself.

Colour

One of the trickiest issues surrounding the production of digital image surrogates of analogue documents, objects and artefacts is the issue of colour accuracy in reproductions. Colour is a mathematically complex construct, and the diverse imaging devices used to capture, create and display image information, using different techniques to stimulate the human visual system, mean that it is a difficult issue to reconcile when creating digital images for both digital and analogue display. A variety of research has been undertaken into digital colour representation, and nowadays a variety of tools and procedures, including colour management software, regular and systematic calibration of equipment, and manual benchmarking of image quality can ensure that the images produced through digitization are valid and useful representations of the original item or document.

Human beings perceive colour when certain wavelengths of visible light (between 400 and 700 nanometres) strike the retina of their eyes. The human eye perceives shades of green and yellow in much more detail than blue and red frequencies of light (see Green 2006, 294). The appearance of colour to humans is affected by perceptual attributes, which can be absolute and measurable (brightness: where an area exhibits more or less light, usually measured in terms of percentage values from 0 to 100; hue, where an area matches a particular mix of red, yellow, green or blue on a colour wheel; and colourfulness, where an area exhibits more or less of a hue). Alternatively, perceived attributes of colour may be relative to other areas in the image (lightness: where an area is judged in relation to the brightness of another; chroma, where colourfulness is judged in proportion to another white or highly illuminated area of the image; and saturation, where the colourfulness is judged in proportion to brightness by establishing the extent to which a colour is a mixture of white). Perceived attributes of colour may be affected by various factors, including viewing conditions and medium. For example, light transmitted from a monitor is perceived differently from light reflected from paper, the accuracy of colour presented on monitors is highly dependent on the quality of the monitor itself, surrounding colours can impact on how specific colours in a part of an image are perceived, and the colour of ambient lighting (known as 'light temperature'), in either the capture or viewing process, affects the way colour is experienced in an image.

Colour is produced in digital display devices, such as television screens and monitors, from an additive palette of red, green and blue (RGB) emitted light. Different colours are created by varying the intensities of these three primary colours at nearby spots on the display (a very different way of handling colour compared to analogue film photography). A full mix of RGB is used to produce white, and altering the levels of intensity at a given spot can give a full 'gamut', the range of colours capable of being produced by a device, from white light to fully saturated colour. However, individual monitors may show colour differently, even when compared with another monitor of the same model from the same manufacturer, due to physical differences in the monitor's construction. Additionally, individual programs running on the same machine can display colour information from the same image very differently (commonly caused by the different ways in which specific programs use colour Look Up tables (see p. 65) or do not take into account colour profiles (see below)).

Printers produce colour differently from monitors and display devices, using the subtractive colours of cyan, magenta, yellow and black (CMYK) to produce a limited gamut of colours within a specific range (which differs from the range available on display devices). As a result, computer operating systems require colour management programs to assist in colour matching and conversion from one model of colour to another, such as from screen to print, but it is difficult for monitors and printers to reproduce each other's colours accurately and consistently. When switching from RGB to CMYK, colours are often dulled. Additionally, the type of ink, toner and wax used for printing varies from one manufacturer to another, producing different shades of colour, and combining with different types of paper in various ways to form other colours.

A related area to colour is the issue of gamma, or contrast, in digital images. Nearly all input and output media are limited in the range of lightness and darkness (or 'dynamic range') they can record or output. Additionally, different devices respond to variations in light intensity in different ways: scanners tend to respond in a linear fashion, where twice the brightness of a sampled pixel will yield a brightness value twice as large, but computer monitors have a non-linear response to the voltage sent: double the mathematical value of light intensity does not mean that it will display a pixel twice as brightly. Due to the difference in light intensity of the various elements in the digitization chain (for example, original contrast in the source painting; contrast of the colour photo of the painting; the gamma of the digital input device; the gamma of the monitor for display; and the gamma controls in the software) images that appear correct in one part of the chain may have mid-tones that are too bright or dark on another display device. Additionally, it is important to note the 'white balance' in images: adjustment of the relative colours and contrast values in an image based on areas of white and black, to ensure that neutral colours in an image are displayed correctly. Test shots are also important when creating digital images in the digitization process; digital cameras tend to burn out highlights very easily when creating images, and as with film, once an area in an image is overexposed, the detail is lost and no amount of gamma or white balance correcting can replace it.

Because of these issues with colour and light, it is difficult to reproduce identical colours on different systems or to accurately produce the same colours in print and display, and in some cases it is impossible. It is also difficult to know how images will be viewed by users and the effect that different systems will have on individual image colour:

> If such production steps as color matching present a certain level of complexity in themselves, the prospect of obtaining a consistent collection of images is greatly compounded in difficulty by the many potential junctures for losing control of how images look. Any time an image is captured, changed, or transferred to another system, medium, or device, the outcome may vary from the intended result. The industry is presently at the stage where no transition can be taken for granted (Ester 1996, 14).

Given that colour often imparts much information of importance in cultural and heritage objects and that providing accurate digital images of documents and objects is central to the usefulness of the digitization process, it is obvious that issues of colour and gamma management must be taken seriously by those creating, managing and delivering digital image material in memory institutions, and 'image digitisation should aim for accurate, repeatable, colour from the input phase through the display and to output' (Grout et al. 2000). Handling these problems is largely a matter of knowing the limitations and behaviour of a medium, and making proper adjustments to the data.

Colour management tools and procedures offer a solution for unambiguous exchange of colour information based on preservation of colour appearance. Originally developed for the reproduction of photographic materials on displays and printers, colour management has become increasingly important in digital environments offering 'a means of controlling colour from a source medium when reproduced on some other medium' with the goals of 'interoperability, consistency, and pleasing colour reproduction' (Green 2006, 11), aiming to accurately reproduce the original object when set viewing conditions are established, producing a recognizable, useful, digital surrogate.

Research into colour management has provided a variety of measures and tools which can aid projects in maintaining colour accuracy. Aside from the subjective, human experience of colour, colour can be measured mathematically by devices which can model the physical attributes of a coloured surface, recording brightness, hue and colourfulness, measuring an object in the same way that it would be viewed by an observer. Systems which mathematically represent colours are called colour models or colour spaces, which assign unique codes to each human perceivable colour. Many colour models exist, such as RGB for computer displays, CMYK for printing or YC_rC_b used in JPEG compression (see pp. 76–79). However, prior to 1995, every computer hardware vendor used their own set up for colour models, which were not standardized until the International Colour Consortium (www.color.org), founded in 1993, began to produce recommendations called 'colour profiles', which describe the colour attributes of a device or viewing environment and compute colour conversions between colour models and devices, allowing for sharing images between systems while maintaining the intended colours. Use of the ICC colour profiles was reasonably well understood by the mid-1990s, forming the basis of a colour management solution for digital workflow and is now an accepted part of digital imaging and colour reprographics.

There are many different ICC profiles in existence, but two which are common include Adobe 1998 (the standard colour profile used for producing images for professional print output, popular with photographers, laboratories and agencies) and sRGB (which has a smaller colour range than Adobe 1998 but is a recommended colour profile for digital display, such as for online graphics). At present, most personal computers are sRGB-based and the default setting for colour printers is sRGB. High end digital cameras can allow users to specify a colour profile to work with: sticking to the same colour profile for capture, processing and output can make dealing with colour accuracy less of a headache for digitization projects.

Most manual colour management procedures, and colour management software which facilitates the accurate reproduction of colour between devices and systems, operate on the basis of colour calibration. Calibration is the process of establishing an instrument's accuracy to known standards, to allow adjustment and correction which will enable the output of the instrument to be trusted. With regards to digitization, the technologies involved: cameras, scanners, monitors and printers; all require calibration to ensure that the outcome of the digitization process is predictable and repeatable. In particular, calibration of colour to a defined standard or profile is necessary to represent colour accurately. Although a time-consuming, and therefore costly, process:

> the effort of implementing this into the normal production cycle is worthwhile, however, as the benefits can quickly be seen. Printing, in particular, becomes a much easier task with less waste and more accurate results (Stevenson 2006, 85).

Calibration of equipment can be achieved by regular, systematic testing. The digitization environment itself can be set up in a specialized manner to meet severe requirements of calibration and workflow, for example, walls can be painted grey to reduce reflectance, fluorescent room lights can have a calibrated colour temperature and atmospheric dust can be kept to a minimum. In addition, the images created by digitization can be accurately reproduced on other, unknown, systems when they are calibrated to 'references' provided within the image itself which will aid users in accurately recreating optimal viewing conditions of the image.

A variety of ISO standards exist to aid in the objective assessment and calibration of monitors, scanners, cameras and the digitization environment as a whole. For example, the noise produced by still picture cameras can be assessed by ISO 15739. The dynamic range of film scanners can be assessed using ISO 21550. The viewing conditions on monitors may be calibrated through use of ISO 3663, 'Viewing Conditions for Graphic Technology and Photography' which provides specifications regarding exactly how monitors and viewing stations should be set up to allow accurate viewing of images when the access to the original for comparison is not possible. ISO 12646 'Graphic Technology – Displays for Colour Proofing – Characteristics and Viewing Conditions', a later specification which complements ISO 3663, provides specific monitor set up when 'soft proofing' – comparing originals with their digital image surrogates (see also benchmarking, below). A list of useful, objective, standard test methods and a discussion of their application, and a recommended approach, can be found in NARA (2004, 24–28).

One of the most common ISO colour management standards (although most people don't realize it is actually an official standard) is known as IT8, which covers a set of standards produced from 1993 onwards that controls colour specifications and aids in calibration. The set of IT8 standards define input test targets: a reflective standard reference consisting of colour bars and greyscales which contains a number of uniform colour patches, to be photographed under the same environmental conditions as the item being captured. The IT8 7.1 is designed, in particular, to aid in colour management between photographic film and scanners, while IT8 7.2 is designed for photographic paper and scanners and IT8 7.3 is designed to enable colour management between input data and the CMYK printing process. These reference charts are produced by a variety of manufacturers, such as Kodak, Alfa, Fuji Film and Wolf Faust. In addition to the IT8 standards, the Macbeth ColorChecker and Gretag Macbeth DC charts are also available, being particularly suited to profiling the use of colour in digital cameras.

Particular reference charts have even been developed for managing colour when photographing stained glass windows (Macdonald et al. 2006, 417–418).

To aid in colour reproduction and management, these standard reference charts should be included in images of digitized material, to create images that can be displayed and printed with accurate colour representation anywhere. After calibration, software can be used to determine the relationship between the ideal measurements of the target and the actual RGB camera or scanner data captured, mapping the characteristics of each device into and out of a standard colour space. Establishing and sustaining a fully calibrated image chain that enables the colour management of digital images created in photo studios to be passed down through a series of 'digital handshakes' to the digital display or printing press is important for maintaining and ensuring image quality.

Additionally, computer monitors should be regularly calibrated (usually monthly and every time the equipment is moved) to ensure that those working with digital images are viewing them under correct colour and lighting conditions. There are various colour calibration software tools for monitors available. The simplest are software-based solutions, such as Adobe Gamma (which comes installed with PhotoShop, www.adobe.com/support/photoshop/) and Apple ColorSync (for Apple Macintosh, www.apple.com/pro/techniques/colorsync/), which create an ICC profile for the individual monitor and can be used to compensate for a monitor's colour display limitations, making adjustments and displaying a consistent result. There are also more complex software and hardware solutions, which use colour correction software in conjunction with a hardware calibrator that fixes onto the monitor, which are more accurate as they measure colour performance in detail. Commonly used packages include those from Colorvision's Spyder range (www.datacolor.eu/en/products/monitor-calibration/) and Gretag Macbeth's EyeOne range (http://usa.gretagmacbethstore.com/). Although more expensive than software solutions, they are worthwhile investments for a digitization project.

Once a monitor is calibrated, and as long as calibration has been used throughout the digitization chain, projects can be confident that the same colour reproduction will be available to any users with a similarly calibrated monitor. Of course, most home computer monitors have never been calibrated, and it is unlikely that they will be: digitization projects can seldom control the user environment in which images are viewed, only providing guidance and instilling best practice in capture to allow individual users who are dependent on accurate colour reproduction to experience it provided they take the time to set up their own work stations correctly. It is here, again, that documentation of the digitization process and the production of technical and managerial metadata (see Chapter 7) are key.

It would seem, then, that although not an exact science, it is understood that colour management is essential to the digitization process, and there are basic procedures that can be undertaken to ensure colour reproduction is as accurate as possible. There are further points which should be noted with regards to colour management in the library, archive, cultural and heritage sector. Because of the various issues presented with colour reproduction, the best quality digital images come from digitizing directly form the source, rather than digitizing from available surrogates, such as transparencies or photographs. Problems can arise with focus and the calibration of true colour if using a surrogate: in effect this is taking a copy of a copy. Although many early digitization projects used already available analogue surrogates as an intermediary to the creation of digital images of documents or artefacts, it is now recommended that the original be used as the digitization source to ensure accurate colour reproduction.

Although it is ideal to include the colour reference target in every digital image created in a digitization project, this tends to create large individual images, simply due to the surface area of the target which needs to be captured in addition to the actual document or artefact. Over the duration of an entire project, which may be digitizing hundreds, if not thousands, of documents, this may add substantial costs to storage and maintenance of the image collection. A workaround for this is to scan or photograph a colour reference target at the start of each digitization session – for example, every day, or when the digitization set up is adjusted – and to refer to the image of the reference target in the metadata of the digitized output. Obviously, this is not as ideal as including the reference in each individual image, but is a suitable compromise for projects with budgetary constraints.

Image Quality

Assessing the quality of images produced by the digitization process is a major issue in digitization projects. Ideally, the digital images produced should be consistently and reliably of the best quality possible. How to actually perceive, understand, measure and benchmark digital image quality is an ongoing topic of research.

Quality can be defined as a sense of fitness for purpose. In the case of images, quality can be assessed by considering how effective the image is in communicating its intended purpose or message to the viewer. An image of poor quality may degrade the effectiveness of communication, but what message that image was to portray can only be decided by the creator and deciphered by the user:

> the meaning of the communication, and the criteria by which its quality should be judged, can only be understood in the context of the intentions of the originator and the needs of the receiver. These may include purposes as diverse as entertainment, advertising, information, education, politics, etc (MacDonald and Jacobsen 2006, 353).

In the case of images created in the digitization process:

> in order to function as intended, digitised surrogates must instil their prospective end-users with the same confidence as (or greater than) earlier forms. This means that the surrogates must prove to be consistently faithful and authentic to the original, having

> captured details in ways that lend confidence to those who would employ the surrogate as they would an original. The digital capture process must be undistorted and reliable (Grycz 2006, 35).

Quality, therefore, can be judged by how accurately the digital image reflects the original artefact it represents, and the relationship of the surrogate to the original. The visual presentation of an image may be affected by its viewing environment (how the observer sees the image, including issues such as lighting and viewing geometry); the medium or device on which the digital image is displayed (issues such as resolution, colour reproduction, colour representation and brightness); characteristics of the image itself (such as tone, sharpness, noise, contrast and identifying technical faults such as moiré patterns[1] and chromatic aberration[2]); and finally the content of the image itself (the composition, stylistic treatment and subject matter, which may be interpreted for meaning) (MacDonald and Jacobsen 2006, 354). Issues of fidelity, usefulness and the perceived quality of the representation can also be used to model image quality (ibid.). As a result, the consistency and accuracy of the image data should be compared with the original photograph or objects, checked for technical errors, optimized for different viewing environments and printed for colour proofing to enable double-checking of colour reproduction.

There are many issues regarding fidelity and representation which are encountered when digitizing collections, not all of which are focused on the technical aspects of the image (such as sharpness and tonal-range). The production of two-dimensional, flat images of often complex, three-dimensional artefacts, can mean it can be difficult to perceive the relative size of objects in their intended environment. Maintaining colour authenticity is problematic (see above). Many art and historical objects were created so that viewers could interact with them from a variety of distances and angles, while the viewer of digital surrogates are often restricted to the static views captured, stored and delivered by the digitization project (the number of images taken of each object may be determined by issues of cost and workflow). Viewing an image of an object, document or artefact can be a very different experience from physically encountering the original and projects have to be careful to frame the objects accordingly, to maintain contextual information. Although there are technical aspects to ascertaining image quality,

1 Many images in books, magazines and articles are printed using a pattern of dots. When scanned or digitally photographed, this pattern can interfere with the arrangement of pixels on the sensor, leading to the creation of visible 'Moiré' patterns in the resulting image, such as wavy lines and false colours.

2 Chromatic Aberration is a lens issue, caused by different wavelengths of light focusing at different distances from the lens, which occurs in both digital and analogue photography. Out of focus subjects in the image can have colour haloes (also known as colour fringing or ghosting).

projects also have to be aware of the wider issues created when presenting digital images to users.

A technique called 'benchmarking' can be used to provide a careful assessment of originals and their digital surrogates to ensure that the attributes of the source material (such as: organization and presentation; size and dimension; detail, tone and colour; and age and condition) are conveyed in the digital reproductions (Chapman 2000, 35). Benchmarks are usually set at the start of digitization projects, where standards of digitization (such as resolution, colour reproduction, etc.) are instigated. Benchmarking then becomes part of the established workflow to ensure that resulting images meet project aims and requirements, and can be viewed as 'a systematic procedure for forecasting a likely outcome' (Kenney and Chapman 1996, iv). The aim of benchmarking is to ensure faithful digital reproductions:

> digital objects that are optimally formatted and described with a view to their *quality* (functionality and use value), *persistence* (long-term access), and *interoperability* (e.g. across platforms and software environments) (Digital Library Federation 2002).

Maintaining quality in digital surrogates is one of the main aims of benchmarking. Image quality can be assessed for single images in isolation or for test images in comparison to a reference image or set of determined criteria, by either human observation, measurement of various attributes or automated computation. Users can also be integrated into the quality assurance workflow, to ensure that their needs have been met within the digitization process (this is especially the case if the images are being created to divert use away from originals towards digital surrogates as a means of preventing handling of fragile or deteriorating documents. The images created would have to be of high enough quality to persuade users that they no longer needed to access the original).

However, although much reference is made to the need for benchmarking, the maintenance of image quality and the integration of benchmarking into digitization project workflow (Hughes 2004, 166), 'ultimately, a human observer must make the visual judgement of whether an image is of acceptable quality' (MacDonald and Jacobsen 2006, 360) and:

> it is still necessary to have knowledgeable and experienced staff to evaluate images visually. At this time, it is not possible to rely entirely on the objective test measurements to ensure optimum image quality. It is still necessary to have staff with the visual literacy and technical expertise to do a good job with digitization and to perform quality control for digital images. This is true for the digitization of all types of archival records, but very critical for the digitization of photographic images (NARA 2004, 25).

Accurate and useful benchmarking and quality assessment is dependent on skilled digitization staff and is limited to the expertise, experience, attention span, mood and even physiological characteristics of the operators undertaking checks against established aims and outcomes: obviously, those undertaking benchmarking should have good eyesight (with or without aids to vision), but less obviously, staff should be checked for colour blindness (which affects around 8 per cent of men, and 0.4 per cent of women, see Birch 2001, 33). Documentation of the benchmarking process should be provided in image or collection metadata (see Chapter 7) to indicate to users that aspects of quality control have been given careful attention in the digitization process.

It should be noted, however, that although ascertaining and maintaining the quality of digital images is not an exact science, our understanding of procedures and techniques to maintain image quality are more sophisticated in the digital realm than they ever were with analogue photography. Film is not an accurate representation of the real world any more than digital is; in both cases a surrogate is produced, but the tools and processes available for checking digital images far exceed the means by which analogue photographs could be benchmarked. A properly managed digital colour and quality workflow can results in improved images above the reproduction capable of traditional film-based imaging: 'image quality, particularly in terms of colour accuracy and dynamic range, were significantly improved over the previous film based process' Hamber (2006, 145). The National Gallery, London, has been taking photographic images of its holdings for curatorial and record keeping purposes from the early twentieth century. Those working in the photographic department have noted that the recent switch to digital photography in the late to mid-1990s has also enabled them to produce consistent high quality images, as the digital imaging technologies allow a range of checks (such as those used to establish colour accuracy) to be undertaken which were not possible with analogue film (White 2007).

Truth and the Digital Image

It has been said that the digital image is 'predicated on fabrication, which can come from a multitude of sources. This changes the role of the photographer from that of a witness to that of an information designer' (Hirsch and Valentino 2001, 218). Some photographic images, taken by a camera, are clearly descended from their analogue ancestors: producing a likeness of something that has a physical presence, through lens and capture-based technology (although distortion of the real world can occur through lens shape and lighting). Others are drawn, or rendered, by computer and are 'digital born': allowing every possible variation and combination of colour, shape and light available, although they may look real to the uninitiated. After creation, computers can be used to affect changes in images which they were not involved in producing.

Early computer-based algorithms developed to process and refine digital images were designed to remove artefacts from photographs, and improve them for human analysis as well as to analyse them automatically (see pp. 21–22). The increasing sophistication and speed of modern computers means that images can now be successfully manipulated on the majority of home computers. In minor cases, this results in the retouching or airbrushing, of simple aspects in images. More worryingly, it facilitates the construction of images of events which never happened, meetings of people which never existed, and allows the removal of unwanted or unwelcome objects and individuals. We have already seen that images are powerful, and that maintaining image accuracy is crucial: manipulated images, whether intentional or accidental, change our understanding of reality and influence our cultural perception.

In some sense this is nothing new. The defacing or erasing of historical personages, documents, artefacts and architecture is well attested: if you control the image, you control the ideology and the information passed on to the viewer. Classical and medieval documents were scraped clean to allow reuse of scarce resources, sculptures in temples and churches defaced to destroy representations of gods to prevent them being viewed by future generations and bodies mutilated on the battlefield to prevent identification (see Dillon 2006 for an overview of the *Revelation of Erasure*). Although the homily 'the camera never lies' is often repeated, photographic and especially digital images, are very easy to manipulate, raising issues of trust, verification and ethics when using them for proof, research or evidence of any kind.

The issue of the relationship between photography and truth, and the outright manipulation of the photographic image, can be traced back to the work of one of the earliest photographers. Hippolyte Bayard's *Self-Portrait of a Drowned Man* (1840) presents the audience with a record of his apparent suicide: a metaphor for his lack of recognition for his photographic discoveries, as the French authorities failed to acknowledge that his own discovery of the photographic process was equal to Daguerre's pioneering work (Sapir 1994). Photographic manipulation became relatively common in the Victorian era: a close-up photographic portrait of Lillie Langtry (1853–1929, society beauty, actress and mistress of Queen Victoria's son Albert Edward (Edward VII)), taken in 1890 by W & D Downey, shows significant retouching to reduce her waist to waspish proportions (Science and Society Picture Library 2004).

Image manipulation was common in advertising during the twentieth century, ranging from brightening colours, to airbrushing, retouching, inserting or deleting information that was never in the original image. The difference with traditional versus digital image manipulation is that it has become so much *easier*, and does not require specialist expertise or expensive technology: image manipulation is achievable on even the most basic of desktop computers. Some manipulated images seem plausible, yet are deceptive, others are obviously faked. Done well, manipulated images are indistinguishable from reality and there is no way of knowing from a digital image whether or not the content has been fabricated. Although the technology behind manipulating images may have changed, the focus often remains depressingly the same: images of the actress Kate Winslet taken to advertise the February 2003 issue of the men's magazine *GQ* were digitally retouched to reduce her thighs by a third (the image is available at DiscoverKate.

com (2003) should you feel the need to see it. Reassuringly, this was accompanied by a media outcry (The Telegraph 2003)). However, in 2006 Hewlett Packard launched a digital camera feature that applied a ‘slimming effect’ to any object in the centre of a picture (‘a subtle effect that can instantly trim off pounds from the subjects in your photos!’ Hewlett Packard 2006). Software exists which is designed to tweak facial images in the direction of the beautiful average face, rejigging the contours of faces to make them more attractive (Anthropics 2006). When images of our own selves are so malleable, what effect does this have on our trust of digital images?

> If it can be assumed that the credibility of photography has rested traditionally on a knowledge of its mechanical rather than manual mode of operation, what will be the ‘truth’ status of images that look convincingly photographic but have actually been constituted from multiple digitised elements and subjected to re-workings by an operator? .. In this sense [digital imaging] reverses the history of imaging technologies and takes photography back to the ontology of the infinitely manipulable medium of painting (Willis 1990, 200–201).

The ethical issues regarding digital image manipulation first came to public attention in February 1982, when Gordon Gahen at National Geographic magazine, long known for its reputation of photojournalism excellence, used expensive digital manipulation software to reposition one of the Great Pyramids at Giza to make a horizontal image fit its vertical cover format. The editors claimed they did not intend to alter the underlying meaning of the subject but their failure to acknowledge that the image had been reworked upset readers who trusted that the National Geographic would deliver accurate photographs. Tom Kennedy, who became the director of photography at *National Geographic* after the manipulated covers were used, said:

> We no longer use that technology to manipulate elements in a photo simply to achieve a more compelling graphic effect. We regarded that afterwards as a mistake, and we wouldn’t repeat that mistake today (personal interview with Carla Hotvedt (1990) cited in Lester 1999, Chapter Six).

The ethics of digital image manipulation are important: ‘The threat to credibility is irreversible if the public starts to mistrust the integrity of the news photograph’ (Lester 1999, Chapter Six). In 1995, The National Press Photographer’s Association added to their Code of Ethics a clause to regulate digital image manipulation:

> It is clear that the emerging electronic technologies provide new challenges to the integrity of photographic images ... in light of this, we … reaffirm the basis of our ethics: Accurate representation is the benchmark of our profession. We believe photojournalistic guidelines for fair and accurate reporting should be the criteria for

> judging what may be done electronically to a photograph. Altering the editorial content ... is a breach of ... ethical standards (NPPA 1995).

Unfortunately, it is becoming even more of a problem:

> The list can go on for pages: NEWSWEEK straightened the teeth of Bobbi McCaughey, the mother of the sextuplets; NEWSDAY ran a photo supposedly showing Nancy Kerrigan and Tonya Harding skating together a day before the event really happened; PEOPLE ran a photo of famous breast cancer survivors made from five separate negatives; The St. Louis Post Dispatch removed a Coke can from a photo of their Pulitzer Prize winner. This just scratches the surface. How many cases have not become known? The cumulative effect is the gradual erosion of the credibility of an entire profession ... We are being bombarded from all sides, from movies, television, advertisements, the Internet, with images that are not real, that are created in computers (Long 1999).

Is this really an issue for the information professional? There is, of course, a difference between images which have been deliberately manipulated to change the information presented to the user and those in which changes happen as part of the production process, perhaps in the resizing, changing of formats or compression (see Chapter 3). Nevertheless, digital images used for pedagogical or research purposes should come with clear provenance and technical and managerial metadata (see Chapter 7) to ensure that the information they display can be trusted. In the field of medical imaging, for example, it is important to retain as accurate a representation of the original as possible. Would you be happy with the use of a medical scan which was only an approximate image as a basis for surgery? The same is true for images which form the basis of expert research. If you were an expert on ancient documents, where the slightest change in marking on the surface of a text can mean the difference between commonly confused words which can give entirely different parses to the same sentence, would you be happy with an approximate representation of a disputed document or would you want the best image possible?

A recent dissertation investigating use and perception of images of digitized medieval manuscript collections highlighted concern over the authority and provenance of digital images: while undergraduate students preferred using digital images to the bother of consulting the originals, postgraduate research students and academics would not base research upon digital images of original manuscripts unless they had been involved in the digitization project themselves and could be sure of the quality of the images they were consulting (Tawse 2003). Findings of the Log Analysis of Internet Resources in the Arts and Humanities (www.ucl.ac.uk/slais/LAIRAH/) project also highlighted that without adequate metadata and technical information, academic researchers in the arts and humanities did not trust online images of artefacts or documents (Warwick et al. 2008). Willis, writing in 1990, predicts a future where digital images cannot be trusted at all, when the photographic medium implodes:

> The archive and history become ruptured. Pictures from the past can no longer be assumed to be a transparent record of the past. An accumulation of imagery travels forward in time as potential raw material for the continual re-invention of history in the present. Conversely it travels backwards as evidence of the archaeology of the technology, thus particular genres, styles, techniques become reference points for photography's own past (206).

If the information profession wishes to ensure the longevity and veracity of digital images, it surely has to engage with such concerns, and be educated in the technological and information infrastructure which underpin the digital imaging medium.

Copyright and Copyright Control

Copyright is the legal right of an author, publisher, individual or institution, to retain ownership of an idea or information and control the production, sale, distribution of reproductions, or derivatives, of the original. Although there are economic grounds for this, there are also moral reasons: original creations should be protected from exploitation from anyone other than the creator.

Understanding, maintaining and exercising copyright rights is a complex activity. In particular, recent advances in the digital information environment do not sit comfortably with established copyright laws and procedures. The fundamental aspects of digital images which make them so attractive to both individuals and institutions pose problems when it comes to copyright:

> The ease with which digital material can be reproduced, disseminated, manipulated, interacted with, stored and compressed at virtually no cost challenge the very concepts at the heart of copyright. This results in a digital landscape where content is very easy to find, but any use of it is restricted within the context of the copyright legislation. Although the copyright legislation is extremely thorough and comprehensive, there are a number of reasons why copyright, as applied to digital images, is neither black nor white and is, more often than not, various shades of grey (TASI 2006f).

Copyright law is highly localized from one country to the next, while the global information environment encourages worldwide use. The legal framework cannot keep up with the pace of technological development. Copyright laws are also full of undefined terms (such as 'original', 'substantial', and 'reasonable'), and case law frequently changes the way legal Acts are understood and applied to changing media. It can be very complicated to manage and clear copyright for items destined for online display, and in the case of digital images, the full impact of copyright law on picture libraries, digitization programs and individual photographers is unclear.

Information professionals often have a duty to care for, and allow access to, other people's works which are in copyright. Additionally, those creating digital image archives will be creating images and databases, each of which have their own copyright considerations, and institutions and individuals will have to consider asserting their own copyright on intellectual effort and the creation of original digital resources. However, the copyright status of images created by the digitization process is uncertain:

> Generally speaking, it is held that if the work is digitized using a scanner and there is no human intervention (like a photocopy), then there is unlikely to be any new copyright created. So a mere scanned copy may not be protected by copyright, but an image that has had a lot of work done on it to enhance its appearance, correct the text, or change the colouring probably will be protected ... But even if they are not [enhanced] ... the actual collection of images may qualify for database right (sic) if they are organized in a systematic and methodical way (Cornish 2004, 7).

It is necessary, and prudent, for institutions dealing in images of copyrighted material, or producing work under their own copyright, to undertake legal advice on the status of their digitized collections and develop a digital knowledge management strategy to ensure they are not compromising the copyright of others, while safeguarding their own rights.

> Protecting and managing copyright, and avoiding infringement, is ultimately more a question of risk management than it is of the law ... Risk management will require considering the benefits of digitisation (wider access, preservation, greater availability of the materials for research) against the potential risks of infringing copyright – and putting materials on the internet makes it that much more likely that the infringement will be discovered ... Where possible, discussing these factors with legal counsel at the outset of a project may help to develop an approach to copyright management that might mitigate any problems throughout the course of a project. Ultimately, certain decisions (such as negotiating with rights holders, or deciding whether or not fees can be paid) will often be made by an institution's legal counsel, who will have the final say in assessing the impact of risk, and deciding how risk averse a project – and the institution – can afford to be (Hughes 2004, 76–78).

Advice should also be taken on other legal issues, such as of publicity (associated with public figures, and the use of likenesses of a well-known person); privacy (designed to protect individuals from intrusion and public disclosure of private information); data protection (regulating the use of information that can identify an individual); and the use of images which may be sensitive, obscene or defamatory (Hughes 2004, 68–71).

An alternative approach to issues of copyright, in the case of asserting copyright for original images and information items, is to look towards the Creative Commons, which is becoming an increasingly popular route for individuals and institutions who wish to assert exactly how the information objects that they are placing online may be used, copied, disseminated and re-appropriated by others. The Creative Commons, a non-profit organization founded in 2001 (http://creativecommons.org/), aims to provide tools for authors and creators which enable copyright holders to grant some or all of their rights to the general public, while withholding others, providing a variety of free licenses which authors can use when releasing their content via the Internet. These licenses can determine how and where content can be used, and if they can be used for profit or commercial gain. Since its launch, the Creative Commons has proved popular: at time of writing there are approximately 60 million digital images licensed with Creative Commons on Flickr (Creative Commons 2008). The use of Creative Commons' licenses is not limited to individuals, as institutions also appreciate the benefits the range of licenses present. Recently, the Wellcome Trust (http://images.wellcome.ac.uk/) made 100,000 digital images from its collection of scientific, research and historical images of '2000 years of Human Culture' available under a non-commercial Creative Commons license, allowing users to download, copy and display JPEG images from their collection, as long as they are used in a non-commercial environment, not altered in any way, and attributed to the Wellcome Trust. Other institutions and initiatives, such as Tufts University Open Courseware (http://ocw.tufts.edu/) and Carnegie Mellon's Open Learning Initiative (www.cmu.edu/oli/) are adopting Creative Commons licenses for the distribution of image, text and other pedagogical material. The control and options offered by the Creative Commons licenses are attractive to both individuals and institutions alike.

This open approach to the delivery of online material can be compared with concerns which dominated early digitization projects: if image material was made freely available online, would this increase the chances of illicit republishing of these materials, where counterfeiters could make a profit from unofficial coffee-table books, greetings cards, tea towels and other unauthorized merchandize? Technical approaches to safeguarding copyright, such as the inclusion of either visible or invisible watermarks, were popular in the late to mid-1990s. Logos, messages or information about how and where the image was accessed were included in the digital image (using a process called digital steganography, literally 'covered writing' in Greek), allowing the image to be traced back to its original source and defacing the image suitably to prevent exploitation:

> A visible watermark can act as an advertisement or as a restriction. For example, you might be willing to give away low-resolution, visibly watermarked images for free, but wish to provide high-resolution unmarked versions of the same images for a fee. Even if the free copies were of the same resolution as the priced ones, the visible watermark can dissuade end-users from improperly misusing them (Mintzner et al. 1997).

The early digitization projects undertaken by the Vatican Library, in conjunction with IBM, used very visible image watermarking (ibid.). The Scottish Cultural

Resources Access Network (SCRAN: www.scran.ac.uk), a nationwide project to digitize the material culture and human history of Scotland, chose to include both visible and invisible watermarking to safeguard their image material:

> [an image is] protected by an invisible 'watermark' (to confirm the resource's copyright status) and 'fingerprint' (to identify who downloaded it and when). To avoid any accusations of 'entrapment', this information is also clearly shown in banners at the top and bottom of the downloaded image (Royan 2000).

However, the inclusion of such watermarks, particularly large, visible, logos, can visibly disrupt the image, threatening its integrity (as pixels are replaced by pixels from the logo), compromising resource quality and preventing users from undertaking valid, useful, advanced research with the image. The images presented in the Mintzner et al. (1997) article as 'good' examples of successful watermarking technology are testament to this. As a result, the use of watermarking has fallen out of favour, and it is now acknowledged that the provision of low resolution, highly compressed JPEG images (see pp. 76–81) or small thumbnail images of digitized holdings, is enough to limit unauthorized repurposing of digital image material, as the quality of image is not high enough to enable professional print-based reproduction. Of course, usable images can still be copied and distributed electronically, but the benefits of providing useful, usable images to researchers and general users far outweighs problems of image integrity and the cost of implementation associated with watermarking technologies.

Access to digital images can also be managed or restricted to prevent unauthorized or unlimited use of materials. Simple methods, such as only allowing users to log on from particular, designated computers within an institution, or from computers with a university or library IP address, can restrict access to those with bona fide reasons for accessing research collections. Likewise, online photo sharing and social networking sites, such as Flickr and Facebook, can allow those uploading digital images to specify groups of users, and limit access to certain images and certain sizes of images. For more advanced control over access, Image Management Systems (IMS, see p. 171) provide facilities for electronic rights management (also known as digital rights management), such as the control of passwords and usernames, managing any subscription payments and different levels of subscription. More contentious facilities available in some IMS (and related digital rights management systems for other types of media) include limiting the number of times images can be accessed, controlling how many times a file may be accessed, opened, copied and printed, and limiting where and how the file may be stored.

Strict Digital Rights Management (DRM) systems have many opponents. Although there are many who advocate the creator's right to prevent unauthorized use of their works, many objectors such as the Free Software Foundation (www.fsf.org) or the Electronic Frontier Foundation (www.eff.org) argue that DRM is often used to attempt to restrict the use of copyrighted material in ways which are not actually covered by the current legal framework (Becker et al. 2003). The use of DRM control is much more prevalent in systems which control access to digital music, film and television than in institutions which primarily provide digital image data to the end user: although institutions should consider issues of access, restriction and control it is unlikely that the digital images created would hold as much interest to counterfeiters as other commercially produced media, and a balance has to be struck between restricting and facilitating access to information and cultural heritage materials.

Sustainability of Collections

A major topic of concern, already covered more fully in Chapter 5, is the issue of sustainability of digital image collections. As with any digital collection, leaving collections of digital images without maintenance and care will mean that access to and use of the collection will become rapidly compromised. This should be of utmost concern to memory institutions undertaking digitization projects, as it is rare that funding is secured to maintain and upkeep a digital collection after project funding ceases. Indeed, many funding bodies, such as the UK's Joint Information System's Committee now insist that, as a requirement of the funding process, institutions will undertake to maintain access to digital projects for a period of up to ten years after the project's end, ensuring that any digitized output will remain available to scholars and the public well after any funding stream has ceased. The maintenance and care of digital collections is time-consuming and costly. Obviously, making any promises to upkeep digital collections requires institutional support and funding, and applicants have to demonstrate that resources are available to ensure sustainability of and access to digital collections.

Other Issues

This chapter has focused on current issues pertinent to those working in professional information environments, such as the production of accurate representations of original documents, objects or artefacts, and the awareness of legal issues such as copyright. Of course, recent changes in the information environment and digital imaging technology have resulted in other issues, some of which have been mentioned or alluded to throughout the book, such as: the proliferation of digital image information and resulting impact on storing and finding image content; the impact the growth of digital imaging has on traditional photographic practice and industry; our changing relationship with images due to the differences afforded by the new capture and networking technologies; the impact digital image technology has had on the modern art sector and creative industries; the changing role of photographic images within our society; the immediacy of digital imaging technologies versus the historicizing nature of analogue photographic technologies;

and so on. Technical issues such as the creation of noise by the sensor in digital imaging, issues in determining the authenticity of digital images and the differing qualities of digital images to film, such as the different treatment of colour and different sensitivities to light, should also be noted. Finally, the expense caused by the regular need to upgrade computing equipment, capture equipment and software when using digital imaging technologies should not be overlooked.

Conclusion

Digital imaging technologies may have seemed to have sprung like Athena, fully formed, from traditional film photography and personal computing technologies in the closing stages of the twentieth century, but the technical, practical, social and theoretical issues which continue to emerge suggest that this is a technology still in development, raising many issues for those handling, storing or facilitating access to images in today's society.

The aim of this text has been to explain the historical background, technical implementation and use of digital imaging technologies, with particular reference to use in and issues concerning the information and cultural and heritage sectors. By understanding and embracing the technological shift in the production of image-based material in modern society, those in the information profession are best placed to create, maintain and deliver high quality image materials in this evolving information environment.

Further Reading

Graham (2005) gives a detailed, though mathematically thorough, introduction to the use of colour in digital imaging. Thorell and Smith (1990) address both practical and theoretical issues when *Using Computer Color Effectively* in an illustrated reference guide. Brown and Shepherd (1995, Chapter 6) give an introduction to colour theory with regard to digital images. Green (2006) provides a useful overview which specifically focuses on the issue of *Colour Management in Heritage Photography*, including a introduction on human colour vision, colorimetry and the characteristics of display devices, before considering the methods and techniques that can be used to ensure accurate colour reproduction.

The National Archives and Records Administration (NARA 2004) provides an excellent, useful overview of how to calibrate a digitization environment and its related technology, providing clear and usable workflows to aid those in setting up their own digitization studio or centre in ensuring the images they capture will be of high quality. Likewise, the Library of Congress guidelines on digitization contain a section on calibration of the digitization environment (2007). MacDonald and Jacobsen (2006) provide a thorough overview of image quality assessment, including technical factors such as tone, sharpness, noise and colour, and image quality metrics.

Lester (1999) and Mitchell (1992) are essential reading for those wishing to know more about the ethics of image manipulation; Willis (1990) is strong on theoretical implications (if technologically rather dated now). Russ (2001) discusses the technical and legal issues regarding the use of digital images as forensic evidence, particularly in court cases. Lipkin (2005) explores the extent to which modern artists are utilizing digital imaging, investigating, in particular, the manipulation of digital images to create photorealistic artworks, and the ethical and artistic concerns this raises.

Cornish (2004) provides an overview of copyright law in the UK, incorporating recent changes in EU law and the consequences this has for the information worker, including recent issues such as electronic rights management and digitization programmes. Norman (2004) is another, readable, general text: Wienand et al. (2000) provide a guide particularly for Museums and Galleries; Padfield's text (2007) is focused on archivists and records managers. TASI (2006f) provides a thorough overview of copyright and digital images, also providing further copyright guides specifically for staff building digital image collections (2006g), and the issue of copyright when using digital images in teaching and research (2006h). Hughes (2004, 53–78) fully explores 'Intellectual property, copyright and other legal issues' with regard to digitization projects. Becker et al. (2003) provides a thorough overview on issues of digital rights management.

Bibliography

Aasbø, K., Ortega García, I., Isomursu, A., Johansson, T. and Klijn, E. (ed.) (2003) 'SEPIADES. Recommendations for cataloguing photographic collections'. European Commission on Preservation and Access, Amsterdam. Accessed 3 March 2008 (www.knaw.nl/ECPA/sepia/workinggroups/wp5/sepiadestool/sepiadesdef.pdf).

Adobe (1992) 'TIFF Revision 6.0. Final' (published online June 3 1992). Accessed 12 April 2007 (http://partners.adobe.com/public/developer/en/tiff/TIFF6.pdf).

Adobe (2004) 'Postscript Turns 20' (published online 2004) Adobe Systems Incorporated. Accessed 15 April 2007 (www.adobe.com/products/postscript/pdfs/postscript_is_20.pdf).

Adobe (2006) 'PDF Reference, Sixth Edition, Version 1.7'. (website, published November 2006) Adobe Systems Incorporated. Accessed 14 April 2007 (www.adobe.com/devnet/acrobat/pdfs/pdf_reference.pdf).

Adobe (2007a) 'Digital Negative (DNG): The public, archival format for digital camera raw data' (website, updated 2007) Adobe Systems Incorporated. Accessed 17 May 2007 (www.adobe.com/products/dng/).

Adobe (2007b) 'Adobe PDF Technology Center, PDF Reference' (website, updated 2007) Adobe Systems Incorporated. Accessed 20 May 2007 (www.adobe.com/devnet/pdf/pdf_reference.html).

Adobe (2007c) 'Create Adobe PDF Online: Convert a File to PDF, Image formats', Adobe Systems Incorporated. Accessed 20 May 2007 (http://createpdf.adobe.com/cgi feeder.pl/formats?BP=&LOC=en_US).

Advanced Imaging Magazine (1991) 'Shuttle mission turns to hands on imaging and image processing', November 1991, 6(11) p. 8.

Aitkenhead, D. (2007) 'Reaching for the stars'. The Guardian Weekend, *The Guardian*, 15 December 2007, pp. 20–33. Accessed 24 February 2008 (www.guardian.co.uk/weekend/story/0,,2226725,00.html).

All the Year Round (1894) 'The Industrial Development of Electricity', 6 October, p. 330.

Anderson, P. (2007) *What is Web 2.0? Ideas, technologies and implications for education*, JISC Technology and Standards Watch, Joint Information Systems Committee. Accessed 3 February 2008 (www.jisc.ac.uk/media/documents/techwatch/tsw0701b.pdf).

Anderson, S., Pringle, M., Eadie, M., Austin, T., Wilson, A. and Polfreman, M. (2006) *Digital Images Archiving Study*, JISC Archiving Study Final Report, Arts and Humanities Data Service. Accessed 4 May 2007 (http://ahds.ac.uk/about/projects/archiving-studies/digital-images-archiving-study.pdf).

Andrews, P., Butler, Y. and Farace, J. (2006) *RAW Workflow, from Capture to Archives. A Complete Digital Photographer's Guide to Raw Imaging.* Oxford: Focal Press.

Andrews, T.J., Halpern, S.D. and Purves, D. (1997) 'Correlated size variations in human visual cortex, lateral geniculate nucleus and optic tract', *Journal of Neuroscience*, 17(6) pp. 2859–66.

Ang, T. (2005) 'Seeing the big picture', The Technology Guardian, *The Guardian*, 24 November 2005, p. 1.

Anthropics (2006) 'Enhance your digital portraits using portrait professional' (website). Accessed 9 January 2007 (www.portraitprofessional.com).

Apple Incorporated (1996) 'About Pictures'. Inside Macintosh: Imaging With QuickDraw. Chapter 7 – Pictures. Accessed 12 May 2007 (http://developer.apple.com/documentation/mac/QuickDraw/QuickDraw-332.html).

Aristotle (n.d.) *De Anima*, translated by J.A. Smith (1931). Oxford: Clarendon Press.

Arts and Humanities Data Service (AHDS) (2005) 'About the Arts and Humanities Data Service' (website, published 16 December 2005). Accessed 27 March 2008 (http://ahds.ac.uk/about/index.htm).

Arts and Humanities Data Service (AHDS) (2006) 'AHDS Timeline'. Accessed 27 March 2008 (http://ahds.ac.uk/about/ahds-timeline.htm).

Arts and Humanities Research Council (AHRC) (2007a) 'Review Activities' (website, updated 12 April 2007) ICT in Arts and Humanities Research. Accessed 13 March 2008 (www.ahrcict.rdg.ac.uk/activities/review/index.htm).

Arts and Humanities Research Council (AHRC) (2007b) 'Important information for applicants to AHRC June deadline' AHRC News/Press Release. Accessed 17 May 2007 (www.ahrc.ac.uk/news/news_pr/2007/information_for_applicants_to_AHRC_june_deadline.asp).

Arts Council of Great Britain (1978) *Pictorial Photography in Britain 1900–1920*, Exhibition Catalogue. London, Arts Council of Great Britain in association with The Royal Photographic Society.

Art Museum Image Consortium (2004) 'AMICO Data Specification: Data Dictionary' (last updated 23 December 2004). Accessed 3 July 2007 (www.amico.org/AMICO library/dataDictionary.html).

Aru, F., Zanuttigh, P. and Cortelazzo, G.M. (2006) 'Visualisation of panoramic images over the internet', in L. MacDonald (ed.) *Digital Heritage, Applying Digital Imaging to Cultural Heritage.* Oxford: Elsevier, pp. 467–87.

Association for Library Collections and Technical Services Task Force on Metadata (2000) 'Final Report'. Committee on Cataloging: Description and Access. Accessed 29 February 2008 (www.libraries.psu.edu/tas/jca/ccda/tf-meta6.html).

Authors Guild (2005) 'Authors Guild Sues Google, Citing "Massive Copyright Infringement, Press Release'. Accessed 26 November 2007 (www.authorsguild.org/news/sues_google_citing.htm).

Baca, M. (ed.) (1998) *Introduction to Metadata, Pathways to Digital Information.* Los Angeles: Getty Information Institute.

Baca, M. (2002a) 'A picture is worth a thousand words: metadata for art objects and their visual surrogates', in W. Jones, J.R. Ahronheim and J. Crawford (eds) *Cataloging the Web, Metadata, AACR and Marc 21.* Lanham, MD: The Scarecrow Press, pp. 131–8.

Baca, M. (ed.) (2002b) *Introduction to Art Image Access Tools, Standards, and Strategies.* Los Angeles: Getty Research Institute. Accessed 23 March 2007 (http://getty.edu/research/conducting_research/standards/intro_aia/).

Baca, M. (2003) 'Practical issues in applying metadata schemas and controlled vocabularies to cultural heritage information', in S.S. Intner, S.C. Tseng and M.L. Larsgaard (eds) *Electronic Cataloguing: AACR2 and Metadata for Serials and Monographs.* Binghamton: The Haworth Press, pp. 47–55.

Baca, M. and Harpring, P. (eds) (2006) *Categories for the Description of Works of Art* (revised 28 August 2006). J. Paul Getty Trust and College Art Association. Accessed 23 March 2007 (http://getty.edu/research/conducting_research/standards/cdwa/index.html).

Baca, M., Harpring, P., Lanzi, E., McRae, L. and Whiteside, A. (eds) (2006) Cataloging Cultural Objects: A Guide to Describing Cultural Works and Their Images (CCO). ALA Editions: American Library Association. Accessed 23 March 2007 (http://vraweb.org/ccoweb/cco/).

Bachelor, L. (2007) 'Hung Out to Dry'. *The Observer Magazine*, *The Observer.* 16 December 2007, pp. 27–32. Accessed 23 January 2008 (http://observer.guardian.co.uk/magazine/story/0,,2226795,00.html).

Balabanović, M., Chu, L.L. and Wolff, G.J. (2000) 'Storytelling with digital photographs', *Proceedings of the SIGCHI conference on Human factors in computing systems.* The Hague, The Netherlands, pp. 564–71. Accessed 14 April 2008 (http://doi.acm.org/10.1145/332040.332505).

Barnett, P. (1991) 'The clearinghouse on art documentation and computerization', in I. Pring (ed.) *ITEM: European Visual Art Information Network (EVAIN) Image Technology in European Museums and Art Galleries Database.* Ipswich: European Visual Arts Centre at Ipswich (EVAC) Issue 1, January 1991, p. iv.

Battilana, M.C. (2004) 'The GIF Controversy: A Software Developer's Perspective' (updated 20 June 2004). Accessed 9 February 2007 (www.cloanto.com/users/mcb/19950127giflzw.html).

BBC (2004) 'Google to scan famous libraries'. BBC News (website, updated 14 December 2004). Accessed 27 February 2007 (http://news.bbc.co.uk/1/hi/technology/4094271.stm).

BBC (2005a) 'Mobiles capture blast aftermath'. BBC News (website, updated 8 July 2005). Accessed 6 April 2007 (http://news.bbc.co.uk/1/hi/technology/4663561.stm).

BBC (2005b) 'Police appeal for bombing footage'. BBC News (website, updated 10 July 2005). Accessed 6 April 2007 (http://newswww.bbc.net.uk/1/hi/uk/4668675.stm).

BBC (2005c) 'Readers take a snapshot of history'. BBC News (website, updated 13 December 2005). Accessed 6 April 2007 (http://news.bbc.co.uk/1/hi/uk/4522014.stm).

BBC (2006) 'Digital cameras "not backed up"'. BBC News (website, updated 3 August 2006). Accessed 25 March 2008 (http://news.bbc.co.uk/1/hi/technology/5241294.stm).

BBC (2007a) Personal Communication to Melissa Terras, 'Re: Freedom of Information Act Request: Pictures Received at yourpics@bbc.co.uk', 15 October 2007.

BBC (2007b) 'Couple lose everything in blaze'. BBC Scotland News (website, updated 24 December 2007). Accessed 23 March 2008 (http://news.bbc.co.uk/1/hi/scotland/north_east/7158949.stm).

Beagrie, N. (2003) *National Digital Preservation Initiatives: An Overview of Developments in Australia, France, the Netherlands and the United Kingdom and of Related International Activity* (published online April 2003) Commissioned for and sponsored by the National Digital Information Infrastructure and Preservation Program, Library of Congress. The Council on Library and Information Resources and the Library of Congress. Accessed 12 January 2008 (www.clir.org/pubs/reports/pub116/contents.html).

Becker, E., Buhse, W., Gunnewig, D. and Rump, N. (eds) (2003) *Digital Rights Management: Technological, Economic, Legal and Political Aspects*. Berlin: Springer-Verlag Berlin and Heidelberg GmbH and Co.

Beckett, N., Schick, B. and Findlater, K. (2006) 'Imaging historical sites for conservation', in L. MacDonald (ed.) *Digital Heritage, Applying Digital Imaging to Cultural Heritage.* Oxford: Elsevier, pp. 377–410.

Benjamin, W. (1936) 'The work of art in the age of mechanical reproduction', in W. Benjamin (1992) *Illuminations: Essays and Reflections.* London: Fontana Press, pp. 211–44.

Benjamin, W. (1992) *Illuminations: Essays and Reflections.* London: Fontana Press.

Bentley, F., Metcalf, C.J. and Harboe, G. (2006) 'Personal vs. commercial content: the similarities between consumer use of photos and music', *Proceedings of the SIGCHI conference on Human Factors in computing systems.* Montréal, Québec, Canada, pp. 667–76. Accessed 17 March 2008 (http://doi.acm.org/10.1145/1124772.1124871).

van den Berg, J., Brandhorst, H. and van Huisstede, P. (1992) 'Image processing and the (art) historical discipline', in M. Thaller (ed.) *Images and Manuscripts in Historical Computing, Proceedings of a workshop at International University Institute, Firenze*, 15 November 1991. Göttingen: Max Planck Institute, pp. 5–40.

Berners-Lee, T. (1999) *Weaving the Web: The Past, Present and Future of the World Wide Web by its Inventor.* London: Texere Publishing.

Bertani, D. and Consalandi, L. (2006) 'High resolution imaging in the near infrared', in L. MacDonald (ed.) *Digital Heritage, Applying Digital Imaging to Cultural Heritage*. Oxford: Elsevier, pp. 212–38.

Besser, H. (1997) 'Image databases: the first decade, the present, and the future', in P.B. Heidorn and B. Sandore (eds) *Digital Image Access and Retrieval*. Urbana-Champaign, IL: University of Illinois at Urbana-Champaign, Graduate School of Library and Information Science, pp. 11–28.

Besser, H., Hubbard, S. and Lenert, D. (eds) (2003) *Introduction to Imaging*, revised edn (published online 2003). Santa Monica: Getty Research Institute. Accessed 17 May 2006 (www.getty.edu/research/conducting_research/standards/introimages/index.html).

Besser, H. and Trant, J. (1994) 'Describing Imaging Files: The Need for a Technical Standard' (published online November 1994). Coalition for Networked Information, Orlando, Florida. Accessed 12 November 2007 (www.archimuse.com/papers/cni.fall.94.html).

Besser, H. and Trant, J. (1995) *Introduction to Imaging, Issues in Constructing an Image Database*. Santa Monica: The Getty Art History Information Program.

Bianchi, C. (2006) 'Making online monuments more accessible through interface design', in L. MacDonald (ed.) *Digital Heritage, Applying Digital Imaging to Cultural Heritage*. Oxford: Elsevier, pp. 444–66.

Birch, J. (2001) *Diagnosis of Defective Colour Vision*, 2nd edn. Oxford: Butterworth-Heinemann Ltd.

Birley, E., Birley, R.E. and Birley, A.R. (1993) *Vindolanda Research Reports, New Series, Volume II, Reports on the auxiliaries, the writing tablets, inscriptions, brands and graffiti*. Hexham: Roman Army Museum Publications for the Vindolanda Trust.

Blyberg, J. (2005) 'ILS Customer Bill-of-Rights: A collection of "must-have's" for doing business in a Web 2.0 world' (website, published online 20 November 2005). Accessed 14 February 2008 (www.blyberg.net/2005/11/20/ils-customer-bill-of-rights/).

Borghoff, U.M., Rodig, P., Scheffczyk, J. and Schmitz, L. (2006) *Long Term Preservation of Digital Documents: Principles and Practices*. Berlin: Springer-Verlag.

Boutell, T. (ed.) (1996) 'PNG (Portable Network Graphics) Specification Version 1.0', *W3C Recommendation* (published online 1 October 1996). Cambridge, MA: World Wide Web Consortium). Accessed 27 February 2007 (www.libpng.org/pub/png/spec/1.0/PNG-Contents.html).

Bowman, A.K. and Thomas, J.D. (2003) *The Vindolanda Writing Tablets Volume III*. London: British Museum Press.

Brown, C.W. and Shepherd, B.J. (1995) *Graphics File Formats*. Greenwich: Manning Publications.

Bruce, V., Green, P.R. and Georgeson, M.A. (1996) *Visual Perception. Physiology, Psychology and Ecology*, 3rd edn. Hove: Psychology Press.

Bryan, P. (2006) 'User requirements for metric survey', in L. MacDonald (ed.) *Digital Heritage, Applying Digital Imaging to Cultural Heritage*. Oxford: Elsevier, pp. 149–73.

Burghart, T. (2006) 'The Impossible Exhibit: Caravaggio in Digital Photos'. *Washington Post* (website, published online 3 January 2006). Accessed 18 March 2008 (www.washingtonpost.com/wpdyn/content/article/2006/01/02/AR2006010201433).

Burnard, L. and Short, H. (1994) *An Arts and Humanities Data Service. Report of a feasibility study Commissioned by the Information Services Sub-committee of the Joint Information Systems Committee of the Higher Education Funding Councils* (published online 31 October 1994). Oxford: Office for Humanities Communication. Accessed 25 January 2008 (http://ahds.ac.uk/about/documents/ahds-feasibility-study.pdf).

Burns, R.W. (1998) *Television, An International History of the Formative Years*, IEE History of Technology Series. London: Institute of Electrical Engineers.

California Digital Library (1999) 'Best Practices for Image Capture' (updated July 1999). Accessed 24 April 2007 (www.gseis.ucla.edu/~howard/MOA2/bp90.doc).

California Digital Library (2007) 'CDL Guidelines for Digital Objects', Version 2.0. (updated January 2007). Oakland, CDL Digital Library Services Advisory Group. Accessed 13 May 2007 (www.cdlib.org/inside/diglib/guidelines/).

Campbell, V. (2007) 'Digital Images and Personal Data', Undergraduate Dissertation. School of Library, Archive and Information Studies, University College London.

Campbell-Kelly, M. and Aspray, W. (2004) *Computer. A History of the Information Machine*, 2nd edn, Sloan Technology Series. Oxford: Westview Press.

Canadian Heritage Information Network (1996) 'Preliminary Digitization Guidelines' (updated 8 December 2002). Accessed 12 April 2006 (www.chin.gc.ca/PM.cgi?pmLANG=English&pmAP=return_full_record&pmLM=Digital_Content&pmPR=FORUM_DIGITIZATION&pmSource=canned&chinKey=33).

Cargill Hall, R. (1977) *Lunar Impact, A History of Project Ranger*, National Aeronautics and Space Administration SP-4210. Washington: NASA History Division. Accessed 11 January 2007 (http://history.nasa.gov/SP-4210/pages/Cover.htm).

Carignan, Y., Evander, J., Gueguen, G., Hanlon, A., Murray, K., Roper, J., Ross, T. and Schreibman, S. (2007) 'Best Practice Guidelines for Digital Collections at the UM Libraries' (published online 6 February 2006, updated June 2006, revised May 2007). College Park, Office of Digital Collections and Research, University of Maryland. Accessed 23 November 2007 (www.lib.umd.edu/dcr/publications/best_practice.pdf).

Carpenter, L., Shaw, S. and Prescott, A. (eds) (1998) *Towards the Digital Library*. London: The British Library.

Carr, R. (2004) 'Oxford-Google digitisation agreement', *Bodleian Library News*. Accessed 30 January 2008 (www.bodley.ox.ac.uk/news/news58.htm).

Cartolano, R., Gertz, J. and Klimley, S. (1995) 'Oversized Color Images: Addressing Issues of Preservation and Access' (updated 2 May 1997). University of Columbia: Phase One Project Report. Accessed 23 May 2007 (www.columbia.edu/dlc/nysmb/reports/phase1.html).

Cassereau, P.M. (1994) 'Wavelet-Based image coding', in A.B. Watson, *Digital Images and Human Vision*. Cambridge, MA: MIT Press, pp. 13–22.

CCITT (1992) *Information Technology: Digital Compression and Coding of Continuous Tone Still Images, Recommendations and Guidelines. Recommendation T.81* (published online September 1992) Terminal Equipment and Protocols for Telematic Services. Geneva: The International Telegraph and Telephone Consultative Committee. Accessed 15 March 2007 (www.w3.org/Graphics/JPEG/itu-t81.pdf).

Ceruzzi, P.E. (2003) *A History of Modern Computing*, 2nd edn. London: MIT Press.

Chad, K. and Miller, P. (2005) 'Do Libraries Matter? The rise of Library 2.0', White Paper, Birmingham, *Talis.com* (published online November 2005). Accessed 23 February 2008 (www.talis.com/applications/downloads/white_papers/DoLibrariesMatter.pdf).

Chalfen, R. (1987) *Snapshot Versions of Life*. Bowling Green, OH: Bowling Green State University Press.

Chalfont, D. (2005) 'Facebook postings, photos incriminate dorm party-goers'. *The Northerner: Independent Student Newspaper of Northern Kentucky University* (website, published online 2 November 2005). Accessed 1 February 2008 (www.thenortherner.com/media/paper527/news/2005/11/02/News/Facebook.Postings.Photos.Incriminate.Dorm.PartyGoers-1042037.shtml).

Chapman, S. (2000) 'Considerations of Project Management', in M.K. Sitts (ed.) *Handbook for Digital Projects: a management tool for preservation and access*, Northeast Document Conservation Center, (updated 4 December 2000). Accessed 29 February 2008 (www.nedcc.org/oldnedccsite/digital/dman2.pdf).

Chun, S., Cherry, R., Hiwiller, R., Trant, J. and Wyman, B. (2006) 'Steve.museum: An ongoing experiment in social tagging, folksonomy, and museums', in J. Trant and Bearman (eds) *Museums and the Web 2006: Proceedings, Toronto: Archives & Museum Informatics* (published online 1 March 2006). Accessed 1 March 2008 (www.archimuse.com/mw2006/papers/wyman/wyman.html).

Clark, R.N. (2001) 'Image Detail (How Much Detail Can You Capture and Scan?)' (updated 8 April 2001) Accessed 8 February 2007 (www.users.qwest.net/~rnclark/scandetail.htm).

Cloud, K.S. (ed.) (1989) *Electronic Imaging Applications in Graphic Arts.* Los Angeles, CA: Proceedings of SPIE, p. 1073.

Coalition for Networked Information (2006) 'About CNI'. Accessed 17 February 2008 (www.cni.org/organization.html).

Colson, F. and Hall, W. (1992) 'Pictorial information systems and the teaching imperative', in M. Thaller (ed.) *Images and Manuscripts in Historical Computing,* Proceedings of a workshop at International University Institute, Firenze, November 15th 1991. Göttingen: Max Planck Institute, pp. 73–86.

CompuServe Incorporated (1987) 'Graphics Interchange Format, A standard defining a mechanism for the storage and transmission of raster-based graphics information'. Accessed 9 February 2006 (www.w3.org/Graphics/GIF/spec-gif87.txt).

CompuServe Incorporated (1990) 'Graphics Interchange Format, version 89a'. Accessed 9 February 2006 (www.w3.org/Graphics/GIF/spec-gif89a.txt).

CompuServe Incorporated (2006) 'About CompuServe'. Accessed 9 February 2006 (www.webcenters.netscape.compuserve.com/menu/about.jsp?floc=DC-0209_06-headnav1).

Consortium of Research Libraries in the British Isles (n.d.) 'CURL'. Accessed 27 January 2008 (www.curl.ac.uk).

Corbis (2007) 'Corbis Partners with the Smithsonian to Offer Celebrated Images of American Culture', press release (published online 24 January 2007). Accessed 15 February 2008 (www.corbis.com/corporate/pressroom/PressReleasesDet.asp?ID=33).

Cornell University Library (2002a) 'Table: Representative institutional requirements for conversion', in Cornell University Library, *Moving Theory Into Practice: Digital Imaging Tutorial*. Accessed 3 February 2008 (www.library.cornell.edu/preservation/tutorial/conversion/table3-1.html).

Cornell University Library (2002b) 'Moving Theory Into Practice: Digital Imaging Tutorial'. Accessed 21 January 2008 (www.library.cornell.edu/preservation/tutorial/index.html).

Cornish, G.P. (2004) *Copyright, Interpreting the Law for Libraries, Archives, and Information Services*, 4th edn. London: Facet Publishing.

Council on Library Resources (1986) 'Brittle Books. Reports of the Committee on Preservation and Access'. Washington, DC: Council on Library Resources. Accessed 5 January 2008 (www.eric.ed.gov/ERICDocs/data/ericdocs2sql/content_storage_01/0000019b/80/1c/04/55.pdf).

Covington, R. (2001) 'Corbis and photographers try to hash out a contract : When art, business and digital rights collide', *International Herald Tribune* (website, published online 29 January 2001). Accessed 28 March 2008 (www.iht.com/articles/2001/01/29/btcorbis.2.t.php).

Cox, A.M. (2007) 'Flickr: What is new in Web 2.0?'. Conference Paper, Towards a Social Science of Web 2.0, University of York, September 2007, University of Sheffield. Accessed 12 March 2008 (www.shef.ac.uk/content/1/c6/04/77/66/flickr%20paper.pdf).

Crawford, W. (2006) 'Library 2.0 and "Library 2.0"', *Cites & Insights: Crawford at Large*, 6 (2). Whole Issue 72. Accessed 10 January 2008 (www.citesandinsights.info/v6i2a.htm).

Creative Commons (2008) 'Content Directories', Creative Commons (website, updated 11 March 2008). Accessed 14 March 2008 (http://wiki.creativecommons.org/Content_Curators).

Crocker, L.D. (1995) 'PNG, the Portable Network Graphic Format', *Dr Dobb's Journal*, 20 (32) July 1995, pp. 36–44.

D'Amato, D.P, and Klopfenstein, R.C. (1996) 'Requirements and Options for the Digitization of the Illustration Collections of the National Museum of Natural History'. National Museum of Natural History's Collections and Research Information System (CRIS) Development Programme. Accessed 24 October 2007 (www.nmnh.si.edu/cris/techrpts/imagopts/).

Dahl, M., Banerjee, K. and Spalti, M. (2006) *Digital Libraries: Integrating Content and Systems*. Information Professional Series. Oxford: Chandos Publishing.

Dale, R. (1999) 'Lossy or Lossless? File Compression Strategies Discussion at ALA', *RLG DigiNews*. Research Libraries Group, 3(1).

DarConte, L.A. (2007) 'Image Storage Solutions Abound Despite Consumer's Slow Adoption Rate', *Picture Business Magazine* (website, published online 1 September 2007). Accessed 15 January 2008 (www.picturebusinessmag.com/story/story.bsp?sid=77913&var=story&publication=Picture%20Business&publicationDate=9/1/07&slug=PB0907_StorageFeature&category=None&section=Unknown&page=1).

Darley, A. (1990) 'From abstraction to simulation: Notes on the history of computer imaging', in P. Hayward (ed.) *Culture, Technology and Creativity in the Late Twentieth Century*. London: John Libbey, pp. 39–64.

Darlington, J., Finney, A. and Pearce, A. (2003) 'Domesday redux: The rescue of the BBC Domesday Project videodiscs', *Ariadne*, Issue 36, July 2003. Accessed 13 November 2007 (www.ariadne.ac.uk/issue36/tna/intro.html).

Datamation (1966) *Product of the Month: IBM Model I*, November 1966, p. 91.

Deegan, M. and Tanner, S. (2002) *Digital Futures: Strategies for the Information Age*. Digital Futures Series. London: Library Association Publishing.

Deegan, M. and Tanner, S. (eds) (2006) *Digital Preservation*, Digital Futures Series. London: Facet.

DigiCULT (2002) 'Digital Asset Management systems for the cultural and scientific heritage sector', *DigiCULT Thematic Issue 2* (published December 2002), European Commission. Accessed 17 January 2008 (www.digicult.info/downloads/html/103951 9224/1039519224.html).

Digital Imaging Group (2001) 'Dig 35 Specification – Metadata for Digital Images'. Version 1.1, Working Draft, (published online 16 April 2001). Accessed 1 April 2008 (http://xml.coverpages.org/FU-Berlin-DIG35-v11WD-010416.pdf).

Digital Library Federation (1998) 'A Working Definition of a Digital Library'. Accessed 23 March 2008 (www.diglib.org/about/dldefinition.htm).

Digital Library Federation (2002) 'Benchmark for Faithful Digital Reproductions of Monographs and Serials', Version 1 (published online December 2002). The

Digital Library Federation Benchmark Working Group. Accessed 14 February 2008 (www.diglib.org/standards/bmarkfin.htm).

Digital Preservation Coalition (2007) 'DPC/BL Joint JPEG 2000 Workshop', 25 June 2007. British Library Conference Centre, St. Pancras, London. Accessed 3 August 2007 (www.dpconline.org/graphics/events/0706jpeg2000wkshop.html).

van Dijck, J. (2007) *Mediated Memories in the Digital Age (Cultural Memory in the Present)*. Palo Alto: Stanford University Press.

van Dijck, J. (2008) 'Digital photography: communication, identity, memory', *Visual Communication*, 7, pp. 57–76.

Dillon, B. (2006) 'The revelation of erasure', *Tate Etc Magazine*, The Tate, Issue 8. Accessed 9 January 2007 (www.tate.org.uk/tateetc/issue8/erasurerevelation.htm).

Dinsdale, A. (1926) *Television.* London: Pitman.

Dinsdale, A. (1927) 'Television demonstration in America: A successful public demonstration of television between Washington and New York' *Wireless World and Radio Review*, Volume XX, pp. 680–6.

DiscoverKate.com (2003) 'Kate Winslet Photos, Home/Magazines/Cover Girl/2003-02 gq uk' (published online 2003). Accessed 9 January 2006 (www.discoverkate.com/gallery/details.php?image_id=5218).

Dobbin, B. (2005) 'Kodak engineer had revolutionary idea: the first digital camera', *Seattle PI* (website, published online 9 September 2005). Accessed 30 January 2007 (http://seattlepi.nwsource.com/business/240048_firstdigital09.html).

Druckery, T. (ed.) (1999) *Ars Electronica: Facing the Future. A Survey of Two Decades.* Cambridge, MA: MIT Press.

Eakins, J. and Graham, M. (1999) 'Content-based Image Retrieval', *JISC Technology Applications Programme, Report 39*, (published online October 1999) London: Joint Information Systems Committee. Accessed 29 March 2008 (www.jisc.ac.uk/uploaded_documents/jtap-039.doc).

Earnshaw, R.A. and Vince, J.A. (2007) *Digital Convergence: Libraries of the Future*. London: Springer-Verlag London Ltd.

Eastman Kodak Company (1994) 'PhotoYCC Color Encoding and Compression Schemes', KODAK Publication PCD-045, White Paper.

Ellis, M. and Kelly, B. (2007) 'Web 2.0: How to stop thinking and start doing: addressing organisational barriers', in J. Trant and D. Bearman (eds) *Museums and the Web 2007: Proceedings* (published online 31 March 2007). Toronto: Archives & Museum Informatics. Accessed 18 March 2008 (www.archimuse.com/mw2007/papers/ellis/ellis.html).

Erway, R. (1996) 'Digital initiatives of the research libraries group', *D-Lib Magazine* (website, published online December 1996). (www.dlib.org/dlib/december96/rlg/12erway.html).

Ester, M. (1996) 'Digital Image Collections: Issues and Practice' (published online December 1996). Washington, DC: Commission on Preservation and Access.

Accessed 7 April 2008 (www.eric.ed.gov/ERICDocs/data/ericdocs2sql/content_storage_01/0000019b/80/14/d8/e8.pdf).

European Commission (2007) 'DigiCULT – Expanding the use of Europe's cultural and scientific resources', Cultural Heritage and Technology Enhanced Learning Unit, (updated 4 August 2007). Accessed 27 August 2007 (http://cordis.europa.eu/fp7/ict/telearn-digicult/digicult_en.html).

Facebook.com (2008) 'Facebook Statistics', Facebook Press Room. Accessed 2 April 2008 (www.facebook.com/press/info.php?statistics).

Farkas, M. (2005) 'Web/Library 2.0 Backlash', *Information Wants To Be Free* (website, published online 1 December 2005). Accessed 28 February 2008 (http://meredith.wolfwater.com/wordpress/index.php/2005/12/01/weblibrary-20-backlash/).

Fetter, W.A. (1964) *Computer Graphics in Communication*, Engineering Graphics Monograph Series. London: McGraw-Hill.

Finley, H. (2007) 'Some Questions About Mum', Personal Communication to M. Terras, via email.

Finney, A. (2007) 'Domesday: The BBC Domesday Project – November 1986' (updated 2007). Accessed 15 February 2008 (www.domesday.org.uk).

Fischer, A. and Swora, T. (1986) *Library of Congress Optical Disk Pilot Program, Optical Disk Print Pilot Project.* Washington, DC: Library of Congress.

Fleischhauer, C. (1998) 'Digital Formats for Content Reproductions', National Digital Library Program, American Memory White Papers (published online 13 July 1998). Washington, DC: Library of Congress. Accessed 12 March 2008 (http://lcweb2.loc.gov/ammem/formats.html).

Flickr.com (2007) 'Two Billionth', (published online 13 November 2007). Accessed 3 February 2008 (www.flickr.com/photos/88646149@N00/2000000000/).

Foster, P. (2007) 'Caught on camera – and found on Facebook', *The Times*, Tech and Web News (website, published online 17 July 2007). Accessed 18 July 2007 (http://technology.timesonline.co.uk/tol/news/tech_and_web/the_web/article2087306.ece).

Frey, F. (2000) 'File Formats for Digital Masters', Guide 5, Guides to Quality in Visual Resource Imaging. Digital Library Federation, Council on Library and Information Resources, Research Libraries Group. Accessed 21 March 2007 (http://chnm.gmu.edu/digitalhistory/links/cached/chapter3/link3.39a.DLFdigitalmastersformats.html).

Future Image Inc (2000) 'Worth 1000 URLs: Visual Strategies for e-Commerce' (published online 1 February 2000). Accessed 25 March 2007 (www.marketresearch.com/product/display.asp?productid=142304&SID=78146590-405723223478590025& kw=worth).

Gargi, U., Deng, Y. and Tretter, D.R. (2002) 'Managing and searching personal photo collections', *Hewlett Packard Technical Report HPL-2002-67* (published online 18 March 2002). Palo Alto Hewlett Packard Laboratories. Accessed 29 April 2006 (www.hpl.hp.com/techreports/2002/HPL-2002-67.pdf).

Giani, A. (2006) 'Image resizing – The limits of image processing', in L. MacDonald (ed.) *Digital Heritage, Applying Digital Imaging to Cultural Heritage*. Oxford: Elsevier, pp. 239–57.

Gibson, H.L. (1978) *Photography by Infrared, Its Principles and Applications*. New York: John Wiley and Sons.

Gill, T. and Miller, P. (2002) 'Re-inventing the wheel? Standards, interoperability and digital cultural content', *D-Lib Magazine* (website, January 2002, 8:1). Accessed 4 April 2007 (www.dlib.org/dlib/january02/gill/01gill.html).

Gilliland-Swetland, A.J. (1998) 'Defining metadata', in M. Baca (ed.) *Introduction to Metadata, Pathways to Digital Information*. Los Angeles, CA: Getty Information Institute, pp. 1–9.

Gilliland-Swetland, A. (2004) 'Metadata – where are we going?', in G.E. Gorman and D. Dorner (eds) *Metadata Applications and Management*, International Yearbook of Library and Information Management 2003–04. London: Facet Publishing, pp. 17–33.

Gladney, H.M. (2007) *Preserving Digital Information*. Berlin: Springer-Verlag.

Gladney, H.M., Mintzer, F. and Schiattarella, F. (1997) 'Safeguarding digital library contents and users: Digital images of treasured antiquities', *D-Lib Magazine*, July/August 1997. Accessed 28 March 2008 (www.dlib.org/dlib/july97/vatican/07gladney.html).

González, P. (1992) 'The digital processing of images in archive and libraries, large scale international projects', in M. Thaller (ed.) *Images and Manuscripts in Historical Computing*. Proceedings of a workshop at International University Institute, Firenze, 15 November 1991. Göttingen: Max Planck Institute, pp. 97–120.

González, P. (1998) 'Computerization of the Archivo General de Indias: Strategies and Results', Council on Library and Information Resources, Pub.76, (published online September 1998). Accessed 6 January 2008 (www.clir.org/pubs/reports/gonzalez/contents.html).

Gonzalez, R.C. and Woods, R.E. (1993) *Digital Image Processing*. Reading, MA: Addison-Wesley Publishing.

Gorman, G.E. and Dorner, D. (eds) (2004) *Metadata Applications and Management*, International Yearbook of Library and Information Management 2003–04. London: Facet Publishing.

Gorman, M. (2003) 'Cataloguing in an electronic age', in S.S. Intner, S.C. Tseng and M.L. Larsgaard (eds) *Electronic Cataloguing: AACR2 and Metadata for Serials and Monographs*. Binghamton: The Haworth Press, pp. 5–17.

Graham, A., Garcia-Molina, H., Paepcke, A. and Winograd, T. (2002) 'Time as essence for photo browsing through personal digital libraries'. *Proceedings of the 2nd ACM/IEEE-CS joint conference on Digital libraries,* Portland, Oregon, USA, pp. 326–35. Accessed 16 March 2008 (http://doi.acm.org/10.1145/544220.544301).

Graham, R. (2005) *The Digital Image*, 2nd edn. Caithness: Whittles Publishing Ltd.

Green, P. (2006) 'Colour management in heritage photography', in L. MacDonald (ed.) *Digital Heritage, Applying Digital Imaging to Cultural Heritage*. Oxford: Elsevier, pp. 293–327.

Greenstreet, R. (2007) 'Q&A', *The Guardian*, Weekend. Accessed 17 November 2007 (www.guardian.co.uk/weekend/story/0,,2210829,00.html).

Gregory, R. (1998) *Eye and Brain: The Psychology of Seeing*, 5th edn. Princeton, NJ: Princeton University Press.

Grimwood, J.M. (1963) 'Project Mercury: A Chronology', *The NASA History Series, NASA SP-4001*. Washington, DC: National Aeronautics and Space Administration History Office. Accessed 19 April 2006 (http://history.nasa.gov/SP-4001/cover.htm).

Grout, C., Purdy, P. and Rymer, J. (2000) *Creating Resources for the Visual Arts: Standards and Good Practice*, Visual Arts Data Service Guide to Good Practice, Section 3, Creating Digital Images, 3.7 Image digitization process: work flow, procedures and good practices. London: Arts and Humanities Data Service. Accessed 20 March 2008 (http://vads.ahds.ac.uk/guides/creating_guide/sect37.html).

Grycz, C.J. (2006) 'Digitising rare books and manuscripts', in L. MacDonald (ed.) *Digital Heritage, Applying Digital Imaging to Cultural Heritage*. Oxford: Elsevier, pp. 33–68.

Guardian (2007) 'Web Watch', *The Guardian,* Guide Magazine, 20 October, p. 31.

Gudivada, V.N. and Raghavan, V.V. (1995) 'Content based image retrieval systems', *Computer*, 28(9) pp. 18–22.

Gudivada, V.N. and Raghavan, V.V. (1997) 'Modeling and retrieving images by content', *Information Processing & Management*, 33(4) pp. 427–52.

Hafner, K. (2007) 'Libraries Shun Deals to Place Books on Web', *New York Times*, (website, published online 22 October 2007). Accessed 9 January 2008 (www.nytimes.com/2007/10/22/technology/22library.html).

Hamber, A. (2006) 'Digitisation in the commercial art world', in L. MacDonald (ed.) *Digital Heritage, Applying Digital Imaging to Cultural Heritage*. Oxford: Elsevier, pp. 115–47.

Hamilton, E. (1992) 'JPEG File Interchange Format', Version 1.02 (published online September 1992). San Jose, CA: C-Cube Microsystems, Inc. Accessed 24 March 2007 (www.jpeg.org/public/jfif.pdf).

Harpring, P. (2002) 'The language of images: Enhancing access to images by applying metadata schemas and structured vocabularies', in M. Baca (ed.) *Introduction to Art Image AccessTools, Standards, and Strategies.* Los Angeles,CA: Getty Research Institute. Accessed 20 February 2008 (www.getty.edu/research/conducting_research/standards/intro_aia/harpring.html).

Harvard University Library (2001) 'Guide to Image Digitization' (published online October 2001). Accessed 9 January 2008 (http://hul.harvard.edu/ois/services/digproj/guide_images.html).

Hayward, P. (ed.) (1990) *Culture, Technology and Creativity in the Late Twentieth Century.* Eastleigh: John Libbey Publishing, pp. 197–208.

Hecker, M. (2007) 'Digital Camera Image Quality'. Accessed 8 February 2007 (www.wyofoto.com/Digital_Image_Quality/Image_Quality.htm).

Heidorn, P.B. and Sandore, B. (eds) (1997) *Digital image access and retrieval.* Urbana-Champaign, IL: University of Illinois at Urbana-Champaign, Graduate School of Library and Information Science.

Henning, T. (2003) 'The Camera–phone phenomenon, a new deal in imaging', Future Image Report Market Research Study. Accessed 30 January 2008 (www.futureimage.com).

Hewlett Packard (2006) 'Slimming photos with HP digital cameras' (updated 2006). Accessed 9 January 2007 (www.hp.com/unitedstates/consumer/digital_photography/tours/slimming/index_f.html).

Higgins, S. (2006) 'What Are Metadata Standards?', Digital Curation Centre Standards Watch Paper. Edinburgh: Digital Curation Centre. Accessed 1 February 2007 (www.dcc.ac.uk/resource/standards-watch/what-are-metadata-standards/).

Hirsch, R.J. (2000) *Seizing the Light, A History of Photography.* London: McGraw Hill.

Hirsch, R. and Valentino, J. (2001) *Photographic Possibilities: The Expressive Use of Ideas, Materials, and Processes*, 2nd edn. Boston, MA: Focal Press, Butterworth-Heinemann.

Hockey, S. and Ross, S. (2008) 'Part 4: Conclusion', in L. Hughes (ed.) *The AHRC ICT Methods Network*. London: Arts and Humanities Research Council, pp. 59–74.

Hoggar, S.G. (2006) *Mathematics of Digital Images: Creation, Compression, Restoration, Recognition.* Cambridge: Cambridge University Press.

Holt, B., Hartwick, L. and Vetter, S. (1995) 'Query by image content, the QBIC Project's applications at Davis's Art and Art History Departments', *Visual Resources Association Journal*, 22(2) Summer, 1995.

Holt, B., Weiss, K., Niblack, W., Flickner, M. and Petkovic, D. (1997) 'The QBIC Project in the Department of Art and Art History at UC Davis', in C. Schwartz and M. Rorvig (eds) *Digital Collections, Implications for Users, Funders, Developers, and Maintainers,* Proceedings of the 60th Annual Meeting of the American Society for Information Science, 1–6 November 1997, Washington, DC. Medford, NJ: Information Today, pp. 189–95. Accessed 11 April 2007 (www.asis.org/annual-97/holt.htm).

van Horik, R. (2005) *Permanent Pixels: Building blocks for the longevity of digital surrogates of historical photographs*. The Hague, DANS Studies in Digital Archiving.

Hourihane, C. (2002) 'It begins with the cataloguer: Subject access to images and the cataloguer's perspective', in M. Baca (ed.) *Introduction to Art Image Access Tools, Standards, and Strategies*. Los Angeles: Getty Research Institute.

Accessed 5 March 2008 (www.getty.edu/research/conducting_research/standards/intro_aia/hourihane).

van House, N.A., Davis, M., Ames, M., Finn, M. and Viswanathan, V. (2005) 'The uses of personal networked digital imaging: an empirical study of cameraphone photos and sharing', *Conference on Human Factors in Computing Systems, Portland, Extended Abstracts*. New York: ACM Press, pp. 1853–6. Accessed 18 February 2008 (http://doi.acm.org/10.1145/1056808.1057039).

Howard, D. (2004) *Sharing Digital Photos, The Future of Memories*. Redmond: Microsoft Press.

Hoyle, B. and Lewis, L. (2006) 'Film camera is killed off by millions of pixels', *The Times* (website, published online 2 March 2006). Accessed 2 February 2007 (http://travel.timesonline.co.uk/article/0,,23209-2066959,00.html).

Hsu, J. and Hwang, A. (2008) 'More functions not resolution key to advancing digital cameras: Q&A with Casio's "digital camera father"', *Digitimes* (website, 24 January 2008). Accessed 17 February 2008 (www.digitimes.com/systems/a20080123PD212).

Huffman, D.A. (1952) 'A Method for the Construction of Minimum-Redundancy Codes', *Proceedings of the Institute of Radio Engineers*, 40(9) pp. 1098–101.

Hughes, L. (2004) *Digitizing collections: strategic issues for the information manager*. London: Facet Publishing.

Hughes, L. (ed.) (2008) *The AHRC ICT Methods Network*. London: Arts and Humanities Research Council.

Image Quality Working Group of ArchivesCom (1997) 'Technical Recommendations for Digital Imaging Projects' (updated 2 April 1997). Accessed 15 March 2008 (www.columbia.edu/acis/dl/imagespec.html).

Infotrends (2005) '2005 Worldwide Consumer Digital Camera Forecast Summary'. Luton: Infotrends Inc. Accessed 6 April 2006 (http://store.infotrendsresearch.com/ProductDetails.asp?ProductCode=67604&Click=631).

Inman, P. (2002) 'Genealogy', *The Guardian* (website, 26 September 2002). Accessed 3 November 2006 (www.guardian.co.uk/internetnews/story/0,,798781,00.html).

International Imaging Industry Association (2005) 'Consumer Photo Archiving Guidelines Idea Description', Version 1.0. (published online 9 January 2005). Accessed 13 March 2008 (http://members.i3a.org/dman/Document.phx?documentId=tv28005114336875&cmd=display).

International Imaging Industry Association (2007) 'Protect your Pictures', Quickstart. Accessed 13 March 2008 (/www.savemymemories.org/quickstart).

International Imaging Industry Association (2008) 'Dig 35: Metadata Standards, a smarter way to look at digital images'. Accessed 13 March 2008 (www.i3a.org/i_dig35.html).

International Organization for Standardization (ISO) (1987) 'ISO 5800:1987: Photography – Colour negative films for still photography – Determination of ISO speed'. Accessed 23 March 2008 (www.iso.org/iso/iso_catalogue/catalogue_tc/catalogue_detail.htm?csnumber=11948).

International Organization for Standardization (ISO) (2006) 'ISO 12232:2006 Photography – Digital still cameras – Determination of exposure index, ISO speed ratings, standard output sensitivity, and recommended exposure index'. Accessed 23 March 2008 (www.iso.org/iso/iso_catalogue/catalogue_tc/catalogue_detail.htm?cs number=37777).

Intner, S.S., Tseng, S.C. and Larsgaard, M.L. (eds) (2003) *Electronic Cataloguing: AACR2 and Metadata for Serials and Monographs.* Binghamton: The Haworth Press.

Jackson, P. (2005) 'VOX PROP: What would you save if the house caught fire?', *The Independent* (website, published online 17 August 2005). Accessed 3 March 2008 (http://findarticles.com/p/articles/mi_qn4158/is_20050817/ai_n14878397).

Jadav, A.D. (2002) *Designing Usable Web Interfaces*. London: Prentice Hall.

Janesick, J.R. (2000) *Scientific Charge Coupled Devices.* Bellingham, WA: SPIE Press.

Japan Electronics and Information Technology Industries Association (JEITA) (2002) 'Exchangeable Image File Format for Digital Still Cameras, Exif version 2.2', Technical Standardization Committee on AV and IT Storage Systems and Equipment, (published online April 2002). Accessed 29 March 2007 (www.exif.org/Exif2-2.pdf).

Jaritz, G. and Schuh, B. (1992) 'Describing the indescribable', in M. Thaller (ed.) *Images and Manuscripts in Historical Computing,* Proceedings of a workshop at International University Institute, Firenze, November 15th 1991. Göttingen: Max Planck Institute, pp. 143–53.

Jeanneney, J-N. (2007) *Google and the Myth of Universal Knowledge, a View from Europe.* London: University of Chicago Press.

Jeffrey, I. (2006) *Photography, A Concise History*, World of Art Series. London: Thames and Hudson.

Jespersen, H.P. and Jespersen, J.K. (2004) 'The problem of subject access to visual materials', *Journal of Educational Media and Library Sciences*, 42(1) pp. 37–48. Accessed 23 March 2008 (http://research.dils.tku.edu.tw/Joemls/42/42-1/37-48.pdf).

JISC Image Digitisation Initiative (2002) 'Metadata Requirements and Guidelines'. London: JIDI. Accessed 28 March 2008 (www.ilrt.bris.ac.uk/jidi/metadata.html).

Joint Funding Council's Libraries Review Group (1993) 'The Follet Report'. A Report for the Higher Education Funding Council for England, the Scottish Higher Education Funding Council, the Higher Education Funding Council for Wales and the Department of Education for Northern Ireland. Accessed 13 January 2008 (www.ukoln.ac.uk/services/papers/follett/report).

Joint Information Systems Committee (JISC) (2007) 'Digitisation Programme' (published online June 2007). London: JISC. Accessed 13 January 2008 (www.jisc.ac.uk/digitisation_home.html).

Joint Photographic Expert Group (2000) 'JPEG2000 Part 1 Final Committee Draft Version 1.0' (published online 16 March 2000). Accessed 28 April 2007 (www.jpeg.org/public/fcd15444-1.pdf).

Jones, C. and Specht, J. (2006) '2006 Raw Survey Report', *OpenRAW.* Accessed 17 April 2007 (http://openraw.org/files/2006rawsurveyreport.pdf).

Jones, W., Ahronheim, J.R. and Crawford, J. (eds) (2002) *Cataloging the Web, Metadata, AACR and Marc 21.* Lanham, MA: The Scarecrow Press.

Jörgensen, C. (1996) 'Indexing images: testing an image description template', *American Society for Information Science Annual Conference Proceedings 1996.* Accessed 23 March 2008 (www.asis.org/annual96/ElectronicProceedings/jorgensen.html).

Joseph, C. (2004) 'Burning questions: Consumer attitudes and fire insurance', *CBCNews* (website, published online 10 October 2004). Accessed 21 March 2008 (www.cbc.ca/consumers/market/files/home/fire/ripley.html).

Jul, E. (2003) 'MARC and mark-up', in S.S. Intner, S.C. Tseng and M.L. Larsgaard (eds.) *Electronic Cataloguing: AACR2 and Metadata for Serials and Monographs.* Binghamton: The Haworth Press, pp. 141–53.

Kaltwasser, F.G. (1971) 'Universal Bibliographic Control', *UNESCO Bulletin for Libraries*, 25 September 1971, pp. 252–9.

Kay, D.C. and Levine, J.R. (1995) *Graphics File Formats.* London: McGraw-Hill.

Kenney, A.R. and Chapman, S. (eds) (1996) *Digital Imaging for Libraries and Archives.* Ithaca, NY: Cornell University Library Press.

Kenney, A.R. and Rieger, O.Y. (1998) 'Using Kodak Photo CD Technology for Preservation and Access, A Guide for Librarians, Archivists, and Curators' (published online 30 April 1998), Department of Preservation and Conservation, Cornell University Library. Accessed 15 January 2008 (www.library.cornell.edu/preservation/kodak/kodak-htm.htm).

Kenney, A.R. and Rieger, O.Y. (2000) *Moving Theory into Practice: Digital Imaging for Libraries and Archives.* Mountain View, CA: Research Libraries Group.

Kiernan, K.S. (1997) *Beowulf and the Beowulf Manuscript.* Ann Arbor: The University of Michigan Press.

Kilbride, W. (2004) 'Why bother with digitisation? Users and using digital resources', *Arts and Humanities Data Service Information Papers* (published online 8 June 2004). London: Arts and Humanities Data Service. Accessed 16 March 2008 (http://ahds.ac.uk/creating/information-papers/why-bother-digitising/index.htm).

Kington, T. (2007) 'Lost Venetian painting is recreated', *The Guardian* (published online 17 September 2007). Accessed 11 April 2008 (http://arts.guardian.co.uk/art/news/story/0,,2169803,00.html).

Kirk, D., Sellen, A.J., Rother C. and Wood, K.R. (2006) 'Understanding photowork', *Proceedings of the SIGCHI conference on Human Factors in Computing Systems*, Montréal, Québec, Canada, pp. 761–70. Accessed 11 April 2008 (http://doi.acm.org/10.1145/1124772.1124885).

Kirsch, R.A. (1998) 'SEAC and the start of image processing at the national bureau of standards', *IEEE Annals of the History of Computing*, 20(2) pp. 7–13.

Kirsch, R.L., Cahn, L.C. and Ray, G.H. (1957) 'Urban experiments with processing pictorial information with a digital computer', *Proceedings of the Eastern Joint Computer Conference*, 9–13 December 1957, Institute of Radio Engineers and Association of Computing Machinists, pp. 221–9. Accessed 19 April 2006 (www.nist.gov/msidlibrary/doc/kirsch_experiments_pict.pdf).

Klein, S.A. (1994) 'Image quality and image compression: A psychophysicists viewpoint', in A.B. Watson, *Digital Images and Human Vision.* Cambridge, MA: MIT Press, pp. 73–88.

Kodak Limited (1961) *How to Make Good Pictures: the Guide for Everyone with a Camera.* London: Kodak.

Kodak Professional Imaging Solutions (2003a) 'Kodak Photo CD Disc: Resolution Information' (updated 13 June 2003). Accessed 15 April 2007 (www.kodak.com/global/en/service/professional/tib/tib7058.jhtml?id=0.1.14.36.3.108&lc=en).

Kodak Professional Imaging Solutions (2003b) 'Kodak Photo CD Disc: Transferring and Viewing Images: How are the Images Compressed?' (updated 19 June 2003). Accessed 15 April 2007 (www.kodak.com/global/en/service/professional/tib/tib7057.jhtml?id=0.1.14.36.3.106&lc=en#SEC6).

Kodak Professional Imaging Solutions (2007) 'Kodak Pro Photo CD System'. Accessed 15 April 2007 (www.kodak.com/global/en/service/professional/products/ekn017045.jhtml).

Koren, N. (2001) 'Understanding Image Sharpness Part 1: Introduction to Resolution and MTF curves' (updated November 18 2001). Accessed 8 February 2007 (www.normankoren.com/Tutorials/MTF.html).

Krogh, P. (2006) *The DAM Book: Digital Asset Management for Photographers.* Sebastapol: O'Reilly Media Inc.

Krug, S. (2005) *Don't Make Me Think!: A Common Sense Approach to Web Usability.* Berkeley: New Riders.

Kuny, T. (1998) 'The digital dark ages? Challenges in the preservation of electronic information', *International Preservation News*, 17 May 1998. Accessed 5 March 2008 (www.ifla.org/VI/4/news/17-98.htm#2).

Kurzweil, R. (2007) 'Ray Kurzweil's Career Summary', Kurzweil Technologies. Accessed 28 January 2007 (www.kurzweiltech.com/raycareersummary.html).

Kustanowitz and Shneiderman (2005) 'Motivating annotation for personal digital photo libraries: Lowering barriers while raising incentives', *Technical Report HCIL-2004-18.* Department of Computer Science: University of Maryland. Accessed 26 March 2008 (http://hcil.cs.umd.edu/trs/2004-18/2004-18.pdf).

Lang, P.J., Greenwald, M.K., Bradley M.M. and Hamm, A.O. (1993) 'Looking at pictures: affective, facial, visceral, and behavioural reactions', *Psychophysiology*, May 1993, 30(3) pp. 261–73.

Lang, P.J., Bradley M.M., Fitzsimmons J.R., Cuthbert, B.N., Scott, J.D., Moulder, B. and Nangia, V. (1998) 'Emotional arousal and activation of the visual cortex: An fMRI analysis', *Psychophysiology*, March 1998, 35(2) pp. 199–210.

Laposky, B.F (1969) 'Oscillons: Electronic Abstractions', *Leonardo*, October 1969, 2(4) pp. 345–54.

Larson, E. (1977) *Telecommunications, A History.* London: Fredrick Muller Limited.

Lazinger, S.S. (2001) *Digital Preservation and Metadata. History, Theory and Practice.* Englewood, CO: Libraries Unlimited, Greenwood Publishing Group.

Lee, S. (2002) *Digital Imaging, a Practical Handbook.* London: Facet Publishing.

Lesk, M. (2005) *Understanding Digital Libraries*, 2nd edn. San Francisco: The Morgan Kaufmann Series in Multimedia Information and Systems, Morgan Kaufmann.

Lester, P.M. (1999) 'Photojournalism, An Ethical Approach'. Digital version of text published in 1991. Hillsdale, NJ: Lawrence Erlbaum Associates, Publishers. Accessed 9 January 2006 (http://commfaculty.fullerton.edu/lester/writings/pjethics.html).

Li, Z-N. and Drew, M.S. (2004) *Fundamentals of Multimedia*. Pearson Education. Upper Saddle River: Pearson Prentice Hall.

Lialina, O. (2007) 'The Vernacular Web 2', *New Network Theory International Conference*, 28–30 June 2007, Amsterdam, The Netherlands. (www.networkcultures.org/networktheory/index.php?onderdeelID=12&paginalD=75). Paper available at (http://contemporary-home-computing.org/vernacular-web-2/) accessed 12 March 2008.

Library of Congress (2001) 'National digital library program reaches goal of 5 million items online'. *News from the Library of Congress*, Library of Congress (website, published online 10 January 2001). Accessed 14 January 2008 (www.loc.gov/today/pr/2001/01-004.html).

Library of Congress (2007) 'Technical Standards for Digital Conversion of Text and Graphic Materials', Library of Congress. Accessed 17 January 2008 (http://memory.loc.gov/ammem/about/techStandards.pdf).

Lipkin, J. (2005) *Photography Reborn, Image Making in the Digital Era.* New York: Harry N. Abrams.

Livingstone, M. (2002) *Vision and Art, The Biology of Seeing.* New York: Harry N. Abrams.

Lojkine, M. (2001) *A Simple Guide to Digital Cameras, Scanning and Using Images.* London: Pearson Education Ltd, Prentice Hall.

Long, J. (1999) 'Ethics in the Age of Digital Photography', National Press Photographers Association. Accessed 3 March 2008 (http://nppa.org/

professional_development/selftraining_resources/eadp_report/digital_manipulation.html).

Lyman, P. and Varian, H.R. (2003) 'How Much Information', School of Information Management and Systems at the University of California at Berkeley (published online 27 October 2003). Accessed 15 May 2007 (www.sims.berkeley.edu/how-much-info-2003).

Lynch, C. (2002) 'Digital collections, digital libraries and the digitization of cultural heritage information', *First Monday*, 5 May 2002. Accessed 20 December 2003 (www.firstmonday.dk/issues/issue7_5/lynch).

Lyon, R.F. (2006) 'A brief history of "pixel"', *Digital Photography II, IS&T/SPIE Symposium on Electronic Imaging*, January 2006, San Jose. Accessed 14 April 2007 (www.foveon.com/files/ABriefHistoryofPixel2.pdf).

Lyra Research Inc (2007) 'The Worldwide Digital Camera Forecast, 2007', Lyra Industry Reports (published online 12 October 2007). Accessed 28 October 2007 (http://lyra.ecnext.com/coms2/summary_0290-761_ITM).

MacDonald, L. (ed.) (2006) *Digital Heritage, Applying Digital Imaging to Cultural Heritage.* Oxford: Elsevier.

MacDonald, L. and Jacobsen, R. (2006) 'Assessing image quality', in L. MacDonald (ed.) *Digital Heritage, Applying Digital Imaging to Cultural Heritage*. Oxford: Elsevier, pp. 351–73.

MacDonald, L., Findlater, K., Tao Song, R., Giana, A. and Suganthan, S. (2006) 'Imaging of stained glass windows', in L. MacDonald (ed.) *Digital Heritage, Applying Digital Imaging to Cultural Heritage*. Oxford: Elsevier, pp. 411–45.

Machover, C. (1998) 'About this issue', *IEEE Annals of the History of Computing*, 20(2) pp. 3–6.

Maney, K. (2007) 'Baby's arrival inspires birth of cellphone camera – and societal evolution'. Technology, *USA Today* (website, published online 23 January 2007). Accessed 1 February 2007 (www.usatoday.com/money/industries/technology/maney/2007-01-23-kahn-cellphone-camera_x.htm).

Manson, P. (1998) 'Telematics for libraries: Actions and initiatives of the European Union', *Beyond the Beginning: The Global Digital Library Conference*, 16–17 June 1997. Accessed 13 January 2008 (www.ukoln.ac.uk/services/papers/bl/blri078/content/repor~14.htm).

Marcellin, M.W., Bilgin, A., Gormish, M.J. and Boliek, M.P. (2000) 'An overview of JPEG-2000', *Proceedings of the Conference on Data Compression,* 28–30 March 2000. Washington, DC: IEEE Computer Society, pp. 523–41. Accessed 25 March 2007 (http://doi.ieeecomputersociety.org/10.1109/DCC.2000.838192).

Marques, O. and Furht, B. (2002) *Content-based Image and Video Retrieval.* Dordrecht, The Netherlands, Multimedia Systems & Applications, Kluwer Academic Publishers.

Martinez, K. and Hamber, A. (1989) 'Towards a colorimetric digital image archive for the visual arts', in K.S. Cloud (ed.) *Electronic Imaging Applications in Graphic Arts* (Proc. SPIE) 1073, pp. 114–21.

Marvin, C. (1988) *When Old Technologies Were New.* New York: Oxford University Press.

Mathes, A. (2004) 'Folksonomies – Cooperative classification and communication through shared metadata'. *Computer Mediated Communication – LIS590CMC* (published online December 2004) Graduate School of Library and Information Science, University of Illinois Urbana-Champaign. Accessed 28 March 2008 (www.adammathes.com/academic/computermediatedcommunication/folksonomies.html).

McConnell, K., Bodson, D. and Urban, S. (1999) *FAX: Facsimile Technology and Systems*, 3rd edn. London: Artech House.

McMahon, K. (2008) 'Digitise your heritage', *Personal Computer World* (website, published online 11 January 2008). Accessed 23 January 2008 (www.pcw.co.uk/personal-computer-world/features/2207012/digitise-heritage-3610584).

Miano, J. (1999) *Compressed Image File Formats: JPEG, PNG, GIF, XBM, BMP.* Reading, MA: ACM Press.

Microsoft Corporation (1993) *Microsoft Win32 Programmer's Reference Volume 5: Messages, Structures, and Macros.* Redmond, WA: Microsoft Press.

Microsoft Corporation (2005) 'MSN Search Announces MSN Book Search'. Press Release, Microsoft, (published online 25 October 2005). Accessed 23 January 2008 (www.microsoft.com/presspass/press/2005/oct05/10-25MSNBookSearchPR.mspx).

Miller, A.D. and Edwards, W.K. (2007) 'Give and take: A study of consumer photo-sharing culture and practice'. *Proceedings of the SIGCHI conference on Human factors in computing systems*, San Jose, CA, pp. 347–56. Accessed 12 February 2008 (http://doi.acm.org/10.1145/1240624.1240682).

Miller, P. (2004) 'Metadata – What it means for memory Institutions', in G.E. Gorman and D. Dorner (eds) *Metadata Applications and Management*, International Yearbook of Library and Information Management 2003–04. London: Facet Publishing, pp. 3–16.

Miller, P. (2005) 'Web 2.0: Building the New Library', *Ariadne*, Issue 45, October 2005. Accessed 21 January 2008 (www.ariadne.ac.uk/issue45/miller/).

Miller, P. (2006) 'Coming Together around Library 2.0, A Focus for Discussion and a Call to Arms', *D-Lib Magazine*, April 2006, 12(4). Accessed 20 January 2008 (http://dlib.org/dlib/april06/miller/04miller.html).

Minerva (2003) 'Summary of Progress'. Coordinating digitization in Europe. Progress report of the National Representatives Group: coordination mechanisms for digitization policies and programmes 2002, European Commission, The Information Society Directorate-General, (updated 6 May 2003). Accessed 16 January 2007 (www.minervaeurope.org/publications/globalreport/globalrep2002.htm).

Minerva (2007) 'Coordinating digitisation in Europe: progress report of the National Representatives Group'. Progress report of the National Representatives Group: coordination mechanisms for digitization policies and programmes, European Commission, The Information Society Directorate-General (updated 13 July

2007). Accessed 16 January 2008 (www.minervaeurope.org/publications/globalreport.htm).

Mintzer, F.C., Boyle, L.E., Cazes, A.N., Christian, B.S., Cox, S.C., Giordano, F.P., Gladney, H.M., Lee, J.C., Kelmanson, M.L., Lirani, A.C., Magerlein, K.A., Pavani, A.M.B. and Schiattarella, F. (1996) 'Toward on-line, worldwide access to Vatican Library materials'. IBM Journal of Research and Development. Volume 40, No. 2. (www.research.ibm.com/journal/rd/402/mintzer.html).

Mintzer, F., Lotspiech, J. and Morimoto, N. (1997) 'Safeguarding digital library contents and users digital watermarking'. *D-Lib Magazine*, December 1997. Accessed 18 January 2008 (www.dlib.org/dlib/december97/ibm/12lotspiech.html).

Misic, V., Kraus, K., Eaves, M., Parker, K.J. and Buckley, R. (2002) 'MRC for compression of blake archive images', in A.G. Tescher (ed.) *Applications of Digital Image Processing*. Seattle, WA: SPIE, pp. 479–90.

Mitchell, W. (1984) 'What is an image?' *New Literary History*, Spring 1984, Image/Imago/Imagination, 15(3) pp. 503–37.

Mitchell, W. (1992) *The Reconfigured Eye: Visual Truth in the Post-Photographic Era.* Cambridge, MA: MIT Press.

Molnar, F. (1997) 'A science of vision for visual art', *Leonardo*, 30(3) pp. 225–32.

Mooney, L. (2006) 'Chaucer's scribe', *Speculum: A Journal of Medieval Studies*, January 2006, 81(1) pp. 97–138.

Moore, M. (2007) 'How Google helped solve canoeist mystery'. *The Telegraph* (website, published online 7 December 2007). Accessed 13 March 2008 (www.telegraph.co.uk/news/main.jhtml?xml=/news/2007/12/06/ngoogle106.xml).

Moore, R.T., Stark, M.C. and Cahn, L. (1964) 'Digitizing pictorial information with a precision optical scanner', *Photogrammetric Engineering*, 30(6) pp. 923–31.

Moorhouse, P. (2004) 'The computerised local image collection at manchester archives and local studies', *Manchester Region History Overview*, 17(1) pp. 62–8. Accessed 28 February 2007 (www.mcrh.mmu.ac.uk/pubs/pdf/mrhr_17i_archives_moorhouse.pdf).

Murray, J.D. and van Ryper, W. (1996) *Encyclopedia of Graphics File Formats*, 2nd edn. Sebastopol: O'Reilly & Associates, Inc.

National Archives and Records Administration (NARA) (1991) *Digital Imaging and Optical Media Storage Systems: Guidelines for State and Local Government Agencies.* Washington DC: National Archives and Records Administration and National Association of Government Archives and Records Administrators.

National Archives and Records Administration NARA (2004) 'Technical Guidelines for Digitizing Material for Electronic Access: Creation of Production of Master Files – Raster Images' (published online June 2004). Washington, DC: US National Archives and Records Administration. Accessed 21 March 2007 (www.archives.gov/preservation/technical/guidelines.pdf).

National Information Standards Organisation (2006) 'Data Dictionary – Technical Metadata for Digital Still Images', Approved Version (published online December 2006). Accessed 28 March 2008 (www.niso.org/standards/resources/Z39-87-2006.pdf).

National Initiative for a Networked Cultural Heritage (NINCH) (2002) 'The NINCH Guide to Good Practice in the Digital Representation and Management of Cultural Heritage Materials' (published online October 2002). Accessed 23 January 2008 (www.nyu.edu/its/humanities/ninchguide/).

The National Press Photographer's Association (NPPA) (1995) 'Digital Manipulation Code of Ethics, NPPA Statement of Principle' (updated June 1995). Accessed 29 March 2008 (http://nppa.org/professional_development/business_practices/digitalethics. html).

Naughton, J. (2000) *A Brief History of the Future: Origins of the Internet.* London: Phoenix Press.

NDIIP (2007a) 'PDF/A-1, PDF for Long-term Preservation, Use of PDF 1.4'. Sustainability of Digital Formats, Planning for Library of Congress Collections (updated 7 March 2007). Accessed 1 April 2007 (www.digitalpreservation.gov/formats/fdd/fdd000125.shtml).

NDIIP (2007b) 'Curator's View for Still Image Content'. Sustainability of Digital Formats, Planning for Library of Congress Collections (updated 7 March 2007). Accessed 1 April 2007 (www.digitalpreservation.gov/formats/content/still_curator.shtml).

Nelson, M. (1995) *The Data Compression Book.* New York: M&T books.

Nielsen, J. (2000) 'End of Web Design', *Alertbox* (website, published online 23 July 2000). Accessed 12 March 2008 (www.useit.com/alertbox/20000723.html).

Nipkow, P. (1884) *Elektrisches Teleskop*, German Patent No. 30105, January 1884.

Nixon, S. (2006) 'Notes on the future of Open RAW formats, and a look at DNG', *OpenRaw* (website, published online 19 April 2006). Accessed 1 May 2007 (www.openraw.org/node/1482).

Noordung, H. (1995) 'The Problem of Space Travel: The Rocket Motor', *The NASA History Series*, NASA SP–4026. Washington, DC: National Aeronautics and Space Administration History Office. Accessed 19 April 2006 (www.hq.nasa.gov/office/pao/History/SP-4026/cover.html).

Norman, S. (2004) *Practical Copyright for Information Professionals: the CILIP Handbook.* London: Facet Publishing.

The Observer (2007) 'Thanks, Jane', Comment Section, 23 October 2007, p. 30.

Ofcom (2007) 'Communications Market Report'. Research Document, Office of Communications (published online 23 August 2007). Accessed 12 March 2008 (www.ofcom.org.uk/research/cm/cmr07/cm07_print/cm07_1.pdf).

Online Computer Library Center (2007) 'About OCLC', *OCLC.* Accessed 23 November 2007 (www.oclc.org/about/default.htm).

Open Content Alliance (n.d.) 'Frequently asked questions', OCA. Accessed 28 November 2007 (www.opencontentalliance.org/faq.html).

Ore, Espen S. (1992) 'A Supra-institutional infrastructure for image processing in the humanities', in M. Thaller (ed.) *Images and Manuscripts in Historical Computing,* Proceedings of a workshop at International University Institute, Firenze, 15 November 1991. Göttingen: Max Planck Institute, pp. 135–42.

O'Reilly, T. (2005) 'What is Web 2.0? Design Patterns and Business Models for the Next Generation of Software', O'Reilly Media Inc (published online 30 September 2005). Accessed 6 February 2007 (www.oreillynet.com/pub/a/oreilly/tim/news/2005/09/30/what-is-web-20.html?page=1).

Oxford English Dictionary (1989a) 'Image', *The Oxford English Dictionary*, 2nd edn, OED Online. Oxford: Oxford University Press. Accessed 11 February 2007 (http://dictionary.oed.com/cgi/entry/50112149?query_type=word&queryword=image&first=1&max_to_show=10&sort_type=alpha&result_place=1&search_id=T80S-Ih9TsJ-4966&hilite=50112149).

Oxford English Dictionary (1989b) 'Resolution', *The Oxford English Dictionary*, 2nd edn, OED Online. Oxford: Oxford University Press. Accessed 27 February 2006 (http://dictionary.oed.com/cgi/entry/50204141?query_type=word&queryword=resolution&first=1&max_to_show=10&sort_type=alpha&result_place=1&search_id=E8Da-E3tkbP-3200&hilite=50204141).

Padfield, T. (2007) *Copyright for Record Managers and Archivists*, 3rd edn. London: Facet Publishing.

Parker, E.B. (1985) 'The Library of Congress non-print optical disk pilot program', *Information Technology and Libraries*, December 1985, 4(4) pp. 289–99.

Peacock, D., Ellis, D. and Doolan, J. (2004) 'Searching For Meaning: Not Just Records', Museums and the Web Conference 2004, in D. Bearman and J. Trant (eds) '*Museums and the Web 2004: Proceedings*'. Toronto: Archives & Museum Informatics. Accessed 12 March 2008 (www.archimuse.com/mw2004/papers/peacock/peacock. html).

Peterson, T.H. (1994) 'Digital-Imaging and Optical Digital Data Disk Storage Systems: Long-Term Access Strategies for Federal Agencies', The Technology Research Staff, The National Archives at College Park (published online July 1994). Accessed 23 May 2007 (www.archives.gov/preservation/technical/imaging-storage-report.html).

Phase One (2006) 'Phase One Introduces Three New Backs', Phase One. Accessed 1 February 2007 (www.phaseone.com/Content/p1digitalbacks/Hotnews/Ultimate%20range.aspx).

PKWare Inc (2007) 'ZIP File Format Specification', Version 6.3.1 (updated 11 April 2007). Accessed 23 April 2007 (www.pkware.com/documents/casestudies/APPNOTE.TXT).

PMA Foresight (2007) 'Data Watch: More households using printing as a method of storing digital images', *PMA Foresight* (webpage, published online 18 December 2007). Accessed 24 December 2007 (http://pmaforesight.

com/2007/12/18/more-households-using-printing-as-a-method-of-storing-digital-images.aspx).

Pointer, M.R. and Attridge, G.G. (1998) 'The number of discernible colours', *Colour Research and Application*, 23(1) pp. 52–4.

Polfreman, M., Broughton, V. and Wilson, A. (2006) 'Metadata Generation for Resource Discovery', Final Report, Arts and Humanities Data Service Metadata Generation Study. London: Arts and Humanities Data Service. Accessed 12 March 2008 (http://ahds.ac.uk/about/projects/metadata-generation/index.htm).

Polikar, R. (2001) 'The Engineer's Ultimate Guide To Wavelet Analysis: The Wavelet Tutorial', Rowan University (updated 12 January 2001). Accessed 4 May 2007 (http://users.rowan.edu/~polikar/WAVELETS/WTtutorial.html).

Politou, E., Pavlidis, G.P. and Chamzas, C. (2004) 'JPEG2000 and dissemination of cultural heritage over the internet', *IEEE Transactions on Image Processing* 13(3) pp. 293–301.

de Polo, A. and Minelli, S. (2006) 'Digital access to a photographic collection', in L. MacDonald (ed.) *Digital Heritage, Applying Digital Imaging to Cultural Heritage*. Oxford: Elsevier, pp. 93–114.

Porter, V. and Thornes, R. (n.d.) 'A Guide to the Description of Architectural Drawings', Architectural Drawing Advisory Group, Foundation for Documents of Architecture. Los Angeles, CA: The Getty Information Institute. Accessed 23 March 2008 (www.getty.edu/research/conducting_research/standards/fda/).

PREMIS Working Group (2005) 'Data Dictionary for Preservation Metadata', Final Report of the Preservation Data: Implementation Strategies Working Group, OCLC and RLG (published online May 2005). Accessed 7 April 2008 (www.oclc.org/research/projects/pmwg/premis-final.pdf).

Prescott, A. (1998) 'Constructing electronic Beowulf. Towards the digital library: the British Library's "Initiatives for Access" programme', in L. Carpenter, S. Shaw and A. Prescott (eds) *Towards the Digital Library*. London: The British Library, pp. 30–49.

Price, J. (1984) 'The Optical Disk Pilot Program at the Library of Congress', *Videodisc and Optical Disc*, November/December 1984, 4(6) pp. 424–32.

Pring, I. (ed.) (1991) *ITEM: European Visual Art Information Network (EVAIN) Image Technology in European Museums and Art Galleries Database,* Issue 1, January 1991. European Visual Arts Centre at Ipswich (EVAC).

Pring, I. (ed.) (1995) *ITEM: European Visual Art Information Network (EVAIN) Image Technology in European Museums and Art Galleries Database*. European Visual Arts Centre at Ipswich (EVAC), 9, May 1995.

Pu, I.M. (2005) *Fundamental Data Compression*. London: Butterworth-Heinemann.

Puglia, S. and Rhodes, E. (2007) 'Digital imaging – How far have we come and what still needs to be done?' *RLG DigiNews* (website, Research Libraries Group, 11 (1) published online 15 April 2007). Accessed 28 October 2007 (www.rlg.org/en/page.php?Page_ID=21033#article2).

Rand, B. (2000) 'Kodak unruffled by photo dot-coms', *Democrat and Chronicle* (website, published online 5 February 2000, http://dbease.democratandchronicle.com/). Cited in S. Vroegindeweij (2002) 'My Pictures: Informal Image Collections'. Hewlett Packard Technical Report, Information Infrastructure Laboratory. Bristol: Hewlett Packard. Accessed 23 November 2007 (www.hpl.hp.com/techreports/2002/HPL-2002-72R1.pdf).

Rao, K.R. and Yip, P. (1990) *Discrete Cosine Transform: Algorithms, Advantages, and Applications*. Boston: Academic Press.

Reilly, J. and Frey, F.S. (1996) 'Recommendations for the Evaluation of Digital Images Produced from Photographic, Microphotographic, and Various Paper Formats', Report to the Library of Congress National Digital Library Project, Imaging Permanence Institute, Rochester Institute of Technology (published online May 1996). Accessed 5 December 2007 (http://lcweb2.loc.gov/ammem/Ipireprt.pdf).

Robinson, J. (2007) Stop the press: the internet is now the first draft of history, *The Observer,* Business and Media section, 22 April 2007, p. 11.

Robinson, P. (1993) *The Digitization of Primary Textual Sources.* Oxford: Oxford University Office for Humanities Communication.

Roelofs, G. (1999) *PNG: The Definitive Guide.* Sebastopol, CA: O'Reilly. Accessed 23 May 2007 (www.libpng.org/pub/png/book/).

Roelofs, G. (2006) 'Current status of PNG', *LibPNG.org.* Accessed 23 May 2007 (www.libpng.org/pub/png/pngstatus.html).

Roelofs, G. (2007a) 'Multiple-image Network Graphics: A PNG-like Image Format Supporting Multiple Images, Animation and Transparent JPEG', *LibPNG.org.* Accessed 23 May 2007 (www.libpng.org/pub/mng/).

Roelofs, G. (2007b) 'Portable network graphics, an open, extensible image format with lossless compression', *LibPNG.org.* Accessed 23 May 2007 (www.libpng.org/pub/png/).

Roelofs, G. (2007c) 'How PNG's two-dimensional interlacing works (JPEG Version with Inlined GIF Animation)' *LibPNG.org*. Accessed 23 May 2007 (www.libpng.org/pub/png/pngpics.html).

Rouse, A. (2005) *Digital SLR Handbook.* Lewes: Photographer's Institute Press, GMC Publications.

Royan, B. (2000) 'Scotland in Europe: SCRAN as a maquette for the European Cultural Heritage Network', *Cultivate Interactive* (website, 1 July 2000). Accessed 14 January 2008 (www.cultivate-int.org/issue1/scran/).

Rubenstein, D. and Sluis, K. (2008) 'A life more photographic, mapping the networked image', *Photographies*, 1 (published online 1 March 2008). Accessed 14 April 2008 (www.informaworld.com/smpp/content~content=a790525007~db=all~order=page).

Rudolf, P. (2006) 'Principles and evolution of digital cameras', in L. MacDonald (ed.) *Digital Heritage, Applying Digital Imaging to Cultural Heritage.* Oxford: Elsevier, pp. 177–209.

Rusbridge, C. (1998) 'Towards the hybrid library', *D-Lib Magazine* (website, July/August 1998). Accessed 13 December 2007 (www.dlib.org/dlib/july98/rusbridge/07rusbridge.html).

Rusbridge, C. (2001) 'After eLib', *Ariadne* (website, 26 January 2001). Accessed 10 December 2007 (www.ariadne.ac.uk/issue26/chris/intro.htm).

Russ, J.C. (2001) *Forensic Uses of Digital Imaging.* London: CRC Press Inc.

Sabbagh, D. (2004) 'Shutters close on Kodak film factory', *The Times* (website, published online 6 October 2004). Accessed 25 November 2007 (www.timesonline.co.uk/tol/news/uk/article490909.ece).

Sagnanet (n.d.) 'The collection and participating libraries', *Saganet.* Accessed 18 November 2007 (http://sagnanet.is/saganet/?MIval=/sgn_start_description_of_data& language=English).

Salomon, D. (2007) *Data Compression: The Complete Reference.* London: Springer-Verlag London Ltd.

Sandore, B. (2000) 'What users want from digital image collections', in A.R. Kenney and O.Y. Reiger (eds), *Moving Theory into Practice: digital imaging for libraries and archives.* Mountain View, CA: Research Libraries Group, pp. 4–5.

Sandore, B. and Dunkelberger, R. (1996) 'The University of Illinois/Kodak Digital Imaging Project: A Report of the Use of the Photo Imaging Workstation and Related Imaging Projects', University of Illinois at Urbana-Champaign Library. Accessed 23 May 2007 (http://images.library.uiuc.edu/projects/Kodak/KODAK.HTM).

Sandore, B. and Shaik, N. (1988) 'Findings of the instructor/ student survey', in C. Stephenson and P. McClung (eds) *Delivering Digital Images: Cultural Heritage Resources for Education*, The Museum Educational Site Licensing Project 1. Los Angeles, CA: The Getty Information Institute.

Sapir, M. (1994) 'The impossible photograph: Hippolyte Bayard's self-portrait as a drowned man', *Modern Fiction Studies*, Fall 1994, 40(3) pp. 619–29.

Saunders, D., Culpitt, J. and Padfield, J. (2006) 'Digital imaging for easel paintings', in L. MacDonald (ed.) *Digital Heritage, Applying Digital Imaging to Cultural Heritage.* Oxford: Elsevier, pp. 521–48.

Scarcella, M.A. (2007) 'Man jailed after nude photo is put on MySpace', *The Herald Tribune* (website, published online 18 February 2007). Accessed 12 March 2008 (www.heraldtribune.com/apps/pbcs.dll/article?AID=/20070218/NEWS/702180336).

Schantz (1982) *The History of OCR, Optical Character Recognition.* Boston: Recognition Technologies Users Association.

Schofield, J. (2002) 'Picture perfect', *The Guardian* (website, published online 21 November 2002). Accessed 12 March 2008 (http://shopping.guardian.co.uk/christmas2002/story/0,,848225,00.html).

Schofield, J. (2005) 'Emerging technology', *The Guardian* (website, published online 24 March 2005). Accessed 11 March 2008 (www.guardian.co.uk/Columnists/Column/0,,1444183,00.html).

Schonfield, R.C. (2003) *JSTOR, A History.* Princeton: Princeton University Press.

Schottlaender, B.E.C. (2003) 'Why metadata? Why me? Why now?', in S.S. Intner, S.C. Tseng and M.L. Larsgaard (eds) *Electronic Cataloguing: AACR2 and Metadata for Serials and Monographs*. Binghamton: The Haworth Press, pp. 19–29.

Schwartz, C. and Rorvig, M. (eds) *Digital collections, implications for users, funders, developers, and maintainers,* Proceedings of the 60th Annual Meeting of the American Society for Information Science, 1–6 November 1997, Washington, DC. Medford, NJ: Information Today, pp. 189–95. Accessed 11 April 2007 (www.asis.org/annual-97/holt.htm).

Science and Society Picture Library (2004) 'Mrs Langtry, 1890'. Inventory No. 1990-5036_6009_0002, Picture Reference: 10428270. Accessed 9 January 2007 (http://scienceandsociety.co.uk/results.asp?image=10428270&wwwflag=2&imagepos=3).

ScienceWatch (1999) 'Citations reveal concentrated influence: some fields have it, but what does it mean?', *ScienceWatch*, January/February 1999. Accessed 25 March 2008 (www.sciencewatch.com/jan-feb99/sw_jan-eb99_page1.htm).

Shatford Layne, S. (2002) 'Subject access to art images', in M. Baca (ed.) *Introduction to Art Image Access Tools, Standards, and Strategies.* Los Angeles: Getty Research Institute. Accessed 20 March 2008 (www.getty.edu/research/conducting_research/standards/intro_aia/layne.html).

Sheridan, A. (2006) 'Pet snake taken by Animal Control', *WCNC.com* (website, published online 25 August 2006). Accessed 21 February 2008 (www.wcnc.com/news/topstories/stories/wcnc-ad-8_25_06-snake.358374bf.html).

Sitts, M.K. (ed.) (2000) *Handbook for Digital Projects: a management tool for preservation and access*, Northeast Document Conservation Center (updated 4 December 2000). Accessed 29 February 2008 (www.nedcc.org/oldnedccsite/digital/dman2.pdf).

Slide.com (2007) 'About slide'. *Slide.com* (website, updated 2007). Accessed 6 February 2008 (www.slide.com/static/about).

Smith, G. (2004) 'Folksonomy: social classification', *Atomiq: a weblog by Gene Smith* (website, published online 3 August 2004). Accessed 21 January 2008 (http://atomiq.org/archives/2004/08/folksonomy_social_classification.html).

Smith, K. (2005) 'NCSU students face underage drinking charges due to online photos', *WRAL.com* (website, published online 29 October 2005). Accessed 21 February 2008 (www.wral.com/news/local/story/121507/).

Smith, N. (2006) 'Digitising documents for public access', in L. MacDonald (ed.) *Digital Heritage, Applying Digital Imaging to Cultural Heritage.* Oxford: Elsevier, pp. 1–31.

Sontag, S. (1979) *On Photography.* London: Penguin.

Soth, A. (2007) 'Where are the great pictures on Flickr?', *Alec Soth, Blog* (website, published online 8 August 2007). Accessed 18 February 2008 (www.alecsoth.com/blog/2007/08/08/where-are-the-great-pictures-on-flickr/).

Sperry Corporation, (1983) 'High speed data compression and decompression apparatus and method', *US Patent, US 4,558,302*. Accessed 9 February 2006 (http://patft.uspto.gov/netacgi/nphParser?Sect1=PTO1&Sect2=HITOFF&d=PALL&p=1&u=/netahtml/srchnum.htm&r=1&f=G&l=50&s1=4,558,302.WKU.&OS=PN/4,558,302&RS=PN/4,558,302>).

Stam, D.S. (1987) 'For data based on art call... A computer information clearinghouse', *Museum News*, June 1987, pp. 67–74.

Stapleton, M. (2006) 'Image databases and access', in L. MacDonald (ed.) *Digital Heritage, Applying Digital Imaging to Cultural Heritage.* Oxford: Elsevier, pp. 259–91.

State Hermitage Museum (2003) 'QBIC Colour and Layout Searches', *State Hermitage Museum* (website, published online 2003). Accessed 23 March 2008 (www.hermitagemuseum.org/fcgibin/db2www/qbicSearch.mac/qbic?selLang=English).

Stephenson, C. and McClung, P. (eds) (1988) *Delivering Digital Images: Cultural Heritage Resources for Education*, The Museum Educational Site Licensing Project, Volume 1. Los Angeles: The Getty Information Institute.

Stevenson, J. (2006) 'Digitisation programmes in the V&A', in L. MacDonald (ed.) *Digital Heritage, Applying Digital Imaging to Cultural Heritage.* Oxford: Elsevier, pp. 69–92.

Stieglitz, A. (1910) 'Photo-Secessionism and its Opponents, Another Letter – The Sixth', New York, 20 October 1910, 8, in Arts Council of Great Britain in association with The Royal Photographic Society (1978) *Pictorial Photography in Britain 1900–1920*, Exhibition Catalogue, 12.

Strunk, L. (2006) 'The RAW problem', *OpenRAW* (website, published online 19 March 2006). Accessed 17 April 2007 (www.openraw.org/info).

Surowiecki, J. (2005) *The Wisdom of Crowds: Why the Many Are Smarter Than the Few.* London: Abacus.

Süsstrunk, S. (1998) 'Imaging production systems at corbis corporation', *RLG DigiNews* (website, published online 15 August 1998) 2(4). Accessed 23 March 2007 (http://digitalarchive.oclc.org/da/ViewObjectMain.jsp?fileid=0000070519:000006286203&reqid=6933#technical).

Swan, T. (1993) *Inside Windows File Formats.* Indianapolis: Sams Publishing.

Swedin, E.G. and Ferro, D.L. (2005) *Computers, the Life Story of a Technology.* London: Greenwood Press.

Tamura, H. and Yokoya, N. (1984) 'Image database systems: A survey', *Pattern Recognition*, 17(1) pp. 29–43.

Tawse, A. (2003) *The Digitisation of Medieval Manuscripts, Success or Failure?* MA Dissertation. London: School of Library, Archives and Information Studies, University College London.

Techical Advisory Service for Images (TASI) (2002a) 'SCRAN Case Study', *TASI* (website) Case Studies of Digitisation Projects. Accessed 15 November 2007 (www.tasi.ac.uk/resources/scran.html).

Techical Advisory Service for Images (TASI) (2002b) 'HELIX case study', *TASI* (website) Case Studies of Digitisation Projects. Accessed 15 November 2007 (www.tasi.ac.uk/resources/helix.html).

Techical Advisory Service for Images (TASI) (2002c) 'About us', *TASI* (website). Accessed 13 November 2007 (www.tasi.ac.uk/about_us.html).

Techical Advisory Service for Images (TASI) (2006a) 'Digital cameras', *TASI* (website). Accessed 1 January 2007 (www.tasi.ac.uk/advice/creating/camera.html).

Techical Advisory Service for Images (TASI) (2006b) 'Generic image workflow: TASI Recommended Best Practice for Digitisation Projects', *TASI* (website). Accessed 17 April 2007 (www.tasi.ac.uk/advice/managing/workflow_generic.html).

Techical Advisory Service for Images (TASI) (2006c) 'Choosing a file format', *TASI* (website). Accessed 23 May 2007 (www.tasi.ac.uk/advice/creating/format.html).

Techical Advisory Service for Images (TASI) (2006d) 'The digital image', *TASI* (website). Accessed 23 May 2007 (www.tasi.ac.uk/advice/creating/image.html).

Techical Advisory Service for Images (TASI) (2006e) 'Sustainability of digital resources', *TASI* (website). Accessed 14 March 2008 (www.tasi.ac.uk/advice/managing/sust.html).

Techical Advisory Service for Images (TASI) (2006f) 'Copyright and digital images', *TASI* (website). Accessed 29 March 2008 (www.tasi.ac.uk/advice/managing/copyright.html).

Techical Advisory Service for Images (TASI) (2006g) 'Roles and responsibilities for staff involved in building digital image collections', *TASI* (website). Accessed 29 March 2008 (www.tasi.ac.uk/advice/managing/copyright-creators.html).

Techical Advisory Service for Images (TASI) (2006h) 'Roles and responsibilities for staff using images for teaching and research', *TASI* (website). Accessed 29 March 2008 (www.tasi.ac.uk/advice/managing/copyright-users.html).

Techical Advisory Service for Images (TASI) (2007a) 'How should you store your digital data?', *TASI* (website). Accessed 13 February 2008 (www.tasi.ac.uk/advice/delivering/storage.html).

Techical Advisory Service for Images (TASI) (2007b) 'Managing your images', *TASI* (website). Accessed 28 March 2008 (www.tasi.ac.uk/advice/delivering/ims.html).

Techical Advisory Service for Images (TASI) (2008) 'Digital preservation and storage', *TASI* (website). Accessed 14 March 2008 (www.tasi.ac.uk/advice/delivering/digital.html).

Techtree.com (2007) 'Mysore varsity texts to be digitised', *Techtree India*, (website, 21 May 2007). Accessed 14 January 2008 (www.techtree.com/India/News/Mysore_Varsity_Texts_to_be_Digitised/551-81217-643.html).

The Telegraph (2003) 'The secret of slimline Kate', *The Telegraph* (website, published online 10 January 2003. Accessed 29 March 2008 (www.telegraph.co.uk/news/main.jhtml?xml=/news/2003/01/10/nkate10.xml).

Terras, M. (2006) *Image to Interpretation: Intelligent Systems to Aid Historians in the Reading of the Vindolanda Texts*, Oxford Studies in Ancient Documents. Oxford: Oxford University Press.

Tescher, A.G. (ed.) (2002) *Applications of Digital Image Processing*. Seattle, WA: SPIE.

Thaller, M. (ed.) (1992a) *Images and Manuscripts in Historical Computing,* Proceedings of a workshop at International University Institute, Firenze, 15 November 1991. Göttingen: Max Planck Institute.

Thaller, M. (1992b) 'The processing of manuscripts', in M. Thaller (ed.) *Images and Manuscripts in Historical Computing,* Proceedings of a workshop at International University Institute, Firenze, 15 November 1991. Göttingen: Max Planck Institute, pp. 41–72.

Theage.com.au (2007) 'Book scans reveal Google's handiwork', *Theage.com.au* (website, published online 6 December 2007). Accessed 29 January 2008 (www.theage.com.au/news/web/bookscansrevealgoogleshandiwork/2007/12/06/1196812901631.html).

Thorell, L.G. and Smith, W.J. (1990) *Using Computer Color Effectively: Illustrated Reference to Computer Colour Interface.* Englewood Cliffs, NJ: Prentice Hall.

Thornton, P. (2004) 'Cost of living index loses a toaster but gains digital camera'. *The Independent* (website, published online 16 March 2004). Accessed 24 February 2008 (www.independent.co.uk/news/business/analysis-and-features/cost-of-living-index-loses-a-toaster-but-gains-digital-camera-566458.html).

Tola, V. and Castellani, C. (2003) 'The future of digital memory and cultural heritage', *Conference Proceedings*, Florence. Accessed 6 April 2006 (www.iccu.sbn.it/PDF/florence_proceedings_2003.pdf).

Trant, J. and Bearman, D. (eds) (2006) *Museums and the Web 2006: Proceedings* (published online 27 March 2006). Toronto: Archives and Museum Informatics. Accessed 15 April 2008 (www.archimuse.com/mw2006/papers/).

Trant, J. and Bearman, D. (eds) (2007) *Museums and the Web 2007: Proceedings* (published online 31 March 2007). Toronto: Archives and Museum Informatics. Accessed 15 April 2008 (www.archimuse.com/mw2007/papers/).

Trefethen, L.N. and Embree, M. (2005) *Spectra and Pseudospectra: The Behavior of Nonnormal Matrices and Operators.* Princeton: Princeton University Press.

Twycross, M. (2006) 'Virtual restoration and manuscript archaeology: A case study'. Audio Recording, *Methods Network Expert Seminar: Virtual History and Archaeology*, University of Sheffield, 19–21 April 2006. Accessed 29 March 2008 (www.arts-humanities.net/audio/meg_twycross_virtual_restoration_manuscript_archae).

UKOLN (2005) 'An introduction to folksonomies', *UKOLN* (website, published online 10 June 2005) QA Focus briefing document 81. Accessed 18 February 2008 (www.ukoln.ac.uk/qa-focus/documents/briefings/briefing-81/).

UKOLN (2006) 'Choosing an appropriate raster image format', *UKOLN* (website, published online 20 April 2006) QA Focus Briefing Document 28. Accessed 23 May 2007 (www.ukoln.ac.uk/qa-focus/documents/briefings/briefing-28/html/).

Valéry, P. (1931) 'Pieces Sur l'Art', *La Conquète de l'Ubiquité*, Paris, translated in W. Benjamin (1936) 'The Work of Art in the Age of Mechanical Reproduction', in W. Benjamin (1992) *Illuminations: Essays and Reflections*. London: Fontana Press, pp. 211–44.

Vasconcelos, N. (2007) 'From pixels to semantic spaces: Advances in content-based image retrieval', *Computer*, 40: 7 July 2007, pp. 20–6. Accessed 18 February 2007 (www.svcl.ucsd.edu/publications/journal/2007/computer/computer07.pdf).

Visual Resources Association (2007) 'Welcome to the VRA Core 4.0', *VRA* (website). Accessed 29 February 2008 (http://vraweb.org/projects/vracore4/index.html).

Vroegindeweij, S. (2002) 'My pictures: informal image collections'. *Hewlett Packard Technical Report*, Information Infrastructure Laboratory. Bristol: Hewlett Packard. Accessed 11 February 2008 (www.hpl.hp.com/techreports/2002/HPL-2002-72R1.pdf).

W3Schools (2007a) 'Browser Statistics: What is the trend in browser usage, operating systems and screen resolution?' *W3Schools* (website). Accessed 23 November 2007 (www.w3schools.com/browsers/browsers_stats.asp).

W3Schools (2007b) 'Browser display statistics', *W3Schools* (website). Accessed 23 November 2007 (www.w3schools.com/browsers/browsers_display.asp).

Warwick, C., Terras, M. Huntington, P., Pappa, N. and Galina, I. (2006) *The LAIRAH Project: Log Analysis of Digital Resources in the Arts and Humanities*, Final Report to the Arts and Humanities Research Council. Accessed 23 March 2008 (www.ucl.ac.uk/slais/claire-warwick/publications/LAIRAHreport.pdf).

Warwick, C., Terras, M., Huntington, P. and Pappa, N. (forthcoming 2008) 'If you build it will they come? The LAIRAH study: quantifying the use of online resources in the Arts and Humanities through statistical analysis of user log data', *Literary and Linguistic Computing*, Accepted.

Waters, D.J. (1991) *From Microfilm to Digital Imagery*. Washington DC: Commission on Preservation and Access.

Watson, A.B. (1994) *Digital Images and Human Vision*. Cambridge, MA: MIT Press.

Weglowska, M. (2006) *Image Management Systems in Academic Libraries and Digitised Collections*, MA Dissertation. London, School of Library, Archive and Information Studies, University College London.

Weibel, P. (1984) 'On the history and aesthetics of the digital image', in T. Druckery (ed.) (1999) *Ars Electronica: Facing the Future. A Survey of Two Decades*. Cambridge, MA: MIT Press, pp. 51–65.

Weibel, S. and Miller, E. (1997) 'Image description on the Internet: a summary of the CNI/OCLC image metadata workshop', *D-Lib Magazine*, January. Accessed 20 March 2008 (www.dlib.org/dlib/january97/oclc/01weibel.html).

Welch, T.A. (1984) 'A Technique for High Performance Data Compression', *IEEE Computer*, 17(6) pp. 8–19.

Wells, J. (2008) 'Understanding & Solutions Ltd Presents Digital Imaging Market Roundup', *Newswire Today* (website, published online 21 January 2008). Accessed 13 February 2008 (www.newswiretoday.com/news/28745/).

WFTV.com (2006) 'Photos on MySpace get family evicted from apartment', *WFTV.com* (website, published online 6 June 2006). Accessed 20 February 2008 (www.wftv.com/news/9331012/detail.html).

White, C. (2007) Personal comments to M. Terras, National Gallery, London.

Wienand, P., Booy, A. and Fry, R. (2000) *A Guide to Copyright for Museums and Galleries*. London: Routledge.

Willis, A.M. (1990) 'Digitisation and the living death of photography', in P. Hayward (ed.) *Culture, Technology and Creativity in the Late Twentieth Century*. Eastleigh: John Libbey Publishing, pp. 197–208.

Wissenberg, A. (2000) 'Digitising journals and the eLib programme', *Proceedings, Digitising Journals: Conference on Future Strategies for European Libraries, 13–14 March 2000, Copenhagen*. Copenhagen: Danish National Library Authority, pp. 11–8. Accessed 15 January 2008 (www.deflink.dk/upload/doc_filer/doc_alle/1113_Digitising %20journals.pdf).

Witten, I. and Bainbridge, D. (2003) *How to Build a Digital Library*, Morgan Kaufmann Series in Multimedia Information and Systems. San Francisco: Morgan Kaufman.

Wray, R. (2007) 'How one year's digital output would fill 16bn iPods', *The Guardian*, 6 March 2007, p. 27.

ZDNet (2004) 'Kodak stops selling film cameras', *ZDNet* (website, published online 14 January 2004). Emerging Tech Toolkit. Accessed 2 February 2007 (http://news.zdnet.co.uk/emergingtech/0,1000000183,39119083,00.htm).

Zellman, T. (2006) 'Image compression and JPEG 2000', in L. MacDonald (ed.) *Digital Heritage, Applying Digital Imaging to Cultural Heritage*. Oxford: Elsevier, pp. 326–50.

Zinkham, H. (1986) *Descriptive terms for graphic materials*, Library of Congress Cataloging in Publication Data, Cataloging Distribution Service. Washington, DC: Library of Congress.

Ziv, J. and Lempel, A. (1977) 'A universal algorithm for sequential data compression', *IEEE Transactions on Information Theory*, 23(3) pp. 337–43.

Ziv, J. and Lempel, A. (1978) 'Compression of individual sequences via variable-rate coding', *IEEE Transactions on information Theory*, 24(5) pp. 530–6.

Index